The Jewish Word Book

The Jewish Word Book

Sidney J. Jacobs

jD | Jonathan David Publishers, Inc.
Middle Village, New York 11379

THE JEWISH
WORD BOOK

Copyright © 1982

by

Jonathan David Publishers, Inc.

Jonathan David Publishers, Inc.
68-22 Eliot Avenue
Middle Village, New York 11379

10 9 8 7 6 5 4 3 2 1

Library of Congress Cataloging in Publication Data

Jacobs, Sidney J.
    The Jewish word book.

    1. Hebrew language—Dictionaries—English.
2. English language—Foreign terms and phrases—Hebrew.
3. Yiddish language—Dictionaries—English.   4. English language—Foreign words and phrases—Yiddish.   I. Title.
PJ4833.J25   492.4'321   81-12641
ISBN 0-8246-0249-8   AACR2

Printed in the United States of America

To
BETTY JANE LAZAROFF JACOBS,
who has enriched the vocabulary
of my life and my love

Preface

Jews have been more preoccupied from the inception of their identity with the flowing rhythm of prose and poesy and less with the "frozen" rhythm of form, line, and dimension. The classic evidence is the Hebrew Bible, more especially the Book of Psalms.

The words Jews have lived by have been, first, those of Hebrew, the tongue of sacred writ and liturgy and, later, the "mother tongue" of Yiddish among Ashkenazic (European) Jews and Ladino in Sephardic (Iberian) Jewry.

There is no "Jewish" language, no "Jewish" newspaper, no "Jewish" theater. There *is* a Jewish people, Jewish civilization, and culture; and when language and vocabulary are to be denoted, the proper adjectives are Hebrew, Yiddish, Ladino.

As a glossary of the vocabulary of Jewish living, *The Jewish Word Book* contains the most familiar articulations of these languages, more precisely Hebrew and Yiddish words, phrases, and idioms that the reader whose primary language is English has often heard but may not understand or be able to define with any degree of precision.

Because there are endless varieties of and distortions in pronunciation, we have attempted to list words and phrases in such a manner that they may be most easily tracked. The reader more familiar with variations and pronunciation eccentricities need only search a bit to trace the term he or she seeks.

* * *

Hebrew, the Semitic language of the Bible and post-biblical Mishna and Midrash, has remained the classic language of Jews throughout the centuries. It was the medium of discourse of the Jewish people until about 100 B.C.E., when it was supplanted as the language of daily use by Aramaic, which was originally brought to the Holy Land by the returnees from the Babylonian Exile.

Revived as a popular tongue with Jewish settlement in Palestine beginning in the last decade of the nineteenth century, Hebrew is the *lingua franca* of the State of Israel with its polyglot population.

Yiddish had its origins in the ninth century in the Rhine Valley, where it was known as *Ivri/Teutsch,* then *Juden/Teutsch,* and still later *Judisch.* From the thirteenth through the seventeenth centuries, it was extended into the kingdom of Poland-Lithuania, where it became the language of the Jewish masses.

Written in Hebrew characters, Yiddish is an amalgam of Hebrew, High German, and Slavic, plus an infusion of words adapted from the vocabulary of each country where it was commonly employed—for example, Polish, Lithuanian, and (from the 1880s) English.

Ladino, also variously called Judezmo, Spaniolish, Haketia, and Jidyo, is the Judeo-Spanish language spoken by Jewry of the Iberian peninsula and the Middle East. (Some scholars distinguish between Ladino as a "translation language" and Judezmo, the spoken language.)

Ladino became especially popular following the expulsion of Jews from Spain in 1492. It rests upon a Spanish linguistic base with the addition of Hebrew, Arabic, Greek, Turkish, French, Italian, and Portugese words, and with Turkish as the most influential.

* * *

The renaissance of the Hebrew language is a miracle of modern Jewish history. For centuries, the language was associated solely with sacred scripture, liturgy, and formal correspondence of primarily religious content.

Its revival began to take shape in the latter decades of the nineteenth century with the emergence both of the Haskalah movement of Jewish Enlightenment in its East European phase and of political and cultural Zionism. From the period of the earliest settlements of Jewish pioneers in the Land of Israel, it came into daily usage. Modernized, it has flourished as the dominant language of science, government, the arts and *belles-lettres* of the State of Israel.

Yiddish is the tongue that will not be silenced. Its obsequies have been legion in the contemporary era, especially since its nourishment in Eastern European Jewry was cut off in the Holocaust, which destroyed the millions and thus strangled their voices.

Nevertheless, Yiddish is living proof that pratfalls should not be confused with rigor mortis. True, the period which witnessed the zenith of Yiddish literature, theater, and press is past. However, four Yiddish theaters were playing simultaneously in New York City as late as the winter of 1980. The YIVO Institute for Yiddish Research reports that Yiddish is being taught in sixty-five institutions of higher learning (and accredited in thirty-five courses) in the United States and Canada as well as in universities in Bergen, Norway; Melbourne, Australia; Ule, Finland; Paris; Frankfurt; Jerusalem, Tel Aviv, and Haifa.

Amazing as is the refusal of this language to accept the funereal fate decreed for it by a legion of pundits, its osmotic effect on American English is only slightly less astounding. Examples proliferate of the infiltration of *mame lawshn* into the vocabulary of Americans of varying creeds and ethnic origins: *shlep, shlemil, oi vei, yentuh, mihsh-mash, chootzpuh (chutzpa), shmaltz, ganef, nash (nosh), nebihsh, gelt, shtihk, blihntz, tuhchuhs (tuches), megihluh (megilla), klawtz (klutz), kihbetz (kibbitz), l'chayihm, meivihn (mayven)*—as well as a host of vulgarisms.

Yiddish is rich in oaths and curses, a circumstance which the editor of *Maledicta: the International Journal of Verbal Aggression* attributes to historic anti-Semitism against which no physical, retaliatory relief was available.

My preference for an example of malediction, which has not lost its vividness over the forty-five years since I first read it, was splashed in a four-column headline in the *Chicago Yiddish Courier* (1887-1944) over a photograph of Nazi Field Marshal Herman Goering, head of Hitler's *Luftwaffe,* beaming at his wife as she held their newborn son.

Characteristic of the personal quality of Yiddish journalism, the headline read, *A Ruach Ihn Zain Taten Arain! Awmein!* ("May an Evil Wind Enter His Father! Amen!"). The concluding word was in keeping with the Yiddish wish, "From your mouth into God's ear!"

I am eternally grateful to the *melamuhd,* my private Hebrew tutor who, on his own initiative, introduced me to the Yiddish word more than a half-century ago. As I moved into adolescence and young adulthood, I heard the language used at meetings, conferences, and conventions of the Zionist movement, especially the Labor Zionists with whom I identified ideologically. *"Ains, tsvai, drai, fir; Poylei Tziyon zainen mir!"*

At one time reviled as the *jargon* of the Jewish masses of Eastern Europe, Yiddish has revealed a capacity for dimension and adaptation that never ceases to astonish: *yentuh* traces her roots to the sultry Spanish *Juanita,* possibly to the French *Gentille; bobe-maise* derives from *Buovo d'Antona,* the Italian version of *Sir Bevis of Hampton!*

In sum, Yiddish is a language of infinite variety. The late and sorely-missed folk humorist Sam Levenson used to compare the English paucity of "ugly . . . uglier . . . ugliest" with the rich Yiddish sequence of *mies . . . nihsht duh gedacht . . . chaluhshes* ("ugly . . . it shouldn't happen here . . . one may faint!").

I shudder when I consider how close I came as a child to the precipice of life without intimacy with Yiddish, once described by a West Coast theater critic as "that peculiar mixture of German and Hebrew designed to maximize the expression of pain and joy at once."

* * *

I am indebted to Rabbi Alfred J. Kolatch, editor-in-chief of Jonathan David Publishers, Inc., both for his suggestion which led to the writing of this book and for his invaluable counsel in the process of its compilation.

SIDNEY J. JACOBS

Culver City, CA
January 16, 1981

Erev Shabbat
12 Shevat 5741 (the 38th *Yahrtzeit* of my father)

How to Use
The Jewish Word Book

Most of the Yiddish and Hebrew words and phrases chosen for inclusion in this book can be "correctly" pronounced in more than one way (varying with local custom and usage). And over the years many different systems have been employed to transliterate these various pronunciations using English characters. All this has been taken into account when planning this book, and every effort has been made to render it as easy as possible for the reader to find the word or phrase in question.

All entries are listed alphabetically. The main entry is printed in boldface type, and is divided syllabically. This is followed by one or more alternate pronunciations, alternate spellings, and as many definitions as apply. The main entry represents the pronunciation of the word as it is most commonly heard. This is not necessarily the spelling most often used in the print media or the pronunciation and spelling as accepted by the scholarly community. The modern Israeli (Sephardic) pronunciation of a given term is indicated by an asterisk (*) placed after the term.

The transliteration system created for *The Jewish Word Book* is a combination of several of the most popular in current use. So that the reader does not have to continually refer to the front matter to recall the basic elements in the system, a complete Key to Transliteration appears at the bottom of each two-page spread of text.

The
Jewish
Word
Book

Key to Transliteration / Pronunciation

a as in f*a*ther
aw as in l*aw*
ai as in *ai*sle
ei as in n*ei*ghbor
e as in b*e*t
i as in vacc*i*ne
ih as in t*i*n
o as in s*o*lar
oi as in v*oi*d
oo as in f*oo*d
u as in p*u*t
uh as in b*u*t
ch as in *ch*utzpa
zh as in *Zh*ivago

* (asterisk) after an entry indicates modern Israeli (Sephardic) pronunciation

A

Ab see *Av*

a-ba*

Also *a-baw, a-buh.*

Also spelled *abba.*

Aramaic form of the Hebrew *av,** meaning "father, dad."

Ab Beth Din see *Av Bet Dihn*

a-bi ge-zoont

Also *a-bi ge-zunt.*

So long as you are (one is) healthy, implying that nothing else matters, nothing else is important.

a-cha-ro-nihm*

Also *ach-ro-nihm, ach-roi-nihm.*

Also spelled *ahronim.*

1. Literally, "the latter ones," referring to post-talmudic rabbinic authorities in contrast with *rishonihm,* "earlier ones."
2. Occasionally refers to the Latter Prophets.

achraiyes see *achrayoot*

ach-rai-yoot*

Also *ach-rai-us, ach-rai-yuhs, ach-rai-yes.*

Also spelled *achrayut.*

1. Responsibility.
2. To assume responsibility.

achronihm see *acharonihm*

a-da-fi-na

The Spanish-Judeo (Ladino) designation for *cholent.* See *cholent.*

a-da-ma*

Also *a-du-muh, a-daw-muh.*

Earth, ground. See also *erd.*

---

a as in father; aw as in law; ai as in aisle; ei as in neighbor; e as in bet; i as in vaccine; ih as in tin; o as in solar; oi as in void; oo as in food; u as in put; uh as in but; ch as in chutzpa; zh as in Zhivago.

a-dam ha-ri-shon*

Also *aw-dawm haw-ri-shon, aw-duhm huh-rishoin*
The first man (Adam) mentioned in the Book of
Genesis.

A-dar*

Also *Oo-duhr.*
Twelfth and final month of the Jewish religious
calendar, the sixth of the Civil calendar, corresponding to February-March. The Purim holiday
occurs on the fourteenth of the month. When a leap
year occurs in the Jewish calendar, an extra month
is added to the year. This is called *Ve-Adar,* meaning "and Adar." The formal Hebrew designation
for the First Adar is *Adar Rishon** and for the
Second Adar, *Adar Sheini (Sheni*).*

Adar Rishon see *Adar*

Adar Sheini see *Adar*

adawmuh see *adama*

Ad-lo-ya-da*

Also *Ad-lo-yaw-da.*
A combination of three Hebrew words: *ad, d'lo,
yada.* Literally, "until one cannot know (tell) the
difference." The annual Purim carnival held in Tel
Aviv and other cities in Israel. The name is derived
from the talmudic dictum that on Purim one should
imbibe until no longer able to distinguish between
the words "blessed is Mordecai" and "cursed is
Haman," that is, between the hero and villain of
the biblical Book of Esther.

A-do-nai*

Also *A-do-noi.*
Also spelled *Adonei.*
1. Literally, "my Lord."
3. Commonly used in the Bible when referring to
God.
2. Used as a substitute for the taboo name Yahweh
(Jehovah), considered too sacred for com-
monplace use. Pronounced by traditional Jews

---

a as in father; aw as in law; ai as in aisle; ei as in neighbor; e as in bet; i as in vaccine; ih as in tin; o as in
solar; oi as in void; oo as in food; u as in put; uh as in but; ch as in chutzpa; zh as in Zhivago.

only during prayer and with heads covered. *Adoshem* and *Hashem* are used as substitutes.

A-don O-lam*

Also *A-don O-lawm.*
1. Literally, "Lord of the universe."
2. The title and opening words of a popular hymn praising the unity and the providence of God and attributed to Solomon ibn Gabirol.

A-do-shem

A combination of two words, *Adonai* and *Hashem* (the Name), used as a substitute for *Adonai* in a nonsacred context. See *Adonai* and *Hashem.*

a-duh-ra-buh

Also *a-de-ra-ba,** *a-de-ra-be.*
Also spelled *aderabbuh.*
An Aramaic word occurring in the Talmud.
1. Not at all.
2. On the contrary.
3. In point of fact.
4. By all means. For special emphasis the word is repeated, as in the phrase *aduhrabuh v'aduhrabuh,* signifying "absolutely," "by all means," or "with the greatest of pleasure."

adumuh see *adama*

af al pi

1. Nevertheless.
2. Despite all.

a-fi-ko-man*

Also *a-fi-ko-muhn.*
Also spelled *afikomen, afikomon.*
From the Greek, meaning "dessert." A piece of *matza* set aside during the early part of the Passover *Seder* to be distributed and eaten at the end of the meal.

a-fi-loo

Also spelled *afilu.*
Even, even if.

---

a as in father; aw as in law; ai as in aisle; ei as in neighbor; e as in bet; i as in vaccine; ih as in tin; o as in solar; oi as in void; oo as in food; u as in put; uh as in but; ch as in chutzpa; zh as in Zhivago.

a-ga-da*
> Also *a-gaw-duh.*
> Also spelled *aggada.*
> 1. The narrative and homiletical portions of the Talmud and Midrash as contrasted with *halacha,* the legalistic portions.
> 2. A legend, tale, fable.

ag-mat ne-fesh*
> Also *ag-mas ne-fesh; ag-muhs ne-fesh.*
> Grief, sadness, depression.

agmuhs nefesh see *agmat nefesh*

a-goo-na*
> Also *a-goo-nuh.*
> Also spelled *aguna, agunah.*
> From the Aramaic, meaning "tied." A woman uncertain of her husband's whereabouts who may not remarry because she was never divorced according to rabbinic law *(halacha).*

a guten Shabes see *gut Shabuhs*

a-ha!
> The expletive "so!" signifying comprehension, surprise, delight, vindication, triumph.

a-hihn awdr a-her
> Also spelled *ahin awder aher.*
> 1. Literally, "here or there."
> 2. Make up your mind!

aidelkeit see *eidlkait*

ai-er kihchl
> Also *ei-er kihchl.*
> Also spelled *aier kichel.*
> Egg cookies.

ailt zihch
> Also *hailt zihch.*
> Also spelled *eilt zich.*
> Hurry up! Rush!

ain-bren
> A roux, a thickener for sauces and stews.

---

a as in father; aw as in law; ai as in aisle; ei as in neighbor; e as in bet; i as in vaccine; ih as in tin; o as in solar; oi as in void; oo as in food; u as in put; uh as in but; ch as in chutzpa; zh as in Zhivago.

ain-fal
Also spelled *einfahl.*
An idea.

ain-ge-fal-en
1. Literally, "fell in."
2. Duped.

ain-ge-machtz
Also spelled *eingemachts.*
Preserves, jam, jelly.

ain-ge-shpart
Also spelled *eingeshpart.*
Obstinate, stubborn, headstrong.

ain-ge-toonkn
Also spelled *aingetunken, eingetunken.*
Dipped in, dunked.

ain haw-re
Also *a-yihn haw-raw, a-yihn ha-ra.**
Also spelled *einhore.*
Literally, "evil eye."

ain-lauf
A soup mix made of egg plus potato or *matza* meal.

ain-red-e-nihsh
Also spelled *einredenish.*
1. Literally, "self-suggestion."
2. Delusion, misconception.
3. Fantasy.

ains, tsvai, drai, fir
Also *eins, tsvei, drai, fir.*
One, two three, four.

Ak-da-moot*
Also *Ak-du-mes, Ak-duh-mes.*
Also spelled *Akdamut.*
An Aramaic prayer recited on Shavuot praising the greatness of God and emphasizing the importance of Torah and the rewards of righteous living.

A-kei-duh
Also *A-kei-da.**
Also spelled *Akeda.*

---

a as in father; aw as in law; ai as in aisle; ei as in neighbor; e as in bet; i as in vaccine; ih as in tin; o as in solar; oi as in void; oo as in food; u as in put; uh as in but; ch as in chutzpa; zh as in Zhivago.

    1. Literally, "the binding."
    2. The name given to the biblical episode (Genesis 22) of Abraham's intended offering of his son Isaac as a sacrifice to God.

alaichem shoolem see *aleichem shalom*

a-lav ha-sha-lom see *awlawv hashawlom*

Al Cheit
    Also spelled *Al Het, Al Chet.*
    Literally, "for the sin of. . . ." A Yom Kippur penitential prayer.

alef see *aluhf*

alef baiz see *aluhf beis*

aleha hashalom see *awlehaw hashawlom*

a-lei-chem sha-lom*
    Also *a-lai-chem shoo-lem, a-lei-chem shaw-lem.*
    1. Literally, "Upon you be peace."
    2. A response to the popular greeting *shalom aleichem,* "peace be unto you."

a-le mai-les huht zi
    Also spelled *alle meiles hot zi.*
    1. She has every good quality.
    2. Refers to a woman who is a suitable mate because she possesses everything a man would want: character, beauty, intelligence, etc.

aleph see *aluhf*

aleph beis see *aluhf beis*

ale shoos-ters gei-en bawr-ves
    1. Literally, "All shoemakers go barefoot."
    2. Refers to a person who doesn't have things you would expect him or her to have.

alevai see *haluhvai*

Al Ha-ni-sihm*
    Also spelled *Al Hanisim.*
    1. Literally, "for the miracles."
    2. The opening words and title of a hymn that is part of the liturgies of Chanukah and Purim, two holidays in which miracles occurred.

---

a as in father; aw as in law; ai as in aisle; ei as in neighbor; e as in bet; i as in vaccine; ih as in tin; o as in solar; oi as in void; oo as in food; u as in put; uh as in but; ch as in chutzpa; zh as in Zhivago.

a-li-ya*
Also *a-li-yuh.*
Also spelled *aliyah.*
1. Literally, "going up" or "ascending."
2. A Torah honor in which one is called to ascend to the reading table to recite the blessings over the Torah.
3. To "go up" to live in Israel, that is, to immigrate to Israel.

alle meiles hot zi see *ale mailes huht zi*

alman see *almuhn*

almana see *almuhne*

al-muhn
Also *al-man.**
Also spelled *almon.*
A widower.

al-muhn-e
Also *al-maw-naw, al-ma-na.**
Also spelled *almoona, almoone.*
A widow.

Al-pha Be-ta
Psalms recited in Sephardic congregations on Saturday afternoons.

al-rait-nihk
Also spelled *alrightnik, alritnik.*
1. An "all right" person, referring to a "greenhorn" who rapidly Americanized. A term popular among Jewish immigrants from Europe.
2. A boastful, ostentatious person; a nouveau riche, parvenu.

alte see *altuh*

alter see *altr*

al-tihsh-kuh
A pet form of *alte.* See *altuh.*

altr
Also spelled *alter.*
Old man. *Altuh* is the feminine form.

---

a as in father; aw as in law; ai as in aisle; ei as in neighbor; e as in bet; i as in vaccine; ih as in tin; o as in solar; oi as in void; oo as in food; u as in put; uh as in but; ch as in chutzpa; zh as in Zhivago.

altr ba-kantr
> Also spelled *alter bakanter*.
> An old acquaintance.

altr bawchr
> Also *al-ter buchr*.
> 1. Literally, "old boy."
> 2. A bachelor.

altr kakr
> Also spelled *alter kaker*.
> 1. Literally, "old defecator."
> 2. Contentious, lecherous.
> 3. A harmless old man.
> Often abbreviated "a.k."

altr truhm-buh-nihk
> Also spelled *alter trombenihk*.
> 1. An old derelict.
> 2. A bum.

al-tuh
> Also spelled *alte*.
> 1. Literally, "old one."
> 2. Old woman.

al-tuh buh-be
> Also spelled *alte bobe, alte bube*.
> 1. Literally, "old grandmother."
> 2. Old woman.

al-tuh ma-cha-shei-fuh
> Also spelled *alte machshayfeh*.
> Old witch.

alt-varg
> 1. Old clothing.
> 2. Something stale, outdated.
> 3. A decrepit person.

altz ihz gut
> 1. Literally, "all is good."
> 2. Everything is fine.

altz vaws (ihz) ihn der kawrt
> 1. Literally, "all that is in the (dealing of a) card."
> 2. Every conceivable bad thing.

---

a as in father; aw as in law; ai as in aisle; ei as in neighbor; e as in bet; i as in vaccine; ih as in tin; o as in solar; oi as in void; oo as in food; u as in put; uh as in but; ch as in chutzpa; zh as in Zhivago.

a-luhf

Also spelled *alef, aleph.*
First letter of the Hebrew and Yiddish alphabet. Its
numerical value is one.

a-luhf beis

Also *a-lef bet.**
Also spelled *aleph bet, aleph beis, aleph bays, alef baiz.*
1. First two consonants of the Hebrew and Yiddish
   alphabet, therefore
2. Basis or beginning of anything.
3. The ABCs.
4. Cf. Greek *alpha beta* and English "alphabet."

am-cha*

Also *am-chu, am-chaw.*
1. Literally, "your (God's) people."
2. Average Jews.
3. The Jewish masses.

a-men*

Also *aw-mein.*
Also spelled *amain.*
1. Literally, "so be it."
2. A response to a prayer.
3. An acronym from the Hebrew words *Eil Melech
   Ne'eman,* meaning "the Lord is a trustworthy
   King."

am ha-a-retz*

Also *am haw-aw-retz.*
1. Literally, "people of the earth, land folk."
2. Farmers.
3. The uneducated.
4. The masses.

am ha-ra-tzut*

Also *am ha-ra-tzus.*
1. Ignorance.
2. Boorishness.

am ha-sei-fer

Also spelled *am hasefer.*
1. Literally, "people of the book."

---

a as in father; aw as in law; ai as in aisle; ei as in neighbor; e as in bet; i as in vaccine; ih as in tin; o as in solar; oi as in void; oo as in food; u as in put; uh as in but; ch as in chutzpa; zh as in Zhivago.

2. A designation for the Jewish people, attributed to Muhammed, founder of Islam.

A-mi-da*
Also *A-mi-duh.*
1. Literally, "stand, standing."
2. A major prayer in the Jewish liturgy recited three times each day in a standing position. Also referred to as the *Tefila* ("prayer") and as the *Shmone Esrei* ("eighteen," the number of benedictions it contains).

a-mood*
Also *aw-mood.*
Also spelled *amud.*
1. A synagogue pulpit.
2. A lectern.
3. One of the posts of the *sukka,* in the Sephardic tradition.

a-mo-ra*
Also *a-mo-ruh.*
A title for Talmudic scholars of the third to sixth centuries in the academies of learning in Palestine and Babylonia.

a-mo-ra-ihm
Plural of *amora.* See *amora.*

a-nav*
Also *aw-nuhv.*
1. A humble person.
2. A poor person.

a nech-tih-ger tawg see *nechtiger tawg*

aninoos see *aninoot*

a-ni-noot*
Also *a-ni-noos, a-ni-nus.*
Also spelled *aninut.*
The period of mourning between the death and burial of a relative.

a-ni-voot*
Also *a-ni-ves, a-ni-voos, a-ni-vus.*
Also spelled *anivut.**
Humility, modesty, meekness.

---

a as in father; aw as in law; ai as in aisle; ei as in neighbor; e as in bet; i as in vaccine; ih as in tin; o as in solar; oi as in void; oo as in food; u as in put; uh as in but; ch as in chutzpa; zh as in Zhivago.

a-noo-sihm
> Also spelled *anusim*.
> 1. Jews forced to covert to another religion, particularly in fifteenth-century Spain and Portugal.
> 2. Marranos.

ant-shool-dihk
> Excuse (me) please!

ant-shool-dihk mihr
> Also *ant-shool-dihkt mihr*.
> Excuse me!

ant-shool-dihkn
> Also spelled *antshuldiken*.
> Pardon (me)! Excuse (me)!

an-uh-ve-nuh
> Also *a nu-ve-ne*.
> 1. Literally, "a small sin." Diminutive of the Hebrew *avon*.
> 2. A mild exaggeration.
> 3. A minor offense.

apikawrsihm*
> Also spelled *apikorsim*.
> Plural of *apikores*. See *apikores*.

a-pi-ko-res
> Also *a-pi-ko-ruhs*.
> Also spelled *apikoros*.
> Akin to the Greek-based word "epicurean."
> 1. A religious heretic.
> 2. A freethinker.
> 3. A skeptic.

a-rain
> Also spelled *arein*.
> 1. In, into.
> 2. Enter. Used most often with *koom* ("come"), as in *koom (kum) arain,* "come in."

a-ra-va*
> Also *a-raw-vuh*.
> 1. A willow.

---

a as in father; aw as in law; ai as in aisle; ei as in neighbor; e as in bet; i as in vaccine; ih as in tin; o as in solar; oi as in void; oo as in food; u as in put; uh as in but; ch as in chutzpa; zh as in Zhivago.

2. One of four species of plants used on the Sukkot
festival.

a-ra-vot*

Also *a-raw-ves, a-ru-ves.*
Plural of *arava.* See *arava.*

arba kanfot see *arba kanfuhs*

ar-ba kan-fuhs

Also *ar-ba kan-fos, ar-ba kan-fot.**
Also spelled *arba kanfes.*
1. Literally, "four corners."
2. The fringes attached to the four corners of a
garment or *talit* (prayer shawl).
3. A garment worn by Orthodox Jews under their
shirts; fringes are attached to the four corners of
the garment. Also called *talit katan,* "a small
talit."

ar-ba ko-sot*

Also *ar-ba ko-sos*
1. Literally, "four cups."
2. The four goblets of wine served at the Passover
Seder.

ar-ba mi-nihm*

1. Literally, "four kinds."
2. The four species of plants used during the obser-
vance of the Sukkot festival: the palm branch,
the citron, willow branches, and myrtle branches.

ar-buhs

Also spelled *arbes.*
Peas.

a-rihbr chapn di maws

Also spelled *ariber chapen di maws.*
To overdo, carry to excess.

arn

To matter, to be of concern. Generally used in the
third person, *"art,"* as in *es art mihr vi di vant,* "it
bothers me (as little) as the wall," that is, "I don't
care a bit."

---

a as in father; **aw** as in law; **ai** as in aisle; **ei** as in neighbor; **e** as in bet; **i** as in vaccine; **ih** as in tin; **o** as in
solar; **oi** as in void; **oo** as in food; **u** as in put; **uh** as in but; **ch** as in chutzpa; **zh** as in Zhivago.

a-rois
> Out! Get out!

a-rois ge-fawr-en
> Also *a-rois ge-foor-en*.
> Travelled away, left.

a-rois ge vawr-fen
> Literally, "thrown out."

a-rois ge-vawr-fe-ne gelt
> 1. Literally, "thrown-out money."
> 2. Wasted expenditure.

a-rois ge-vawr-fe-ne yawr-en
> Also spelled *arois gevorfeneh yoren*.
> 1. Literally, "wasted years."
> 2. Wasted time.

a-ron*
> Also *aw-ron*.
> 1. A chest, a box.
> 2. A coffin.
> 3. A short form of *aron hakodesh*. See below.

A-ron Ha-ko-desh*
> 1. Literally, "Holy Ark."
> 2. A cabinet that houses the Torah scrolls in a synagogue.

art see *arn*

art mihch vi di vant
> 1. Literally, "it bothers me as (little as) the wall."
> 2. I don't care a bit.

a-rum
> Around.

a-rum guh-val-guhrt
> Also spelled *aroom gevalgert*.
> Wandered around, loafed.

a-rum loifr
> 1. A street urchin.
> 2. A runaround.
> 3. A philanderer.

aruves see *aravot*

---

a as in father; aw as in law; ai as in aisle; ei as in neighbor; e as in bet; i as in vaccine; ih as in tin; o as in solar; oi as in void; oo as in food; u as in put; uh as in but; ch as in chutzpa; zh as in Zhivago.

ar-viht*
Also *ar-vihs.*
1. Evening.
2. Evening prayers, vespers. Also referred to as *tefilat arviht.**

A-sa-ra b'Tei-veit*
Also *A-saw-raw b'Tei-veis.*
Also spelled *Asara b'Tevet.*
1. The tenth day of the Hebrew month Tevet, a fast day.
2. Anniversary of the start of the siege of Jerusalem in the sixth century B.C.E.

A-se-ret Ha-dihb-rot*
Also *A-se-res Ha-dihb-ros.*
1. Literally, "the ten statements."
2. The Ten Commandments, the Decalogue.

A-se-ret Y'mei T'shoo-va*
Also *A-se-res Y'mei T'shoo-vaw.*
Also spelled *Aseret Yemei Teshuvah.*
1. Literally, "Ten Days of Penitence."
2. The ten-day period in the Jewish calendar beginning with Rosh Hoshana and ending with Yom Kippur.

ashir see *awshir*

Ash-ke-na-zi
1. Literally, "German."
2. A Jew of East European extraction, originally from Germany, in contradistinction to a Sephardi, a Jew of West European extraction, principally from Spain or Portugal. *Ashkenazim* is the plural form. *Ashkenazic* is the adjectival form.

Ashkenazim see *Ashkenazi*

Av
Also spelled *Ab.*
The fifth month of the Jewish religious calendar, corresponding to July-August.

---

a as in father; aw as in law; ai as in aisle; ei as in neighbor; e as in bet; i as in vaccine; ih as in tin; o as in solar; oi as in void; oo as in food; u as in put; uh as in but; ch as in chutzpa; zh as in Zhivago.

Av Bet Dihn*
Also spelled *Av Bet Din, Ab Beth Din.*
1. Vice-president of the *Sanhedrin* in Second Temple days.
2. Chief rabbi of an ecclesiastical court.

av-dut*
Also *av-duhs, av-dus.*
Slavery, enslavement.

aveilus see *aveilut*

a-vei-lut*
Also *a-vei-loos, a-vei-lus, a-vei-luhs.*
Also spelled *aveloot, avelut.*
1. Mourning.
2. A period of mourning.
3. The act of mourning.

a-vei-ra*
Also *a-vei-raw, a-vei-ruh.*
Also spelled *avera.*
1. A sin, a transgression.
2. A pity, in the sense of a waste.
Often mispronounced *"naveira,"* from the two words "an *aveira."*

(an) a-vei-ruh daws gelt
1. Literally, "a sin for the money."
2. A waste of money.

a-vek
Away, as in *gei avek,* meaning "go away."

a-vek fihr-en ihn bawd a-rain
1. Literally, "to lead one into the bathhouse."
2. To lead astray, deceive, dupe.

a-vel*
Also *aw-veil, oovl.*
A mourner, after the funeral.

avelus see *aveilut*

avelut see *aveilut*

avera see *aveira*

a-vihv*
Also *aw-vihv*

---

a as in father; aw as in law; ai as in aisle: ei as in neighbor; e as in bet; i as in vaccine; ih as in tin; o as in solar; oi as in void; oo as in food; u as in put; uh as in but; ch as in chutzpa; zh as in Zhivago.

Also spelled *aviv.*
1. Spring.
2. Springtime.

aviv see *avihv*

av-la*
Also *av-luh.*
1. A sin.
2. A crime.
3. A wrong, injustice, injury, grievance.

a-vo-da*
Also *a-vo-daw.*
1. Work.
2. Worship.
3. The main service performed in the Holy of Holies by the High Priest on the Day of Atonement.

a-vo-da za-ra*
Also *a-vo-daw zaw-raw.*
1. Literally, "strange, foreign worship."
2. Idolatry.

Av-ra-ham a-vi-noo*
Also *Av-raw-hawm aw-vi-noo.*
Also spelled *Avraham avinu.*
Literally, "Abraham, our father," referring to the biblical patriarch.

awch un vei
Also spelled *och oon vai.*
1. Alas and alack!
2. Tough luck! Too bad!

awdawm hawrishon see *adam harishon*

aw-duhm na-kuht
Also spelled *odem-naket.*
1. Literally, "as naked as Adam."
2. Stark naked.

awlawv hashawlom see *awluhv hashawluhm*

aw-le-haw ha-shaw-lom
Also *a-le-ha ha-sha-lom.**
The feminine form of *awlawv hashawlom.*
1. Literally, "Peace be upon her."

---

a as in father; aw as in law; ai as in aisle; ei as in neighbor; e as in bet; i as in vaccine; ih as in tin; o as in solar; oi as in void; oo as in food; u as in put; uh as in but; ch as in chutzpa; zh as in Zhivago.

2. May she rest in peace.

aw-luhv ha-shaw-luhm
Also *aw-lawv ha-shaw-luhm, a-lav ha-sha-lom.**
Also spelled *olav hasholem.*
1. Literally, "Peace be upon him."
2. May he rest in peace.

awmein see *amen*

awmood see *amood*

awn-ge-blaw-zen
Also spelled *ongeblozen.*
1. Literally, "blown up, inflated."
2. Conceited.
3. Peevish, sulky, pouting.

awn-ge-blaw-zen-er man
A conceited man.

awn-ge-patsh-ket
Also spelled *ongepatshket.*
1. Overdone, overdecorated.
2. Cluttered, littered.
3. Disordered, sloppy.

awn-ge-shtawpt
Also spelled *ongeshtopt.*
1. Stuffed, packed.
2. Overeaten, bloated.

awn-ge-shtawpt miht gelt
Also spelled *ongeshtopt mit gelt.*
1. Literally, "stuffed with money."
2. Very wealthy.

awn-ge-vawrfn
Also spelled *ongevorfen.*
Cluttered, disordered.

awn-shihk-uh-nihsh
Also spelled *onshikenish.*
1. A hanger-on.
2. A pest, nuisance.

awp-ge-flihkt
Also spelled *opgeflikt.*

---

a as in father; aw as in law; ai as in aisle; ei as in neighbor; e as in bet; i as in vaccine; ih as in tin; o as in solar; oi as in void; oo as in food; u as in put; uh as in but; ch as in chutzpa; zh as in Zhivago.

1. Literally, "plucked, defeathered."
2. Done in, suckered, taken.

awp-ge-hiht
   Also spelled *opgehit.*
   Careful, guarded.

awp-ge-hihtn
   Also spelled *opgehiten.*
   1. Careful, cautious.
   2. Pious, observant of the commandments.

awp-ge-kraw-chen-e s'choiruh
   Also spelled *opgekrochene s'choireh.*
   1. Shoddy merchandise.
   2. Wornout merchandise.

awp-ge-krawchn
   Also spelled *opgekrochen.*
   Shoddy, rotten.

awp-ge-lawzn
   Also spelled *opgelozen.*
   1. Careless, negligent.
   2. Shabby.
   3. Slipshod.

awp-ge-nart
   Also spelled *opgenart.*
   Cheated, fooled.

awp-hihtn
   Also spelled *ophiten.*
   1. To watch out for, guard against.
   2. To take care of, keep.

awp-nar-en zihch
   Also spelled *opnaren zich.*
   1. Literally, "to fool oneself, to kid oneself."
   2. To be disappointed.

awnuhv see *anav*

awn-zaltzn
   Also spelled *onzaltzen.*
   1. Literally, "to salt."
   2. To bribe.
   3. To sweet-talk, snow-job.

---

a as in father; aw as in law; ai as in aisle; ei as in neighbor; e as in bet; i as in vaccine; ih as in tin; o as in solar; oi as in void; oo as in food; u as in put; uh as in but; ch as in chutzpa; zh as in Zhivago.

awp-nar-er
Also spelled *opnarer.*
1. Trickster.
2. Shady operator.

awp-tshepn
Also spelled *optshepen.*
To get rid of, shake off.

aw-rem
Also spelled *orem.*
Poor.

aw-re-man
Also spelled *oreman.*
Poor man.

aw-rem-kait
Also spelled *oremkeit.*
Poverty.

aw-rem-uh-lait
Also spelled *oremeleit, oremalit.*
Poor people. Plural of *awreman.*

awron see *aron*

aw-shir
Also *a-shir.**
1. A wealthy person.
2. Wealth, riches.

awveil see *avel*

aw-vent
Also spelled *ovent.*
1. Evening.
2. Night.

awvihv see *avihv*

Aw-vi-noo Mal-kei-noo
Also *A-vi-noo Mal-kei-noo.**
Also spelled *Avinu Malkenu.*
1. Literally "our Father, our King."
2. A popular prayer in the High Holiday liturgy.

aydem see *eidm*

---

a-yihn
> Also spelled *ayin.*
> Sixteenth letter of the Hebrew alphabet; an un-
> sounded letter with a numerical value of seventy.

ayihn hara see *ain hawre*

az awch un vei
> Also spelled *az och oon vai.*
> 1. Alas and alack!
> 2. Tough luck! Too bad!

az a yawr oif mir
> 1. Literally, "May I have such a year."
> 2. I swear it!
> 3. May I have no luck if what I say is not true!

a-za-zel*
> Also *a-zaw-zeil.*
> 1. The evil spirit thought to live in the wilderness of
>   Judea, to which the scapegoat was sent during
>   the Temple ceremonies on the Day of Atone-
>   ment.
> 2. Hell.

**az drai zawgn m'shu-guh, darf der fer-ter zawgn
"bihm bam"**
> 1. Literally, "When three say something crazy, the
>   fourth must go along by uttering a nonsensical
>   phrase (like *bihm bam*)."
> 2. Majority rules.

az es klingt, iz mihs-ta-muh choo-ge
> 1. Literally, "When there is a ringing (of bells), it's
>   probably a festival."
> 2. Where there's smoke, there's fire.

a-zes paw-nihm see *azoot panim*

Az-ha-rot*
> 1. Literally, "warnings."
> 2. Special prayers for Shavuot in the Sephardic
>   liturgy.

a-zoi
> 1. So really!
> 2. Is that so?

---

a as in father: aw as in law; ai as in aisle; ei as in neighbor; e as in bet: i as in vaccine; ih as in tin: o as in
solar: oi as in void; oo as in food; u as in put; uh as in but; ch as in chutzpa: zh as in Zhivago.

3. So!
4. That's how it is!

a-zoi geit es
So it goes; that's the way things are.

a-zoi gihch?
So soon? So fast?

a-zoi ret men tzoo a tatn?
Is that how you talk to your father?

a-zoi vert daws kihchl tze-brawchn
That's how the cookie crumbles.

a-zoi zawgst doo!
1. That's what you say!
2. Really! You don't say!

a-zoot pa-nim*
Also *a-zoos pawnim, a-zes paw-nihm.*
Also spelled *azut panim.*
An impudent, insolent person.

B

ba-al*
>Also *bal.*
>1. Master, owner.
>2. Husband.

ba-al a-ga-la*
>Also *ba-al a-goo-luh, ba-al a-gaw-law.*
>Also spelled *balagoleh.*
>1. A teamster, a wagon driver.
>2. Occasionally, an uncouth person.
>3. An ignoramus.

ba-al ga-a-va*
>Also *bal gai-vuh.*
>1. A haughty or arrogant person.
>2. A showoff, braggart.

ba-al ha-ba-yiht*
>Also *ba-al ha-ba-yihs.*
>Also spelled *baal habayit.*
>1. Literally, "master of the house."
>2. The owner, landlord.
>3. The male head of the household.
>4. A male employer.

ba-al ko-rei*
>Also spelled baal *koray.*
>A Torah reader in the synagogue.

ba-al m'law-chaw
>Also *ba-al m'la-cha,* * *ba-al me-luh-chuh.*
>Also spelled *bal maluchah.*
>1. A laborer, a workman.
>2. A craftsman.

ba-al moo-sawf
>Also *ba-al moo-saf.* *
>Also spelled *bal musaf.*
>One who leads the second half of the Sabbath and
>holiday synagogue services.

---

a as in father; aw as in law; ai as in aisle; ei as in neighbor; e as in bet; i as in vaccine; ih as in tin; o as in solar; oi as in void; oo as in food; u as in put; uh as in but; ch as in chutzpa; zh as in Zhivago.

ba-al shach-riht*
Also *ba-al shach-rihs, ba-al sha-cha-rihs, ba-al sha-cha-rit.**
Also spelled *bal shachrit.*
One who leads the first half of the Sabbath or holiday synagogue services.

Ba-al Shem Tov*
Literally, "master of the good name," referring to Israel ben Eliezer, eighteenth-century founder of the Chasidic movement.

ba-al sihm-chaw
Also *ba-al sihm-cha*, ba-al sihm-chuh.*
Also spelled *bal simcha.*
1. A celebrant at a festivity.
2. An honoree.

ba-al t'fi-la*
Also *bal t'fi-luh, ba-al t'fi-law.*
Also spelled *baal tefillah.*
One who leads a group in prayer.

ba-al To-raw
Also *ba-al To-ra.**
Also spelled *bal Torah.*
1. Literally, "master of Torah," the equivalent of *ben Tora.*
2. A scholar.
3. A student.

ba-al t'shoo-vuh
Also *ba-al t'shoo-va.**
Also spelled *bal t'shuva.*
A returnee to the practice of Judaism.

ba-al tz'da-ka*
Also *ba-al tz'daw-kaw.*
Also spelled *bal tzedaka, baal tsedakah.*
A philanthropist, charitable person.

bab-kuh
Also spelled *bobke.*
A sweet cake, a coffeecake.

ba-choor*
Also *baw-choor.*

---

a as in father; aw as in law; ai as in aisle; ei as in neighbor; e as in bet; i as in vaccine; ih as in tin; o as in solar; oi as in void; oo as in food; u as in put; uh as in but; ch as in chutzpa; zh as in Zhivago.

Also spelled *bachur.*
1. A young man.
2. A *yeshiva* student.
3. An unmarried man.

badchan see *badchn*

bad-chaw-nihm
Also *bad-cha-nihm.**
Also spelled *badchanim.*
Plural of *badchn.* See below.

badchn
Also *bad-chan,** *bad-chawn.*
Also spelled *badchen.*
1. A professional jester or entertainer.
2. A master of ceremonies at Jewish weddings in Eastern Europe from the Middle Ages to modern times.

ba-dekn
Also spelled *badeken.*
1. Literally, "to cover."
2. Covering the bride with a veil before the wedding ceremony.

ba-geg-nen
Also *ba-geig-nen.*
To meet, to encounter.

bagel see *beigl*

ba-grawbn
Also *ba-groobn.*
1. To bury.
2. Buried, interred.

bailik see *beilihk*

bai mir bihst doo shein
Also spelled *bai mir bist du shayn.*
1. Literally, "to me you are beautiful."
2. The name of a popular Yiddish/English song of the 1930s.

bai mir poilst doo
It's agreeable to me; its O.K. with me.

bain in haltz see *bein ihn haltz*

---

a as in father; aw as in law; ai as in aisle; ei as in neighbor; e as in bet; i as in vaccine; ih as in tin; o as in solar; oi as in void; oo as in food; u as in put; uh as in but; ch as in chutzpa; zh as in Zhivago.

bais see *bet*

baitza see *beitza*

ba-kakt
1. Literally, "dirtied with feces."
2. All fouled up.

ba-kan-te
Also *ba-kan-tuh*.
An acquaintance.

ba-ka-sha*
Also *ba-koo-shuh*.
1. A supplication, plea, request.
2. A petitionary prayer that is part of the Sephardic High Holiday liturgy.

ba-kvem
Convenient, handy, comfortable.

bal see *baal*

bal-a-ba-tihsh
Also spelled *balebatish*.
Respectable, refined, well-mannered, decent.

bal-a-ba-tih-she Yihdn
1. Respectable Jews.
2. Sometimes, Jews of means.

balagoleh see *baal agala*

balebatihm see *balebaws*

balebatish see *balabatihsh*

bal-e-baws
Also *bal-e-boos*.
Also spelled *balebos*.
Derived from the Hebrew *baal habayiht.**
1. Literally, "head of the household, master of the house."
2. A landlord.
3. A male employer.
Balebawstuh (baleboostuh) is the feminine form.
Balebatihm is the plural form.

balebooste see *balebaws*

baleboste see *balebaws*

---

a as in father; aw as in law; ai as in aisle; ei as in neighbor; e as in bet; i as in vaccine; ih as in tin; o as in solar; oi as in void; oo as in food; u as in put; uh as in but; ch as in chutzpa; zh as in Zhivago.

bal gaivuh see *baal gaava*

bal maluchah see *baal m'lawchaw*

bal musaf see *baal moosawf*

bal shachrit see *baal shachriht*

bal simcha see *baal sihmchaw*

bal t'filuh see *baal t'fila*

bal Torah see *baal Toraw*

bal tzedaka see *baal tz'daka*

ban-diht
    1. A bandit.
    2. A mischievous child, a rascal.

bang
    1. Pain.
    2. Sorrow.

bang tun
    Regret, be sorry.

ban-kuhs
    Also spelled *bankes, bankis.*
    1. Cupping, in which a cup or glass was used (by doctors and also by barbers) in order to draw blood to the surface, presumably for remedial purposes.
    2. A useless activity, as in the expression, *es vet helfen vi a toiten bankuhs,* meaning "it will help as much as treating a dead man with *bankuhs* (cupping)."

bar
    1. The Aramaic word for the Hebrew *ben,* meaning "son."
    2. A contraction of *ben reb,* meaning "son of Mr. ———."

bar-a-ban
    A drum.

bar-chuhs
    Also spelled *barches.*
    The German word for *challa,* a Sabbath bread.

---

a as in father; aw as in law; ai as in aisle; ei as in neighbor; e as in bet; i as in vaccine; ih as in tin; o as in solar; oi as in void; oo as in food; u as in put; uh as in but; ch as in chutzpa; zh as in Zhivago.

ba-redn
>Also spelled *vareden;*
>1. Gossip.
>2. Backbiting.

barg
>A mountain.

ba-rihmr
>A braggart, a showoff.

Bar Mihtz-va*
>Also *Bar Mihtz-vuh, Bar Mihtz-vaw.*
>Also spelled *Bar Mitzva, Bar Mitzvah.*
>1. Literally, "son of the commandment," referring to a Jewish boy, aged 13, who is obligated to assume his place as an adult member of the Jewish religious community.
>2. Name of the ritual induction ceremony of a boy who has attained religious maturity, usually at age 13.

Bar Mitzvah see *Bar Mihtzva*

ba-ruch*
>Also *baw-ruch.*
>Also spelled *barukh.*
>1. Blessed.
>2. Praised.

ba-ruch Da-yan E-met*
>Also *baw-ruch La-yan T-mes;*
>Literally, "blessed is the true Judge (God)," an expression uttered upon hearing of a death. Also pronounced by the immediate family during the service at the funeral parlor or at the graveside.

ba-ruch Ha-Sheim
>Also *ba-ruch Ha-Shem,* baw-ruch Ha-Shem.*
>1. Literally, "blessed is the Name (God)"
>2. Thank God!

ba-ruch she-p'ta-ra-ni*
>Also *baw-ruch she-p'taw-ra-ni.*
>Literally, "blessed is He who freed me of my obligation," a prayer recited by the father of a Bar Mitzvah.

a as in father; aw as in law; ai as in aisle; ei as in neighbor; e as in bet; i as in vaccine; ih as in tin; o as in solar; oi as in void; oo as in food; u as in put; uh as in but; ch as in chutzpa; zh as in Zhivago.

barukh see *baruch*

ba-shert
Preordained, fated, inevitable.

Bas Mihtzva see *Bat Mihtzva*

batlan* see *batln*

bat-lawn-ihm Plural of *batlan*. See above.

batln
Also *bat-lan*, bat-lawn*.
1. A lazy person, a loafer, a good-for-nothing.
2. An alms-seeker in a synagogue.

Bat Mihtz-va*
Also *Bas Mihtz-va, Bas Mihtz-vuh*.
Also spelled *Bat Mitzva, Bat Mitzvah*.
1. Literally, "daughter of the commandment," the female equivalent of *Bar Mihtzva*.
2. The ceremony inducting girls into the Jewish fold.

ba-va
Literally, "a gate" in Aramaic.

ba-vaibt
Also spelled *baveibt*.
A married man.

baw-be see *buhbuh*

bawchoor see *bachoor*

bawd
Also *buhd*.
Also spelled *bod*.
1. A bath.
2. A bathhouse.

bawrd
Also spelled *bord*.
A beard.

baw-re-kes
Also spelled *borekes*.
Cheese-filled pastries popular among Sephardic Jews.

---

a as in father; aw as in law; ai as in aisle; ei as in neighbor; e as in bet; i as in vaccine; ih as in tin; o as in solar; oi as in void; oo as in food; u as in put; uh as in but; ch as in chutzpa; zh as in Zhivago.

bawrsht
>Also spelled *borscht, borsht.*
>A variety of soups, usually sweet-sour, the most popular of which are made of beets, cabbage, or spinach.

Bawrsht Belt
>Also spelled *Borsht Belt.*
>Name given to the Catskill Mountain area in New York State, where hotels cater to a preponderantly Jewish clientele and where many Jewish comedians got their start.

bawruch see *baruch*

bawruch Dayan Emes see *baruch Dayan Emet*

bawruch Ha-shem see *baruch Ha-Sheim*

bawruch shep'tawrani see *baruch shep'tarani*

bawr-vuhs
>Also *boor-ves.*
>Barefoot.

ba-yiht*
>Also *ba-yihs.*
>Also spelled *bayit, bayis.*
>A house, home.

bayis see *bayiht*

baylick see *beilihk*

bays see *bet*

bays chayim see *bet chayihm*

bays din see *bet dihn*

ba-zuchn
>1. To visit.
>2. To investigate.

b'chor*
>Also spelled *bechor.*
>Eldest male child in a family.

b'di-kat cha-metz*
>Also *b'di-kas cha-meitz.*
>Also spelled *bedikat chametz.*

---

a as in father; aw as in law; ai as in aisle; ei as in neighbor; e as in bet; i as in vaccine; ih as in tin; o as in solar; oi as in void; oo as in food; u as in put; uh as in but; ch as in chutzpa; zh as in Zhivago.

1. Literally, "searching for the leavened bread."
2. A ceremony held prior to Passover.

B.C.E.
Abbreviation for Before Common Era, used by
Jews instead of B.C., "Before Christ." See also C.E.

behema see *b'heima*

beigl
Also spelled *bagel*.
A hard-crusted roll shaped like a doughnut.

bei-lihk
Also *bei-lihg*.
Also spelled *bailik, baylick*.
The white meat of a fowl, usually of a chicken.

bein ihn haltz
Also spelled *bain in haltz*.
1. Literally, "a bone in the throat."
2. An obstruction, a nuisance.

beis see *bet*

beis chayihm see *bet chayihm*

beis din see *bet dihn*

beis hakneses see *bet hakneset*

beis hamedruhsh see *bet hamihdrash*

beis hamihkdawsh see *bet hamihkdash*

beis hatefilaw see *bet hat'fila*

beis medruhsh see *bet hamihdrash*

beis olawm see *bet olam*

bei-tza*
Also *bei-tzaw*.
Also spelled *baitza*.
1. An egg.
2. The name of one of the sixty-three tractates of
the Talmud.

beiz
Angry.

bei-zuh cha-yuh
Also spelled *beize chaye*.

---

a as in father; aw as in law; ai as in aisle; ei as in neighbor; e as in bet; i as in vaccine; ih as in tin; o as in
solar; oi as in void; oo as in food; u as in put; uh as in but; ch as in chutzpa; zh as in Zhivago.

1. Literally, "angry animal."
2. An angry person.
3. A disagreeable person.

beli naider see *b'li neidr*

ben
1. Son, son of.
2. Used to denote age, as in *ben chamishihm shana,* "50 years of age" (literally, "a son of 50 years").
3. Used to designate affiliation or status, as a person being a *ben Tora.*

Bar is the Aramaic form of *ben.*

ben To-ra*
Also *ben To-raw.*
Also spelled *ben Torah.*
Literally, "son of the Torah," a student of the Bible and Talmud. Synonymous with *baal Tora.*

bentshn
Also spelled *bentshen.*
1. To bless.
2. To pronounce a benediction.
3. Grace After Meals. Often Anglicized as "*bentshing.*"

bentshn lihcht
Also spelled *bentshen licht.*
Literally, "blessing the lights," pronouncing a prayer over the candles to usher in Sabbaths and holidays. Also referred to as *lihcht bentshn.*

beracha levatala* see *b'racha l'vatala*

ber-ches
A *chala,* a Sabbath bread.

bereshit see *b'reishiht*

bergl
A small mountain, a hill. A diminutive form of *barg.*

berit see *briht*

ber-yuh
Also spelled *berya.*

---

a as in father; **aw** as in law; **ai** as in aisle; **ei** as in neighbor; **e** as in bet; **i** as in vaccine; **ih** as in tin; **o** as in solar; **oi** as in void; **oo** as in food; **u** as in put; **uh** as in but; **ch** as in chutzpa; **zh** as in Zhivago.

1. A Yiddish form of the Hebrew *b'ria,* meaning "creature."
2. An efficient, skillful, competent homemaker.

bes medruhsh see *beis medruhsh*

beser see *besr*

besomim see *b'samihm*

besomim biksl see *b'sawmihm biksl*

besr
> Also spelled *beser.*
> Better.

bet*
> Also *beis.*
> Also spelled *bais, bays.*
> The second letter of the Hebrew alphabet, having the numerical value of two.

bet cha-yihm*
> Also *beis cha-yihm.*
> Also spelled *bays chayim.*
> 1. Literally, "house of life."
> 2. A euphemism for "cemetery."

bet dihn*
> Also *beis dihn.*
> Also spelled *bays din, beis din, beth din.*
> 1. Literally, "house of judgment."
> 2. A court.

bet-guh-vant
> Bedding.

bet ha-knes-et*
> Also *beis haknes-es.*
> 1. Literally, "house of assembly."
> 2. A synagogue.

bet ha-mihd-rash*
> Also *beis ha-med-ruhsh, beis ha-mihd-rawsh, beis med-ruhsh.*
> Also spelled *bet hamidrash.*
> 1. Literally, "house of study."
> 2. A study room, often in the synagogue.
> 3. A teachers' institute.

---

a as in father; aw as in law; ai as in aisle; ei as in neighbor; e as in bet; i as in vaccine; ih as in tin; o as in solar; oi as in void; oo as in food; u as in put; uh as in but; ch as in chutzpa; zh as in Zhivago.

bet ha-mihk-dash*
> Also *beis ha-mihk-dash, beis ha-mihk-dawsh.*
> Also spelled *bet hamikdash, beis hamikdash.*
> The Holy Temple, referring to the First and Second
> Temples in Jerusalem. The First Temple was de-
> stroyed in 586 B.C.E. by the Babylonians; the Sec-
> ond Temple was destroyed in 70 C.E. by the
> Romans.

bet ha-t'fila*
> Also *beis ha-te-fi-law.*
> Also spelled *bet hatefila, beth hatefila.*
> 1. Literally, "house of prayer."
> 2. A synagogue.

beth din see *bet dihn*

bet o-lam*
> Also *beis o-lawm.*
> 1. Literally, "eternal house."
> 2. A euphemism for "cemetery."

betoola see *b'toola*

betula see *b'toola*

b'ez-rat Ha-shem*
> Also *b'ez-ras ha-Shem.*
> Literally, "with God's help."

B.H
> An abbreviation for *b'ezrat Ha-Shem,* often used
> by traditional Jews on legal documents and on
> personal or business stationery.

b'hei-ma*
> Also *b'hei-maw.*
> Also spelled *behema.*
> 1. A beast.
> 2. A head of cattle.
> 3. An uncouth human being.
> 4. A fool.

bi-a*
> Also *bi-aw.*
> Sexual intercourse.

bialy see *b'yali*

---

a as in father; aw as in law; ai as in aisle; ei as in neighbor; e as in bet; i as in vaccine; ih as in tin; o as in solar; oi as in void; oo as in food; u as in put; uh as in but; ch as in chutzpa; zh as in Zhivago.

bih-d'eved
Literally, "after the fact." See also *lechatchilaw*.

bihl-bul
Also spelled *bilbul*.
1. A mixup.
2. Libel.

bihl-bul ha-dam*
Blood libel.

bih-lihg
Also *bih-lihk*.
Also spelled *bilig*.
Cheap, inexpensive.

bih-lihg vi borsht
Also spelled *bilig vi borscht*.
1. Literally, "as cheap as beet soup."
2. Very cheap.

bihmuh see *bima*

bihntl
Also spelled *bintl, bintel*.
A bundle, a batch. See also *bihntl brif*.

bihntl brif
Also spelled *bintel brief*.
1. A pack of letters.
2. The name of a column that appeared in the Yiddish newspaper *Forverts,* in which letters from readers were answered.

bihrkas Ko-ha-nihm see *birkat Kohanihm*

Bihr-kat Ei-roo-sihn*
Also *Bir-kas Ei-roo-sihn*.
Also spelled *Birkat Erusin*.
Betrothal blessings recited during the marriage ceremony.

Bihr-kat Ha-go-meil*
Also *Bir-kas Ha-go-meil*.
Also spelled *Birkat Hagomel*.
Literally, "Prayer of Thanksgiving," recited after recovery from a severe illness or accident or upon the safe return from a journey.

---

a as in father: aw as in law; ai as in aisle; ei as in neighbor; e as in bet; i as in vaccine; ih as in tin: o as in solar; oi as in void; oo as in food; u as in put; uh as in but; ch as in chutzpa: zh as in Zhivago.

Bihr-kat Ha-ma-zon*
Also *Bir-kas Ha-maw-zon.*
Also spelled *Birkat Hamazon.*
Grace After Meals.

Bihr-kat Ko-ha-nihm*
Also *Bir-kas Ko-ha-nihm.*
Also spelled *Birkat Kohanim.*
Priestly blessings uttered in Temple times and later incorporated into the prayerbook.

bihsl
Also spelled *bisl, bisel.*
1. Little bit.
2. Small amount.

bihs-lech-vaiz
A little bit at a time; little by little.
Also expressed as *tzoobihslach.*

bihst m'shu-guh?
Also spelled *bist meshuga?*
Are you crazy?

bihst oif ein fus?
1. Literally, "Are you (standing) on one foot?"
2. What's your hurry?

bih-te-re ge-lechtr
Also spelled *bittere gelechter.*
1. Literally, "bitter laughter."
2. Laughter through tears.

bih-tuh
Also spelled *bitte.*
1. Please.
2. Excuse me.

bihz hun-dert und tzvan-tzihg
Literally, "until one hundred and twenty (years)," said after mentioning a person's age and expressing the hope that one will live a long life.

bi-koor cho-lihm*
Also *bi-kur choi-lihm*
Also spelled *bikur cholim.*

---

a as in father; aw as in law; ai as in aisle; ei as in neighbor; e as in bet; i as in vaccine; ih as in tin; o as in solar; oi as in void; oo as in food; u as in put; uh as in but; ch as in chutzpa; zh as in Zhivago.

1. Literally, "visiting the sick."
2. An organization whose members visit the sick.

bi-koo-rihm
Also spelled *bikurim, bikkurim.*
First fruits brought to the Temple in Jerusalem in
Bible times.

bilbul see *bihlbul*

bilig see *bihligh*

bilig vi borscht see *bihlihg vi borsht*

BILU
1. An acronym for the biblical verse, *Beit Yaakov
l'choo v'neilcha,* "O House of Jacob, come and let
us go" (Isaiah 2:5).
2. The name of a movement organized in 1882 for
agricultural settlement and pioneering in Palestine.

bi-ma*
Also *bih-muh, bi-maw.*
Also spelled *bimah.*
1. A platform, a stage.
2. In a synagogue, the pulpit from which services
are conducted.

bintel see *bihntl*

bintel brief see *bihntl brif*

Birkas Hamawzon see *Bihrkat Hamazon*

Birkat Erusin see *Bihrkat Eiroosihn*

Birkat Hagomel see *Bihrkat Hagomeil*

Birkat Kohanim see *Bihrkat Kohanihm*

bisel see *bihsl*

bisl see *bihsl*

bist meshuga see *bihst m'shuguh*

bi-taw-chon*
Also *bi-ta-chon.*
1. Hope, faith.
2. Truth.

bitte see *bihtuh*

---

a as in father; aw as in law; ai as in aisle; ei as in neighbor; e as in bet; i as in vaccine; ih as in tin; o as in
solar; oi as in void; oo as in food; u as in put; uh as in but; ch as in chutzpa; zh as in Zhivago.

bittere gelechter see *bihtere gelechtr*
blat
> A sheet (of paper), a page. See also *bletl*.

blech
> 1. Tin.
> 2. A sheet of tin kept on the stove to keep food warm on the Sabbath.

bletl
> Also spelled *bletel*.
> 1. A page, a sheet (a diminutive form of *blat*).
> 2. The fine dough wrapping for blintzes or crepes.

blet-lach
> Plural of *blat* and *bletl*. See *blat* and *bletl*.

blihntz
> Also *blihntz-e*.
> Also spelled *blintz, blintzeh*.
> A crepe filled with cheese, potato, or fruit and then baked or fried. *Blihntzes (blintzes)* is the plural form.

b'li neidr
> Also *b'li nedr*.*
> Also spelled *beli naider*.
> Without taking a vow. A person makes a promise but excludes it from the category of a vow.

blintz see *blihntz*
blintzes see *blihntz*
blo
> Also *bloi*.
> Blue.

bloom
> Also *bloo-me*.
> Also spelled *blum*.
> A flower.

bloot
> Also spelled *blut*.
> Blood.

blote see *bluhte*

---

a as in father; aw as in law; ai as in aisle· ei as in neighbor; e as in bet; i as in vaccine; ih as in tin; o as in solar; oi as in void; oo as in food; u as in put; uh as in but; ch as in chutzpa; zh as in Zhivago.

bluhn-jen
Also spelled *blunjn.*
1. To ramble, wander.
2. To be mixed up in one's thinking, as in *ferblunjen.* See *ferblunjen.*

bluhte
Also spelled *blote.*
1. Mud, filth.
2. A mess.

bluhz-en foon zihch
Also *bluzn fun zihch.*
1. Literally, "to blow oneself up."
2. To be haughty.

bluhzn
Also *bluz-en.*
Also spelled *bluhzen.*
1. To blow
2. To be angry.

blum see *bloom*

blunjn see *bluhnjen*

blut see *bloot*

B'nai B'rith see *B'nei B'rith*
Preferred spelling by the international organization.

B'nai Yisrael see *B'nei Israel*

B'nei B'rith
Also *B'nei Brihs, B'nei Briht.**
Also spelled B'nai Brith, B'nai Bris, B'nai Brit.
1. Literally, "sons of the covenant."
2. An international Jewish fraternal organization founded in New York in 1843.

B'nei Is-ra-el
Also *B'nei Yihs-ra-eil, B'nei Yihs-ra-el.**
Also spelled B'nai Israel, B'nai Yisrael.
1. Literally, "Children of Israel."
2. The sons of the biblical Jacob, whose offspring became known as the "Children of Israel," also called the "tribes of Israel."

---

a as in father; aw as in law; ai as in aisle; ei as in neighbor; e as in bet; i as in vaccine; ih as in tin; o as in solar; oi as in void; oo as in food; u as in put; uh as in but; ch as in chutzpa; zh as in Zhivago.

3. The Jewish community in India, sometimes known as "the brown Jews of India."

B'not Is-ra-el
Also *B'nos Yihs-ra-eil, B'not Yihs-ra-el.**
Also spelled *B'not Yisrael, B'nos Yisrael.*
Literally, "Daughters of Israel." Plural of *Bat Mitzva.*

Bo-az
1. Literally, "with strength, strong."
2. Ruth's second husband (Ruth 2:1).
3. The name of one of the two pillars that held up the Temple in Jerusalem (the other was Jachin).

bobe see **buhbuh**

bobe meise see *buhbe maise*

Bobe Yachne see *Bube Yachne*

bobke see *babke* and *buhbkuh*

bobkes see *buhbkes*

bod see *bawd*

boich
Belly, abdomen.

boich vei-tihk
Also *boich vei-tihg.*
Also spelled *boich vaytik.*
Stomachache.

boi-dem
An attic.

boikr see *boker*

boi-tsihk
Also spelled *boitchik.*
A little boy. A Yiddishized diminutive form of "boy."

bo-ker*
Also *boikr.*
Morning.

bo-ker tov*
"Good morning," a greeting.

---

a as in father; aw as in law; ai as in aisle· ei as in neighbor; e as in bet; i as in vaccine; ih as in tin; o as in solar; oi as in void; oo as in food; u as in put; uh as in but; ch as in chutzpa; zh as in Zhivago.

bokser see *buhkser*

boobe see *buhbuh*

bool-be
>Also spelled *bulba, bulbe.*
>Potato.

bool-ka-lach
>Also spelled *bulkalach.*
>Little rolls. Plural of *boolke.*

bool-ke
>Also spelled *bulke, bulken.*
>A roll.

bool-van
>Also spelled *bulvan.*
>A rude person, a boor.

boor-e-kes
>Also *bur-e-kes, bur-e-kus.*
>Beets.

boortsh
>1. Complain.
>2. Protest.
>See also *boortshn.*

boortshn
>Also spelled *boortchen, burtchen.*
>To grumble, mutter, complain.

boorves see *bawrvuhs*

boosha see *busha*

bord see *bawrd*

borekes see *bawrekes*

borscht see *bawrsht*

Borsht Belt see *Bawrsht Belt*

borves see *bawrves*

bra-cha*
>Also *braw-chaw.*
>Also spelled *beracha, berakha.*
>A blessing, a benediction.

---

bra-cha l'va-ta-la*
> Also *b'raw-chaw l'va-taw-law.*
> Also spelled *beracha levatala.*
> A wasted blessing, an unnecessary blessing.

branfn
> Also *brawnfn.*
> Also spelled *branfen, bronfen.*
> Whiskey, liquor.

brav
> Brave, bold.

(a) brawch
> Also spelled *(a) broch.*
> 1. A break, a fracture.
> 2. A curse, equivalent to "hell!" or "damn!"

brawchaw see *beracha*

brawchaw l'vatawlaw see *bracha l'vatala*

(a) braw-chaw oif dain kuhp
> 1. Literally, "(a) blessing on your head."
> 2. God bless you.

(a) brawch tzoo mihr
> Also spelled *(a) broch tzu mir.*
> 1. Literally, "a curse to me."
> 2. Woe is me!

brawnfn see *branfn*

brech a foos
> Also *brech a fus.*
> Break a foot (leg)!

brechn
> Also spelled *brechen.*
> 1. Break.
> 2. Vomit.

breingn
> Also spelled *breingen, brengen.*
> To bring, fetch. See also *(a) farbrengung.*

brei-ra*
> Also *brei-raw, brei-ruh.*
> A choice, option, alternative.

---

a as in father; aw as in law; ai as in aisle; ei as in neighbor; e as in bet; i as in vaccine; ih as in tin; o as in solar; oi as in void; oo as in food; u as in put; uh as in but; ch as in chutzpa; zh as in Zhivago.

(a) brei-ruh hawb ihch?
> Do I have a choice?

brei-shiht*
> Also *b'rei-shihs.*
> Also spelled *bereshit.*
> 1. Literally, "in the beginning."
> 2. The first word in the Bible.
> 3. The name of the first *sidra* (section) and of the first book (Genesis) of the Bible.

brei-ter vi lein-ger
> 1. Literally, "wider than longer."
> 2. A fat person.
> 3. A big smile.

bren
> Burn.

(a) bren
> 1. Literally, "a burn."
> 2. An energetic person, one always on the go.

bren-en
> 1. Burn (fire).
> 2. Heartburn.

brengen see *breingn*

brent
> Past tense of *brenen,* as in *es brent a fire,* "a fire is raging," or *es brent mihr oonteren hartzen,* "I have heartburn." See also *brenen.*

brief see *brif*

brif
> Also spelled *brief.*
> A letter.

brihs see *briht*

Brihs Milaw see *Briht Mila*

brihst see *broost*

briht*
> Also *brihs.*
> Also spelled *brit, bris, berit.*
> 1. Covenant.
> 2. Abbreviated form of *Briht Mila.* See *Briht Mila.*

---

a as in father; aw as in law; ai as in aisle; ei as in neighbor; e as in bet; i as in vaccine; ih as in tin; o as in solar; oi as in void; oo as in food; u as in put; uh as in but; ch as in chutzpa; zh as in Zhivago.

Briht Mila*

>   Also *Brihs Milaw*.
>   Also spelled *Brit Mila*.
>   1. Literally, "covenant of circumcision."
>   2. A ritual circumcision performed on the eighth day after the birth of a Jewish boy in which the child becomes a part of the Jewish people.

bris see *briht*

brit see *briht*

broch see *brawch*

(a) broch tzu mir see *(a) brawch tzoo mihr*

broi-ges

>   1. Angry.
>   2. Sullen.
>   3. Insulted, offended.

broin

>   Brown.

broit

>   Bread.

broit-ge-ber

>   1. Literally, "breadgiver."
>   2. Breadwinner.
>   3. Head of the family.

bronfen see *brawnfn*

broodr

>   Also *bru-der*. *Brider* is the plural form.
>   1. Brother.
>   2. Buddy.

broost

>   Also *brihst*.
>   Also spelled *brust*.
>   1. Breast.
>   2. Breast of beef.

broost dekl

>   Also spelled *brust dekel*.
>   Breast of beef, brisket.

bruder see *broodr*

---

a as in father; aw as in law; ai as in aisle; ei as in neighbor; e as in bet; i as in vaccine; ih as in tin; o as in solar; oi as in void; oo as in food; u as in put; uh as in but; ch as in chutzpa; zh as in Zhivago.

brust see *broost*

brust dekel see *broost dekl*

b'sa-mihm*
>Also *b'saw-mihm.*
>Also spelled *besomim, besamim.*
>Spices, usually those placed in the spicebox used at the *Havdala* ceremony on Saturday night.

b'saw-mihm biksl
>Also spelled *besomim biksl.*
>Spicebox.

b'sula see *b'toola*

b'too-la*
>Also *b'soo-law.*
>Also spelled *betula, b'sula, betoola.*
>1. A young woman.
>2. A girl.
>3. A virgin, a maiden.

bub see *buhb*

bubbe see *buhbuh*

bu-be-le
>A term of endearment.

bubke see *buhbke*

buch
>A book.

buhb
>Also *bub.*
>A bean. See also *buhbkuh.*

buh-be mai-se
>Also *bu-be mai-se.*
>Also spelled *bobe meise.*
>1. Literally, "a grandmother's story."
>2. An old wives' tale.

Buh-be Yach-ne
>Also spelled *Bobe Yachne, Bube Yachne.*
>The name of a witch in a play by Abraham Goldfaden (1840-1908), father of the Yiddish theater. See *Yachne.*

---

a as in father: aw as in law; ai as in aisle; ei as in neighbor; e as in bet: i as in vaccine: ih as in tin: o as in solar: oi as in void; oo as in food; u as in put; uh as in but; ch as in chutzpa: zh as in Zhivago.

buhb-kes
>Also spelled *bubkes, bobkes.*
>Plural of *buhbkuh.*
>1. Beans.
>2. Something worthless, a trifle.

buhb-kuh
>Also spelled *bubke, bobke.*
>A bean. See also *buhb.*

buh-buh
>Also *baw-be, buh-be, boo-be.*
>Also spelled *bobe, bube, bubbe.*
>1. Grandmother.
>2. Old lady.

buhd see *bawd*

buhksr see *bukser*

buhm-er-ke
>Also spelled *bummerkeh.*
>1. An evil woman.
>2. A prostitute.

buk-ser
>Also spelled *bokser.*
>Carob, St. John's bread.

bulba see *boolbe*

bulkalach see *boolkalach*

bulkeh see *boolke*

bulvan see *boolvan*

bummerkeh see *buhmerke*

burekes see *boorekes*

burtchen see *boortshn*

burtsh see *boortsh*

bu-sha*
>Also *boo-sha, bu-shuh, bu-shaw.*
>Shame, disgrace.

b'va-ka-sha*
>Also *b'va-kaw-shaw.*
>Please; if you please.

---

a as in father; aw as in law; ai as in aisle· ei as in neighbor; e as in bet; i as in vaccine; ih as in tin; o as in solar; oi as in void; oo as in food; u as in put; uh as in but; ch as in chutzpa; zh as in Zhivago.

b'ya-li
>Also *bi-a-li.*
>Also spelled *bialy.*
>A flat hard roll.

C

Cabbalah see *Kabala*

caftan* see *kaftan*

canary
> A popular Anglicized form of *kein ayin hara.*

campote see *kampot*

C.E.
> Abbreviation for Common Era. Used by Jews instead of the Latin A.D., *Anno Domini,* "in the year of the Lord." See also B.C.E.

Cha-bad
> 1. An acronym formed from the initials of *cha-chma* (wisdom), *bina* (understanding), and *dei'a* or *daat* (knowledge).
> 2. A chasidic sect founded in Russia by Shneour Zalman of Ladi (Liady).

chacham see *chawchm*

chag
> Also spelled *hag.*
> A holiday.

chai
> 1. Literally, "life."
> 2. A charm worn on a neckchain, consisting of the two Hebrew letters *chet* and *yad,* considered by some to bring good luck.

chala see *chaluh*

chalav Yisrael see *chawlawv Yihsrawel*

chale see *chaluh*

cha-lef*
> Also *cha-luhf.*
> 1. A knife used by a *shochet* (ritual slaughterer).
> 2. A butcher knife.

---

a as in father; aw as in law; ai as in aisle; ei as in neighbor; e as in bet; i as in vaccine; ih as in tin; o as in solar; oi as in void; oo as in food; u as in put; uh as in but; ch as in chutzpa; zh as in Zhivago.

cha-ler-yuh
>Also *cha-ler-ye.*
>Also spelled *cholera, cholerya.*
>1. Literally, "cholera," a plague.
>2. A curse.

(a) cha-ler-yuh zawl dihr chapn
>Also spelled *a chalerye zol dir chapen.*
>1. May you be struck by cholera!
>2. May the plague get you!

chalesh see *chaluhsh*

cha-li-la*
>Also *chaw-li-law.*
>Also spelled *cholileh.*
>God forbid!

chalila v'chas see *chawlilaw v'chas*

cha-li-tzuh
>Also *cha-li-tza,* cha-li-tzaw.*
>Also spelled *halitza* and *halitzah.*
>A religious ceremony by which an unmarried brother is freed from the biblical obligation of marrying his brother's childless widow. The procedure is detailed in Deuteronomy 25:5-10.

cha-lootz*
>Also spelled *halutz.*
>1. Literally, "pioneer."
>2. A pioneer who settled in Palestine between the 1880s and the establishment of the State of Israel in 1948.

cha-loo-tza*
>Also spelled *chalutza, halutza, chalootzah.*
>Feminine form of *chalootz,* "a pioneer." See *chalootz.*

cha-loo-tzihm*
>Also spelled *chalutzihm, halutzim.*
>Plural of *chalootz.* See *chalootz.*

cha-lootz-i-yoos
>Also *cha-lutz-i-yut.**
>Also spelled *halutziyut.*

---

a as in father; aw as in law; ai as in aisle; ei as in neighbor; e as in bet; i as in vaccine; ih as in tin; o as in solar; oi as in void; oo as in food; u as in put; uh as in but; ch as in chutzpa; zh as in Zhivago.

"The pioneer spirit" in the Land of Israel before the creation of the State in 1948.

cha-loo-tzot*
> Also *cha-loo-tzos.*
> Also spelled *halutzot.*
> Plural of *chalootza.* See above.

chaloshes see *chaluhshes*

cha-luh
> Also *cha-la,* *cha-law,* *cha-le.*
> 1. A Sabbath loaf, a braided white bread.
> 2. The priest's share of the dough in Temple times.
> 3. A tractate of the Talmud.

chaluhf see *chalef*

cha-luhsh
> Also *cha-lesh.*
> From the Hebrew *chalash,** meaning "weak, faint."

cha-luh-shes
> Also spelled *chaloshes.*
> 1. Weakness, faintness, feebleness.
> 2. Something obnoxious.

chalutz see *chalootz*

chalutza see *chalootza*

chalutzihm see *chalootzihm*

chalutziyut see *chalootziyoos*

chalutzot see *chalootzot*

chamalyeh see *chmalye*

chametz see *chawmetz*

chametzdihg see *chawmetzdihg*

cha-mihn
> A synonym for *cholent* used by Sephardim. See *cholent.*

cha-mor*
> 1. Literally, "a jackass, a donkey."
> 2. A fool.

---

a as in father; aw as in law; ai as in aisle; ei as in neighbor; e as in bet; i as in vaccine; ih as in tin; o as in solar; oi as in void; oo as in food; u as in put; uh as in but; ch as in chutzpa; zh as in Zhivago.

cha-ni-fuh
> Also *cha-ni-faw* and *cha-ni-fa.**
> Also spelled *chanife.*
> Flattery.

cha-noo-kas ha-ba-yihs
> Also *cha-nu-kat ha-ba-yit.**
> Also spelled *hanukat habayit.*
> 1. Literally, "dedication of the house."
> 2. Housewarming.

cha-noo-ki-yaw
> Also *cha-noo-ki-ya.**
> Also spelled *hanukia.*
> A special nine-branched candelabrum *(menora)* equipped with cups to hold oil or candles. Used on the eight days of Chanuka. The ninth candle is the server *(shamash)* used to light the other candles.

Cha-nu-ka
> Also *Cha-noo-kaw, Cha-noo-ka.**
> Also spelled *Hannuka, Hanuka, Hanukah, Hanuk-kah, Chanukah.*
> A Jewish holiday that usually falls in the month of December, commemorating the victory of the Maccabees in 165 B.C.E. over the Syrian-Greek rulers of Palestine in a struggle for their religious freedom. Celebrated for eight days beginning with the twenty-fifth day of the Hebrew month Kislev.

Cha-nu-ka gelt
> Also *Cha-noo-ka gelt, Cha-noo-kaw gelt.*
> Also spelled *Chanukah gelt, Hanukah gelt, Hanuk-kah gelt.*
> Literally, "Chanuka money," distributed as gifts during the Chanuka festival.

chap
> Also *chapn*
> To catch, to grab.

chap a gang
> 1. Literally, "Catch a walk!"
> 2. Beat it! Go away!

---

a as in father; aw as in law; ai as in aisle; ei as in neighbor; e as in bet; i as in vaccine; ih as in tin; o as in solar; oi as in void; oo as in food; u as in put; uh as in but; ch as in chutzpa; zh as in Zhivago.

chap a-rain
1. Literally, "to grab in."
2. To take advantage of a situation.

chapn see *chap*

chapn a me-tzi-uh
Also spelled *chapen a metziye.*
Literally, "to grab a bargain," to get a bargain.

chap niht
1. Literally, "Don't grab!"
2. Take it easy! Not so fast!

cha-ro-ses
Also *cha-roi-ses, cha-ro-set.**
Also spelled *haroset.*
A paste –made from wine, nuts, apples, and spices—served at the Passover Seder, symbolic of the mortar used by the Hebrew slaves in Egypt to make bricks for their masters.

chasan see *chawsn*

Cha-san B'rei-shihs
Also *Cha-tan Be-rei-shiht,* Cha-san B'rei-shit.*
Also spelled *Chatan B'reshit.*
1. Literally, "Bridegoom of the Beginning."
2. Title given to the man awarded the honor of reading the Tora and/or reciting the Tora blessing for the reading of the first chapter of Genesis (Breshit) on Simchat Tora.

Cha-san To-ruh
Also *Cha-tan To-ra,* Cha-san To-raw.*
1. Literally, "Bridegroom of the Torah."
2. Title given to the man chosen to read the concluding section of the Book of Deuteronomy at the Simchat Tora service.

chasene see *chasuhnuh*

chaser deia see *chuhsr deiuh*

chasid see *chuhsihd*

cha-si-dei Ash-ke-naz
Also spelled *hasidei Ashkenaz.*

---

a as in father; aw as in law; ai as in aisle: ei as in neighbor; e as in bet; i as in vaccine; ih as in tin; o as in solar; oi as in void; oo as in food; u as in put; uh as in but; ch as in chutzpa; zh as in Zhivago.

1. A pietist movement among Jews of medieval Germany.
2. Members of the movement.

cha-si-dei oo-mos haw-o-lawn
> Also *cha-si-dei oo-mot ha-o-lam.**
> Literally, "the righteous among the nations of the world," used particularly in modern times to describe Gentiles who aided Jews during the Holocaust.

chasihd see *chuhsihd*

cha-sihd-ihzm
> Also *ha-sihd-ihzm.*
> Also spelled *chasidism, hasidism.*
> 1. A religious movement revolving around the person of Israel Baal Shem Tov in the first half of the eighteenth century.
> 2. Popular mysticism.
> Often capitalized.

cha-suh-nuh
> Also *cha-se-ne, cha-too-na,** *cha-soo-naw.*
> A wedding.

chas v'chaw-li-luh
> Also *chas v'chaw-li-law, chas v'cha-li-la.**
> God forbid! Perish the thought!
> The same as *chaw-li-law v'chas,* except in reverse form.

chas v'shaw-luhm
> Also *chas v'shaw-lom, chas v'sha-lom.**
> God forbid!

chatan see *chawsn*

chatchke see *tzatzke*

chatoona see *chasuhnuh*

chatshke see *tzatzke*

Cha-tzi Ka-dihsh
> Also spelled *Hatzi Kaddish, Chatzi Kaddish.*
> Literally, "half Kaddish," a short form of the full Kaddish. See *Kadihsh.*

chaver see *chawvr*

---

a as in father; aw as in law; ai as in aisle; ei as in neighbor; e as in bet; i as in vaccine; ih as in tin; o as in solar; oi as in void; oo as in food; u as in put; uh as in but; ch as in chutzpa; zh as in Zhivago.

cha-ve-ra*

Also *cha-vei-raw.*
Also spelled *havera.*
Feminine of *chaver.* See below.

cha-voo-ra*

Also *cha-voo-raw.*
Also spelled *chavura, chavurah, havura.*
1. A friendship cluster.
2. A small group organized to celebrate Jewish holidays and traditions, usually without a rabbi. The first such group organized in Somerville, Massachusetts, in 1968.

chawchm

Also *cha-cham,** *chaw-chawm.*
1. A wise person, a sage.
2. Sarcastically, a "wise guy."
3. The title of the spiritual leader of a Sephardic congregation or community.

chawch-me

Also *chuch-muh, chawch-maw, chawch-muh, chach-ma.**
Also spelled *chochma, hokhma.*
1. Wisdom.
2. A witty saying, a joke.
3. A facetious remark.

chawchm einr

Also spelled *chawchawm einer.*
1. A wise guy.
2. A fool.

chaw-lawv Yihs-raw-el

Also *cha-lav Yis-ra-el.**
1. Literally, "milk of Israel."
2. Milk that has been processed under the scrutiny of a qualified Jewish supervisor.

chaw-lent

Also *cho-lent.*
A Sabbath dish of meat, beans, peas, and other ingredients cooked before sunset on Friday and kept hot until ready to be eaten on Saturday, to avoid violating the Sabbath by cooking.

---

a as in father; aw as in law; ai as in aisle; ei as in neighbor; e as in bet; i as in vaccine; ih as in tin; o as in solar; oi as in void; oo as in food; u as in put; uh as in but; ch as in chutzpa; zh as in Zhivago.

chawlilaw see *chalila*

chaw-li-law v'chas see *chas v'chawliluh*

chaw-metz
Also *cha-metz,* *chaw-meitz.*
Also spelled *chometz, hametz.*
1. Leavened food.
2. Food or utensils not kosher for Passover.

chaw-metz-dihk
Also *chaw-metz-dihg.*
Also spelled *chometzdig, chometzdik.*
The adjectival form of *chametz.* See *chametz.*

chawsawn see *chawsn*

chawseir deiaw see *chuhsr deiuh*

chaw-shevr mentsh
Also spelled *choshever mensh.*
A prominent person, a celebrity.

chawsihd see *chuhsihd*

chawsn
Also *cha-san, cha-tan.**
Also spelled *chawsen.*
Bridegroom.

chawsn ka-luh
Also *chaw-sawn ka-law, cha-tan ka-la.**
Bridegroom and bride.

chawsn ka-luh mazl tuhv
Also *chaw-sawn ka-law ma-zawl tov, cha-tan ka-la
ma-zal tov.**
Literally, "Bridegroom and bride: congratulations!"

chawvr
Also *chaw-veir, cha-ver.**
Also spelled *haver.*
1. A friend.
2. A comrade, colleague, member of a group.

chaw-zawk see *chazak*

cha-ye
Also *cha-ya,* *cha-yaw, cha-yuh.*

---

1. An animal.
2. A feminine personal name.

cha-yihm
Also spelled *chayim, hayim, hayyim.*
Plural of *chai,* "life." A masculine personal name.

Cha-yihm Yank-kel
Also spelled *Chaim Yankel, Chaim Yonkil.*
1. A combination of two very ordinary names.
2. A non-entity.
3. A nobody.

chayn see *chein*

cha-zak*
Also *chaw-zawk.*
1. Strong.
2. Be strengthened!
3. A strong person.

cha-zak cha-zak v'nihs-cha-zeik
Literally, "Be strong and you will be strengthened!" Repeated by the congregation as the reading of each of the Five Books of Moses is completed in the synagogue.

chazak u'va-ruch*
Also *cha-zak u'ba-ruch.*
Literally, "Be strong and blessed!" Used by Sephardim to express congratulations.

chazan see *chazn*

cha-za-nihm*
Also spelled *chazanim, chazonim.*
Cantors. Plural of *chazan.*

cha-za-niht
Also spelled *chazanit, hazanit.*
A woman cantor. See also *chazntuh.*

cha-zaw-ras ha-shatz
Also *cha-za-rat ha-shatz.**
Literally, "repetition of the *Amida* [by the reader]."

cha-ze-rai
Also *cha-zuh-rai.*

    1. Pig-like food, distasteful food, junk food.

    2. A mess, filth, anything rotten or unpalatable.

(a) cha-zihr-she tawg

    1. Literally, "a piggish day."

    2. A miserable day.

chazir see *chazr*

chazn

    Also *cha-zan,** *cha-zawn.*

    Also spelled *hazan, chazzen.*

    A male cantor, also referred to as a *shaliach tsibur.*

chazn-tuh

    Also *chazn-te.*

    1. A cantor's wife.

    2. A woman cantor. See also *chazaniht.*

chazr

    Also *cha-zir.**

    1. A pig.

    2. A person who behaves like a pig, a glutton.

(a) chazr blaibt a chazr

    1. Literally, "once a pig always a pig."

    2. One doesn't change easily.

chazuhrai see *chazerai*

chazzen see *chazn*

cheidr

    Also *che-der.**

    Also spelled *heder.*

    1. A room.

    2. An elementary Jewish school.

cheilv

    Also *chei-lev, che-lev.**

    Fat (of an animal).

chein

    Also *chen.**

    Also spelled *chayn.*

    Grace, charm.

chei-nev-dihk

    A person who exudes charm.

---

a as in father; aw as in law; ai as in aisle; ei as in neighbor; e as in bet; i as in vaccine; ih as in tin; o as in solar; oi as in void; oo as in food; u as in put; uh as in but; ch as in chutzpa; zh as in Zhivago.

chei-rem
>   Also spelled *cherem, herem.*
>   Excommunication, ostracism.

cheit
>   Also *chet.**
>   Also spelled *het.*
>   1. A sin.
>   2. A transgression.

chelev see *cheilv*

Chelm
>   A fictitious town inhabited by foolish people.

cherem see *cheirem*

ches
>   Also *chet.**
>   The eighth letter of the Hebrew alphabet.

che-sed
>   Also spelled *hesed.*
>   Favor, grace, benevolence.

cheshbn
>   Also *chesh-bon.**
>   Reckoning, computation, accounting.

chesh-bon ha-ne-fesh*
>   1. Literally, "inventory of the soul."
>   2. Soul-searching, taking spiritual inventory.

Cheshvn
>   Also *Chesh-van.**
>   Also spelled *Heshvan.*
>   The eighth month of the Jewish religious calendar,
>   second of the Civil, corresponding to October-
>   November. Also called *Mar-Cheshvn,* "bitter
>   *Cheshvn,*" because it is a month in which there are
>   no Jewish holidays.

chesron see *chisawroin*

chet see *ches* and *cheit*

chev-ruh
>   Also *chev-ra,** *chev-raw.*
>   1. A group.
>   2. A club, fellowship, association.

---

a as in father; aw as in law; ai as in aisle; ei as in neighbor; e as in bet; i as in vaccine; ih as in tin; o as in solar; oi as in void; oo as in food; u as in put; uh as in but; ch as in chutzpa; zh as in Zhivago.

Chev-ruh Che-sed V'e-mes
Also *Chev-ra Che-sed V'e-met.**
1. Literally, "Society of Benevolence and Truth," a
euphemism for Burial Society. The name of volunteer burial societies among Sephardic Jews
(of Iberian and Middle Eastern descent), similar
to the Ashkenazic *Chevruh Kadishuh.*

Chev-ruh Ka-di-shuh
Also *Chev-ra Ka-di-sha.**
Also spelled *Hevra Kaddisha.*
Literally, "Sacred Society."
General name for a volunteer burial society in
Ashkenazic (European Jewish) communities.

Chev-ruh Shas
Also spelled *Chevra Shas.**
A Talmud study group.

Chev-ruh T'h-lihm
Also spelled *Chevra Tehilim.**
A group devoted to reading or studying the Book of
Psalms.

chi-lool ha-Sheim
Also *chi-lul ha-Shem.**
Also spelled *hilul haShem.*
1. Literally, "profanation of the [Divine] Name."
2. Blasphemy.

chi-lool Shab-bes
Also *chi-lul Sha-baws, chi-lul Shabuhs, chi-lul Sha-
bat.**
Also spelled *hilul Shabbat.*
Literally, "desecration of the Sabbath."

chi-saw-roin
Also *chi-sa-ron,** *ches-ron.*
A flaw, defect, deficiency.

(a) chi-saw-roin, di ka-le iz tzoo shein
1. Literally, "The bride's defect is that she is too
beautiful," used sarcastically.
2. An unwarranted complaint.

chlaw-pe
Also spelled *chloppeh.*

---

a as in father; aw as in law; ai as in aisle; ei as in neighbor; e as in bet; i as in vaccine; ih as in tin; o as in
solar; oi as in void; oo as in food; u as in put; uh as in but; ch as in chutzpa; zh as in Zhivago.

    1. To rain in torrents.
    2. A downpour.

Chmel-nihtz-ki's yaw-ren
    1. Literally, "Chmelnitzki's years," a reference to
    the seventeenth-century Ukrainian anti-Semite.
    2. Long ago.

chochma see *chawchme*

cho-desh
    Also spelled *hodesh*.
    Month.

choi-tei
    Also *cho-tei*.*
    A sinner.

choi-tei oo-poi-shei
    An outrageous sinner.

choi-zek machn
    Also *choi-zihk ma-chen*.
    To ridicule, to poke fun.

cholent see *chawlent*

cholerya see *chaleryuh*

Chol Ha-mo-eid
    Also spelled *Chol Hamoed*,* *Hol Hamoed*.
    The intermediary days of Passover and Sukkot.

cholileh see *chalila*

chometz see *chawmetz*

choo-kas ha-go-yihm
    Also *chu-kat ha-goyim*.*
    1. Literally, "the custom (or law) of the nations."
    2. A practice forbidden to Jews (Leviticus 20:23).

choolem see *chulm*

choopa see *chupuh*

choorban see *choorbn*

choor-ban ba-yihs ri-shon
    Also *choor-ban ba-yit ri-shon*.*
    Literally, "destruction of the First Temple."

---

a as in father; aw as in law; ai as in aisle; ei as in neighbor; e as in bet; i as in vaccine; ih as in tin; o as in solar; oi as in void; oo as in food; u as in put; uh as in but; ch as in chutzpa; zh as in Zhivago.

choor-ban ba-yihs shei-ni
> Also *choor-ban ba-yit shei-ni.*
> Literally, "destruction of the Second Temple."

choor-ban beis ha-mihk-dawsh
> Also *chur-ban bet ha-mik-dash*.
> Literally, "destruction of the Temple."

choorbn
> Also *choor-ban.*
> Also spelled *churban, hurban.*
> 1. Literally, "destruction."
> 2. Specifically, destruction of the First and Second
>   Temples in Jerusalem.

chootz la-a-retz*
> 1. Literally, "outside of the land (of Israel)."
> 2. Countries of exile.
> 3. The Diaspora.

chootz-pe-nihk
> Also spelled *chutzpenik.*
> An impudent person.

chootz-puh
> Also *chootz-pa,* *chootz-paw.*
> Also spelled *chutzpa, hutzpa.*
> Gall, impudence, nerve, impertinence.

choshever mensh see *chawshevr mentsh*

chotei see *choitei*

chrawpe see *chruhpuh*

chrawpn
> To snore.

chrein
> Also spelled *chrain, chrayn.*
> Horseradish.

chremzl
> Also spelled *chremzel, chremsl.*
> A pancake, usually made of potato or matzo meal.

chrupuh
> Also *chraw-pe.*
> Snore.

---

a as in father; aw as in law; ai as in aisle; ei as in neighbor; e as in bet; i as in vaccine; ih as in tin; o as in solar; oi as in void; oo as in food; u as in put; uh as in but; ch as in chutzpa; zh as in Zhivago.

chuchmuh see *chawchem*

chuhn-te
> A prostitute.

chuh-sihd
> Also *cha-sihd, chaw-sihd, cha-sid.**
> Also spelled *hasid.*
> 1. A pietist, a very pious person.
> 2. A fan, a buff, a follower of an ideology.
> 3. In the first and second centuries, one of the militants who were fiercely anti-Roman.
> 4. A follower of the eighteenth-century Israel Baal Shem Tov in Eastern Europe.
> Often capitalized.

chuhsr dei-uh
> Also *chaw-seir dei-aw, cha-ser dei-a.**
> 1. Literally, "deficient of judgment."
> 2. Insane.
> 3. Feebleminded.

chukat hagoyim see *chookas hagoyihm*

chulm
> Also *choo-lem, cha-lom.**
> A dream.

chulmen
> Also *choo-lem-en.*
> To dream.

Chumash see *Chumuhsh*

Chu-muhsh
> Also *Chu-mash.**
> Also spelled *Chumesh, Humash.*
> The Pentateuch, the Five Books of Moses.

chu-puh
> Also *chu-pe, choo-pa,** *choo-paw, choo-pe.*
> Also spelled *huppa, hupaw.*
> 1. A bridal canopy.
> 2. The wedding ceremony.

churban see *choorban*

chutzpa see *chootzpuh*

---

a as in father; aw as in law; ai as in aisle; ei as in neighbor; e as in bet; i as in vaccine; ih as in tin; o as in solar; oi as in void; oo as in food; u as in put; uh as in but; ch as in chutzpa; zh as in Zhivago.

chutz-pe-dihk
> 1. An audacious person.
> 2. Brazen.

chutzpenik see *chootzpenihk*

cloistr
> Also *clois-ter*.
> A church.

Cohen see *Kohein*

Con-ver-so
> Spanish for Jews and Moors who converted to Christianity under duress during the Inquisition in fifteenth-century Spain and Portugal.

cronkite see *krankhait*

D

dai-ge
>Also *da-a-ga**
>1. Worry.
>2. Concern.
>3. Anxiety.

(a) dai-ge hawb ihch
>1. I should worry!
>2. I couldn't care less!

dai-ge nihsht
>Don't worry!

Daitsh
>Yiddish for *Deutsch,* meaning "German."

da-let*
>Also *da-lihd.*
>Fourth letter of the Hebrew alphabet.

dam briht*
>Also *dam brihs.*
>Literally, "blood of the covenant," referring to the
>rite of circumcision.

Dan
>1. The northermost city of biblical Israel.
>2. A son of Jacob.
>3. One of the twelve tribes.

(a) dank
>Thanks!

(a) dank aich
>Thank you!

dankn
>Also spelled *danken.*
>To thank someone.

dar
>1. Thin, slender.
>2. Dried (fruit).

---

darfn
> Also spelled *darfen.*
> To need, require.

dar-kei shaw-lom
> Also *dar-kei sha-lom.***
> Literally, "ways of peace."
> See also *mipnei darkei shalom.*

dar oond kvar
> Thin and haggard.

dar-shan*
> Also *dar-shawn, dar-shuhn.*
> A preacher. *Darshanim* is the plural form.

dar-shan-ihm
> Also spelled *darshanim.*
> The plural of *darshan.* See above.

darshn
> Also spelled *darshenen.*
> To preach.

davn
> Also *da-ven.*
> To pray.

dav-nen
> Also *dav-en-en.*
> To pray.

Daw-ner-shtihg
> Also *Daw-ner-shtihk.*
> Thursday.

dawrf
> Also spelled *dorf.*
> A village.

dawrsh-tig
> Also *dawrsh-tik.*
> Thirsty.

daws gelt ihz tze-roon-en ge-vawr-en
> 1. Literally, "the money trickled out."
> 2. The money went down the drain (wasted).

daws hartz hawt mihr ge-zawgt
1. Literally, "my heart told me."
2. I predicted it.

daws ihz altz
That's all.

da-yan*
Also *da-yawn*.
Also spelled *dayyan, dayen*.
A judge. *Dayanim* is the plural form.

dayanim
Plural of *dayan*. See above.

(a) dei-uh hawbn
Also *(a) dei-a ha-ben*.
To have an opinion.

de-rech a-gav
Incidentally, by the way.

de-rech e-retz
1. Literally, "way of the land."
2. Respect, courtesy, politeness, decency, good manners.

der Ei-ber-shter ge-loibt
To praise God, thank God.

der-nihd-er-ihken
To embarrass someone.

der-shtihkt zawlst doo ve-ren
You should only choke!

devar Torah see *d'var Tora*

devekut see *d'veikoot*

d'harg-et
Killed, was killed.

Diaspora
An English word for the Hebrew *gawloos* or *galut.**
1. The dispersion of Jews to countries outside the Land of Israel.
2. The location of Jews living outside Israel.

dibbuk see *dihbook*

---

di e-me-se s'choi-re
>   1. Literally, "the true merchandise."
>   2. The real thing.

di Far-ein-ihg-te Felk-er
>   The United Nations.

di Far-ein-ihg-te Shtatn
>   The United States.

dih-book
>   Also spelled *dybuk, dybbuk, dibbuk.*
>   1. Literally, "to cleave, to hold to."
>   2. In Jewish folklore, the spirit of a dead person that enters the body of a living person and assumes control over it.
>   3. In Jewish mysticism, a soul condemned to wander the world because of its sins.

dihn
>   Also spelled *din.*
>   1. Judgment.
>   2. Law.
>   3. Jewish religious law.

dihn To-raw
>   Also *dihn To-ra.**
>   Also spelled *din Torah.*
>   1. Literally, "judgment of the Torah."
>   2. Arbitration of a dispute according to rabbinic law.

dihv-rei To-raw
>   Also *dihv-rei To-ra.**
>   Also spelled *divre Torah.*
>   1. Literally, "words of Torah."
>   2. A brief Torah-study session.

din see *dihn*

di-na d'mal-choo-ta di-na*
>   Also *di-naw d'mal-choo-saw di-naw.*
>   Literally, "the law of the land is the law."

dingn
>   Also spelled *dingen.*
>   1. Rent, lease.

---

a as in father; aw as in law; ai as in aisle; ei as in neighbor; e as in bet; i as in vaccine; ih as in tin; o as in solar; oi as in void; oo as in food; u as in put; uh as in but; ch as in chutzpa; zh as in Zhivago.

2. To bargain.

3. Hire, engage.

divre Torah see *dihvrei Toraw*

doochn
> Also *du-chan.**
> Also spelled *duchen.*
> 1. The platform in front of the Holy Ark in the synagogue.
> 2. Ceremony in which Jews of priestly (Aharonic) descent mount the synagogue platform to pronounce the Priestly Benediction at religious services (popularly referred to as *duchening).*

doom kawp
> Literally, "dumb head," dunce.
> From the German *"Dumkopf."*

doo-nam*
> Also *doo-nawm.*
> Also spelled *dunam.*
> A plot of land approximately one-quarter of an acre.

dorf see *dawrf*

draikop see *dreikawp*

dreidl
> Also spelled *draydl, dreidel, dredel.*
> A four-sided top used on the Chanuka holiday.

drei-en
> To turn, twist.

drei-en a kawp
> 1. Literally, "to turn one's head."
> 2. To confuse someone.
> 3. To annoy someone.

drei-en miht dem tzoong
> 1. Literally, "twisting with one's tongue."
> 2. To hem and haw.

drei-en mihtn gruh-ben fihn-ger
> 1. Literally, "to twist with one's thick finger [thumb]."

a as in father; aw as in law; al as in aisle; ei as in neighbor; e as in bet; i as in vaccine; ih as in tin; o as in solar; oi as in void; oo as in food; u as in put; uh as in but; ch as in chutzpa; zh as in Zhivago.

2. To force an argument.

3. To infer something unwarranted.

drei-kawp

Also spelled *draikop, dreikop, draykop.*

1. Literally, "twist-head."

2. Scatterbrain.

3. Busybody.

drei mihr niht kein kawp

1. Literally, "Don't turn my head."

2. Don't confuse me!

3. Don't pester me!

drei zihch

1. Literally, "turn yourself."

2. Keep moving!

drek

1. Feces, manure, excrement, "crap."

2. Inferior merchandise or work.

3. Insincere talk or excessive flattery.

drerd

A contraction of *der erd,* meaning "the earth."

(ihn) drerd main gelt

1. Literally, "My money is in the earth."

2. My money is lost.

(ihn) droisen ihz a glihtsh

Literally, "It's slippery outside."

duchan see *doochn*

dunam see *doonam*

d'var To-ra*

Also *d'var To-raw.*

Also spelled *devar Torah.*

1. Literally, "a word of Torah."

2. A Torah lesson.

3. A study session.

d'vei-koot*

Also *d'vei-koos.*

Also spelled *d'vekut, devekut.*

1. Literally, "attachment, adhesion."

2. Devotion to and communion with God.

---

a as in father; aw as in law; ai as in aisle; ei as in neighbor; e as in bet; i as in vaccine; ih as in tin; o as in solar; oi as in void; oo as in food; u as in put; uh as in but; ch as in chutzpa; zh as in Zhivago.

dybbuk see *dihbook*
dzhlob see *zhlawb*

E

edel see *eidl*

edelkeit see *eidlkait*

efn
> Also spelled *efen*.
> Open.

ef-nen
> To open.

efshr
> Also *ef-shar,* ef-shawr*.
> Also spelled *efsher*.
> Perhaps, maybe, possibly.

(der) Ei-bihsh-ter
> Also *der Ih-ber-shter*.
> 1. Literally, "the Most High."
> 2. God.

eidelkait see *eidlkait*

eidem see *eidm*

eides zawgn see *eiduhs zawgen*

eidl
> Also spelled *edel, aydel*.
> 1. Courteous, refined, genteel, polite.
> 2. Sometimes used sarcastically, as in *eidl ge-patchket,* meaning "overparticular, perfectionist."

eidl-kait
> Also spelled *eidelkait, edelkeit, aidelkait*.
> Gentility.

eidm
> Also *ei-duhm*.
> Also spelled *eidem, aidem, aydem*.
> Son-in-law.

---

eidm oif kest
> Literally, "a son-in-law who boards," referring to one who continues his studies while being supported by his in-laws.

ei-duhs zawgen
> Also spelled *eides zawgen, eidus zogen.*
> Testify, bear witness.

ei-er kih-chel
> Also *ai-er kih-chel.*
> Egg biscuit.

ei-ge-ne bloot oon fleish
> Also *ai-ge-ne blut oon flaish.*
> 1. Literally, "one's own blood and flesh."
> 2. A relative.

Ei-li-ya-hoo Ha-na-vi*
> Also *Ei-li-yaw-hu Ha-naw-vi.*
> Also spelled *Eliahu Hanavi.*
> Elijah the Prophet.

Eil Maw-lei Ra-cha-mihm
> Also *El Ma-le Ra-cha-mihm.**
> 1. Literally, "God abundant in compassion."
> 2. The memorial prayer recited at funerals, unveilings, and on special occasions in the synagogue.

eilt zich see *ailt zihch*

einbren see *ainbren*

einfahl see *ainfal*

eingemachts see *aingemachts*

eingeshpart see *aingeshpart*

eingetunken see *aingetoonken*

einhore see *ain hawre*

ein klein-ih-keit
> Also *ain klain-ih-kait.*
> Also spelled *ein kleinikait.*
> 1. Some trifle!
> 2. Is that so!
> 3. Wow!

---

a as in father; aw as in law; ai as in aisle; ei as in neighbor; e as in bet; i as in vaccine; ih as in tin; o as in solar; oi as in void; oo as in food; u as in put; uh as in but; ch as in chutzpa; zh as in Zhivago.

ein oond ein-tsih-ke
1. Literally, "a one and only."
2. A rarity.
3. An only child

ein-red-e-nihsh see *ainredenihsh*

Ein Sof
Also *En Sof.**
1. Literally, "without end."
2. Eternal.
3. A kabbalistic reference to a hidden aspect of God.

eins, tsvei, drai, fir see *ains, tsvai, drai, fir*

ei-ruv
1. The "mixing" (literally) of that which is permitted and that which is prohibited on the Sabbath. By a symbolic action, that which is generally prohibited on the Sabbath becomes permissible.
2. In popular usage, the term refers to an enclosure created around a given area in the public domain in order that individuals may carry on the Sabbath.

ei-ruv tav-shi-lihn
1. Literally, "the merging (mixture) of foods."
2. A religious procedure to enable one to prepare food on a holiday when the Sabbath follows immediately after the holiday.

ei-sek
Also *e-sek.**
1. Business.
2. Occupation.
3. Dabbling.
4. Involvement.

ei-shes cha-yihl
Also *ei-shet cha-yihl.**
Also spelled *eshet chayil.*
1. Literally, "woman of valor" (Proverbs 31:10).
2. The proverbial Jewish woman, respected for her devotion to husband and family.

---

a as in father; aw as in law; ai as in aisle; ei as in neighbor; e as in bet; i as in vaccine; ih as in tin; o as in solar; oi as in void; oo as in food; u as in put; uh as in but; ch as in chutzpa; zh as in Zhivago.

ei-tzuh
> Also *ei-tza.**
> Also spelled *ai-tze.*
> Advice, counsel.

ei-ver
> Also *e-ver.**
> 1. Appendage (part of the body), limb.
> 2. Penis (slang).

eizl
> Also spelled *eizel.*
> 1. Literally, "a goat."
> 2. A fool.

ek velt
> 1. Literally, "the edge of the earth."
> 2. The other side of the world.
> 3. Far away.

El Male Rachamim see *Eil Mawlei Rachamihm*

E-lo-hihm
> Also spelled *Elohim*
> God.

E-lool
> Also spelled *Elul.*
> Sixth month of the Jewish religious calendar, the twelfth and final month of the Civil calendar, corresponding to August-September.

e-mes
> Also *e-met**
> Truth.

(der) e-mes ge-shprawch-en
> 1. Literally, "the truth was spoken."
> 2. The absolute truth.

emet see *emes*

En Sof see *Ein Sof*

e-puhs
> Also spelled *epes, eppes.*
> 1. Something, somewhat.
> 2. An interjection used for emphasis.

---

a as in father; aw as in law; ai as in aisle: ei as in neighbor; e as in bet; i as in vaccine; ih as in tin; o as in solar; oi as in void; oo as in food; u as in put; uh as in but; ch as in chutzpa; zh as in Zhivago.

er
> He, him.

erd
> Earth, ground. See also *drerd,* a combination of *der* (the) and *erd* (earth).

er est vi nuhch a krenk
> Literally, "he eats like one who just recovered from an illness," that is, heartily.

E-retz Yihs-raw-eil
> Also *E-retz Yis-ra-el.**
> The Land of Israel.

e-rev*
> Also *e-ruhv.*
> Evening.

e-rev Sha-bes
> Also *e-rev Sha-baws, e-rev Sha-buhs, erev Sha-bat.**
> Sabbath Eve (Friday at sundown).

e-rev Yom Tov
> The eve of a holiday.

er far-macht niht daws moil
> 1. He doesn't close his mouth.
> 2. He doesn't stop talking.

es
> 1. It.
> 2. Eat.

esen see *esn*

es far-drihst mihr
> 1. It saddens me.
> 2. It disturbs me.

es felt a bihsl fefr
> 1. Literally, "Some pepper is missing."
> 2. It's not just right.
> 3. It's bland.

es felt a bihsl seichel
> 1. Literally, "Some brains are lacking."
> 2. Reference to a stupid person.

---

a as in father; aw as in law; ai as in aisle; ei as in neighbor; e as in bet; i as in vaccine; ih as in tin; o as in solar; oi as in void; oo as in food; u as in put; uh as in but; ch as in chutzpa; zh as in Zhivago.

es felt a bihsl zaltz
>   1. Literally, "Some salt is missing."
>   2. It's not just right.
>   3. It's bland.

es ge-zoonte heit
> Also spelled *es gezunte hait.*
>   1. Literally, "Eat in a healthy condition."
>   2. Eat hearty! Enjoy your meal!

eshet chayil see *eishes chayihl*

es-ihg
> Also *es-ihk.*
> Vinegar.

es-ihg fleish
> Also spelled *esig flaish.*
>   1. Literally, "vinegar meat."
>   2. A stew with vinegar as one of its ingredients.

es main kihnd
> Also spelled *es mein kind.*
> Literally, "Eat, my child!"

esn
> Also *es-en.*
>   1. To eat.
>   2. Food.

esn teg
> Also spelled *esen teg.*
> Literally, "eating days," referring to *Yeshiva* (seminary) students of Eastern Europe who ate in different homes.

esn vi a chazr
> Also spelled *esen vi a chazer.*
> To eat like a pig.

esn vi a ferd
> To eat like a horse.

esn vi nawch a kihm-piht
>   1. Literally, "to eat like one who just got over a pregnancy."
>   2. To eat like a glutton.

---

a as in father; aw as in law; ai as in aisle; ei as in neighbor; e as in bet; i as in vaccine; ih as in tin; o as in solar; oi as in void; oo as in food; u as in put; uh as in but; ch as in chutzpa; zh as in Zhivago.

esn vi nawch a kreink
1. Literally, "to eat like one after an illness."
2. To eat heartily.

es past niht
1. It's not suitable.
2. It's not fitting.

es ret zihch a-zoi
1. Literally, "It speaks that way."
2. It seems that way.
3. So it says (I don't believe it).

es-rihg
Also *es-rog, et-rog.**
Also spelled *esrig*.
A citron, used on the Sukkot holiday.

esrog see *esrihg*

essn see *esn*

etrog see *esrihg*

ez-ras naw-shihm
Also *ez-rat na-shim.**
Women's section in an Orthodox synagogue.

---

a as in father; aw as in law; ai as in aisle; ei as in neighbor; e as in bet; i as in vaccine; ih as in tin; o as in solar; oi as in void; oo as in food; u as in put; uh as in but; ch as in chutzpa; zh as in Zhivago.

F

fahrdrayen see *fardreien*

(a) fai-er zawl ihm trefn
> Also spelled *a feier zol im trefen.*
> 1. Literally, "A fire should happen to him."
> 2. Let him disappear!

faifn
> Also spelled *feifen, faifen.*
> To whistle.

faifn oif
> 1. Literally, "to whistle on (at) someone."
> 2. To show contempt.

faifn oifn yam
> Also spelled *feifen oifen yam.*
> 1. Literally, "to whistle on the ocean."
> 2. To waste breath, to waste effort.

faifr
> Also spelled *feifer, fifer.*
> One who whistles.

faigel see *feigel*

faigele see *feigele*

faind
> Also spelled *faint, feind.*
> Enemy, foe.

faind hawbn
> Also *faint hawbn.*
> Also spelled *feind hoben.*
> To hate, loathe, abhor.

faind krihgn
> Also spelled *faint krign, feint krigen.*
> To hate, abhor, dislike, detest.

fain-kuchn
> Also spelled *fainkuchen, feinkuchen.*

---

1. Literally, "fine cooking."
2. An omelet.

fain-shmekr
Also spelled *fainshmeker, feinshmeker.*
1. Literally, "fine-sniffing."
2. Elite, uppity.

faint see *faind*

Falashas
Dark-skinned Jews who live in Ethiopia.

fangn uhn
Also spelled *fangen un.*
1. Literally, "to start in."
2. To begin.
3. To create a scene.
Also expressed in reverse: *uhn-fangn.*

fang shoin un
1. Literally, "Begin already!"
2. Stop procrastinating!

fangst shoin uhn?
Are you starting in again? Are you starting trouble
again?

fan-taz-yawr
A visionary, a dreamer.

far-ain
Also spelled *farein.*
1. From the German *verein,* "an organization."
2. A social group.
3. A club.

far-baitn di Yoitz-res
Also spelled *farbeiten di Yoitzruhs.*
1. Literally, "to confuse the *Yotzer* prayers" (part
of the morning prayer service), that is, to recite
them in the wrong order.
2. To mix things up.

far-baitn
Also spelled *farbaiten, farbeiten.*
1. To supplant, replace, exchange.
2. To mix up.

far-bihs-en
> Also spelled *farbissen.*
> Embittered, bitter, caustic, angry.

far-bihs-enr
> Also spelled *farbisener.*
> 1. An embittered person.
> 2. A mean person.

far-blun-jet
> Also spelled *farblonjet.*
> 1. Lost.
> 2. Misguided.
> 3. Bewildered, confused.

far-breing-en
> Also *far-braing-ung.*
> Also spelled *farbraingen, farbraingung.*
> 1. To get together, to celebrate
> 2. A Chasidic cultural and social gathering with
>   the *rebbe.*

far-brentr
> Also spelled *farbrenter.*
> 1. Literally, "a burnt one."
> 2. A devotee, disciple, fan.

far-dai-get
> 1. Worried, anxious.
> 2. Distressed.
> 3. Careworn.

far-dart
> Dried out, withered.

fardihnen
> Also spelled *fardinen.*
> 1. To earn.
> 2. To be deserving.

far-dih-nen a mihtz-vuh
> Also spelled *fardinen a mitzvah.*
> To earn (merit) a good deed.

far-dih-ner
> Also spelled *fardinr, fardiner.*
> A provider, breadwinner.

---

a as in father; aw as in law; ai as in aisle: ei as in neighbor; e as in bet; i as in vaccine; ih as in tin; o as in solar; oi as in void; oo as in food; u as in put; uh as in but; ch as in chutzpa; zh as in Zhivago.

fardraien see *fardreien*

far-draws
>Also *far-drus*.
>Also spelled *fardross*.
>1. Distress, annoyance.
>2. Chagrin, resentment. Used with *hawbn* (to have): *hawbn fardraws* or *fardrus*, "to be distressed."

far-drei-en
>Also *far-drai-en*.
>Also spelled *fardrayen, fardrehen*.
>1. To turn, twist.
>2. To distort, misrepresent.

far-drei-en a kawp
>Also spelled *fardrehen a kop*.
>1. Literally, "to twist a head."
>2. To confuse.

far-drei-e-nihsh
>1. A bothersome situation.
>2. Confusion created by another person.

far-drei zihch dain ei-ge-ne kawp
>1. Literally, "twist your own head."
>2. Drive yourself crazy!
>3. Don't bother me!

far-drihs
>Also *far-dris*.
>1. Hurt, irked, peeved, distressed.
>2. A sad situation.

far-drihsn
>Also *far-dris-en*.
>To aggravate, distress, as in *es fardrihst mihr*, "it distresses me."

fardross see *fardraws*

fardrus see *fardraws*

farein see *farain*

far-faln
>Also spelled *farfalen*.

---

a as in father; aw as in law; ai as in aisle; ei as in neighbor; e as in bet; i as in vaccine; ih as in tin; o as in solar; oi as in void; oo as in food; u as in put; uh as in but; ch as in chutzpa; zh as in Zhivago.

1. Doomed, lost.
2. Hopeless.

farfel see *farfl*

farfl
Also spelled *farfel*.
1. Broken-up pieces of *matza*.
2. Noodle dough chopped or grated into barley-like pieces.

far-foiln
Also spelled *farfoilen*.
Rotten, decayed, putrid.

far-froi-ren
Frozen.

far-ge-ni-gen
Also *far-ge-nihgn*.
A pleasure, delight.

far-gesn
Also spelled *fargesen*.
Forgotten.

far-gloost
Also *far-glust, far-gluhst*.
1. To desire.
2. To crave.

far-kawchn a ka-she
1. Literally, "to cook up a pot of *kashe* (buckwheat kernels)"
2. To cook up a storm.
3. To make a mess.

far-kert
1. Opposite.
2. Vice versa.
For emphasis *punkt farkert* is used. See *punkt farkert*.

far-kil-en
1. To cool.
2. To catch cold.

far-libt
Also *far-lihbt*.

---

a as in father; aw as in law; ai as in aisle; ei as in neighbor; e as in bet; i as in vaccine; ih as in tin; o as in solar; oi as in void; oo as in food; u as in put; uh as in but; ch as in chutzpa; zh as in Zhivago.

1. To fall in love with someone.
2. To fall in love with a thing.

far-mach daws moil
1. Literally, "shut your mouth."
2. Shut up!

far-machn
Also spelled *farmachen.*
To close, to shut.

far-matrt
Also spelled *farmatert.*
Weary, tired.

far-mihshn
Also spelled *farmishen.*
To mix up, confuse.

far-mihsh niht di Yoitz-res
1. Literally, "Don't mix up the prayers."
2. Don't mix things up.
See also *farbaiten di Yoitzres.*

far-mihsht
Mixed up, confused, befuddled.

far-mut-shet
Fatigued, exhausted, worn out.

far-nemt zihch
Beat it! Go away!

far-patsh-ket
Also spelled *farpotshket.*
1. Messed up.
2. Sloppy.
3. Mixed up.

far-pootzt
Also spelled *farputzt.*
1. Dressed up.
2. Adorned, decorated.

(a) far-shlep-te kreink
Also spelled *(a) farshlepte krenk.*
1. A drawn-out sickness.
2. A chronic condition.

---

a as in father: **aw** as in law; **ai** as in aisle; **ei** as in neighbor; **e** as in bet; **i** as in vaccine; **ih** as in tin; **o** as in solar; **oi** as in void; **oo** as in food; **u** as in put; **uh** as in but; **ch** as in chutzpa; **zh** as in Zhivago.

far-shmai-et
Busy, active.

far-shmai-e-ter
One who is always on the go.

far-shnawsh-ket
Drunk, tipsy.

far-shtawpt
Also spelled *farshtopt*.
1. Stuffed, cluttered, clogged.
2. Constipated.

far-shtawp-te kawp
1. Literally, "a clogged head."
2. Dumb, stupid.

far-shtei-en
To understand, comprehend.

far-shteist?
Do you understand?

farshtinken see *farshtoonken*

far-shtoonk-en
Also *far-shtin-ken*.
Also spelled *farshtunken*.
Stinking, smelly.

farshtopt see *farshtawpt*

far-shvihtzt
Also spelled *farshvitzt*.
Sweated, sweaty.

far-tihg
Also spelled *fartig*.
1. Ended, completed.
2. It's all over.

far-tih-ge-heit
1. In the end.
2. Eventually.

far-tshad-et
1. Confused.
2. Charmed, taken in.
3. Surprised.

---

a as in father; aw as in law; ai as in aisle: ei as in neighbor; e as in bet; i as in vaccine; ih as in tin; o as in solar; oi as in void; oo as in food; u as in put; uh as in but; ch as in chutzpa; zh as in Zhivago.

far-tutst
　　Bewildered, confused.

fartz
　　A fart.

fartzen see *fartzn*

fartzn
　　Also spelled *fartzen*.
　　To fart.

far-zawr-ger
　　Also spelled *farzorger*.
　　1. Literally, "a provider."
　　2. Head of the family.

far-zawrgn
　　Also spelled *farzorgen*.
　　1. To be concerned.
　　2. To be angry.
　　3. To be upset.

far-zooch-en
　　Also spelled *farzuchen*.
　　1. To examine.
　　2. To taste.

farzorgen see *farzawrgn*

fawdm
　　Also spelled *fawdem*.
　　A thread.

fawlg mihch a gang
　　1. Literally, "It follows me on a walk."
　　2. It's worthless, a waste of time.
　　3. Some distance!
　　Also expressed as *s'fawlgt* (or *es fawlgt*) *mihch a gang*.

fawlgn
　　Also spelled *folgn* and *folgen*.
　　1. To follow.
　　2. To obey.

fawlks-mensh
　　Also spelled *folks-mentsh*.

---

a as in father; aw as in law; ai as in aisle; ei as in neighbor; e as in bet; i as in vaccine; ih as in tin; o as in solar; oi as in void; oo as in food; u as in put; uh as in but; ch as in chutzpa; zh as in Zhivago.

1. Literally, "a folk-person," a folksy person.
2. An average person.

fawnfn
> Also spelled *fawnfen, fonfen.*
> 1. To speak with a nasal twang.
> 2. To mumble.
> 3. Double-talk.

fawnfn oon-ter
> Also spelled *fonfen unter.*
> To incite, instigate.

fawnfr
> Also spelled *fawnfer, fonfer, fuhnfr.*
> 1. One who speaks with a twang.
> 2. A mumbler, one who speaks unclearly.

fawr-shpais
> Also spelled *forshpeis.*
> An appetizer.

fawr-shtel-oong
> Also spelled *forstellung.*
> A performance, a play.

fawrt ge-zoont-er-heit
> Also spelled *fort gezunter hait.*
> 1. Literally, "travel in good health."
> 2. Have a good trip!

fawrt vaiter
> Also spelled *fort veiter.*
> 1. Literally, "travel further."
> 2. Move ahead! Go on!

fawr-vertz see *Forvets*

fawtr
> Also spelled *foter.*
> Daddy, father.

faygehleh see *feigele*

fe
> Also spelled *feh.*
> 1. An expression of distaste.
> 2. Phooey!

---

a as in father; **aw** as in law; **ai** as in aisle: **ei** as in neighbor; **e** as in bet; **i** as in vaccine; **ih** as in tin; **o** as in solar; **oi** as in void; **oo** as in food; **u** as in put; **uh** as in but; **ch** as in chutzpa; **zh** as in Zhivago.

fees-e-lach
> Also *fihs-e-lach.*
> Small feet.

fefr
> Also spelled *feffer.*
> Pepper.

feh see *fe*

(a) feier zol im trefen see *a faier zawl ihm trefn*

feifen see *faifn*

feifer see *faifr*

fei-gel see *feigl*

fei-ge-le
> Also spelled *faygeleh, faigele.*
> 1. Literally, "little bird."
> 2. A gay, a homosexual (slang).

feigl
> Also spelled *feigel, faigel.*
> A bird.

feilen
> 1. To fail.
> 2. To be missing.

feilt
> Past tense of *feilen,* as in *es feilt a bihsl zaltz,* "A bit of salt is missing."

fein see *fain*

feind see *faind*

feind hoben see *faind hawbn*

feinkuchen see *fainkoochen*

feinshmeker see *fainshmekr*

feint see *faind*

feint krigen see *faint krihgn*

feln
> Also spelled *felen.*
> 1. To be wanting.
> 2. Missing.

---

a as in father; aw as in law; ai as in aisle; ei as in neighbor; e as in bet; i as in vaccine; ih as in tin; o as in solar; oi as in void; oo as in food; u as in put; uh as in but; ch as in chutzpa; zh as in Zhivago.

fenstr
Also spelled *fenster*.
A window.

ferd
1. A horse.
2. A boor.
3. A fool.

fer-gihn-en
To begrudge.

fer-machn di moil
1. Literally, "Close the mouth."
2. Shut up!

fet
Fat, greasy.

fetr
Also spelled *feter*.
Uncle.

fifer see *faifr*

fih-lan-trup
A philanthropist.

fihnf
Also *fih-nef*.
Five.

(a) fihnfer
A fiver, a five-dollar bill.

(a) fihn-ste-ren sawf
1. Literally, "a dark ending."
2. (May you have) a miserable end (to your life).

(a) fihn-ste-re yawr
1. Literally, "a dark year."
2. A miserable year.

fihn-ster-nihsh
1. Darkness.
2. A plague, a curse.

fihnstr
Also spelled *finster*.
1. Dark.

---

a as in father; aw as in law; ai as in aisle; ei as in neighbor; e as in bet; i as in vaccine; ih as in tin; o as in solar; oi as in void; oo as in food; u as in put; uh as in but; ch as in chutzpa; zh as in Zhivago.

2. Sinister.
3. Bleak.
4. Foreboding.

fihnstr ihn di oi-gen
Also spelled *finster in di oigen.*
1. Literally, "dark in the eyes."
2. Faint, fainting.
3. Hopeless.

fihnstr oond glihtch-ihk
1. Literally, "dark and slippery."
2. Miserable.

fihselach see *feeselach*

flaishig see *fleishihg*

flaishik see *fleishihg*

flankn
Also spelled *flanken.*
1. A cut of meat from the side (flank) of the animal.
2. Short ribs.

fleish-e-dihg
A variant form of *fleishihg.* See *fleishihg.*

fleish-ihg
Also *fleish-ihk.*
Also spelled *flaishig, flaishik, flayshig.*
Meat or meat products as well as utensils that have been used in the preparation or serving of meat products. In contrast to *mihlchihk.* See *mihlchihk.*

fligel
Wing of fowl.

flihgn ihn nuhz
Also spelled *fligen in nuz.*
1. Literally, "flies in one's nose."
2. An uppity person.

floim
A plum.

fluden
Dessert made by alternating layers of thin pancakes *(crepes)* with a filling.

---

a as in father; aw as in law; ai as in aisle; ei as in neighbor; e as in bet; i as in vaccine; ih as in tin; o as in solar; oi as in void; oo as in food; u as in put; uh as in but; ch as in chutzpa; zh as in Zhivago.

foiln zihch
>Also spelled *foilen zich*.
>To be lazy.

foilr
>Also spelled *foiler*.
>A lazy person.

folgn see *fawlgn*

folksmentsh see *fawlksmensh*

fonfen see *fawnfn*

fonfer see *fawnfr*

foon
>Also spelled *fun*.
>From.

foon ai-er moil ihn Gawtz oi-ren
>1. Literally, "From your mouth into God's ears."
>2. May God hear you!

foon dest-veign
>Also spelled *fun destvegen*.
>1. Nevertheless, however.
>2. Still, yet.

foon va-nen
>Also *fun vanen*.
>From where?

foos
>Also spelled *fus*.
>Foot, leg.

forshpeis see *fawrshpais*

forstellung see *fawrshteloong*

fort gezunter hait see *fawrt gezoonterheit*

fort veiter see *fawrt vaiter*

Forverts
>A Yiddish newspaper founded in New York City in
>1897. Pronounced: *Fawr-vertz*. English: *Forward*.

foter see *fawtr*

fra-ge
>Question, query.

---

a as in father; aw as in law; ai as in aisle; ei as in neighbor; e as in bet; i as in vaccine; ih as in tin; o as in solar; oi as in void; oo as in food; u as in put; uh as in but; ch as in chutzpa; zh as in Zhivago.

frai
> Also spelled *frei*.
> 1. Free, no charge.
> 2. Not enslaved.

fraid see *freid*

frailich see *freilihch*

fraind
> Also spelled *freind*.
> Friend.

Frankists
> Followers of the Sabbatean pseudomessiah Joseph Frank (1726-1791), who eventually converted to Catholicism.

frask
> Also spelled *frosk*.
> A strong slap, usually in the face.

a frask ihn fressr
> Literally, "a smack in the eater (face)."

frau see *froi*

freg
> Ask, inquire

fregn
> Also spelled *fregen*.
> To ask.

frei see *frai*

freid
> Also spelled *fraid*.
> Happiness, delight, joy.

freilach
> 1. Happy, cheerful, merry.
> 2. A Jewish folk dance.

frei-lihch
> Also spelled *frailich*.
> Cheerful, merry.

freind see *fraind*

fremdr
> Also spelled *fremder*.

---

a as in father; aw as in law; ai as in aisle; ei as in neighbor; e as in bet; i as in vaccine; ih as in tin; o as in solar; oi as in void; oo as in food; u as in put; uh as in but; ch as in chutzpa; zh as in Zhivago.

1. A stranger
2. A foreigner, an alien.

fres

To eat like a glutton. See also *fresn*.

fresn

Also spelled *fresen*.
1. To devour.
2. To gorge oneself.

fresn vi a ferd

1. Literally, "to eat like a horse."
2. To gorge oneself.

fresr

Also spelled *fresser*.
1. A big eater.
2. A glutton.

frihtz

Also spelled *fritz*.
1. A novice.
2. A blockhead.

fri-shtihk

Also spelled *frishtik*.
Breakfast.

froi

Also spelled *frau*.
1. Woman.
2. Wife.

froocht

Also spelled *frucht*.
Fruit.

froom

Also spelled *frum*.
1. Devout, pious.
2. A religious person.

froom-ak

Also spelled *frumak*.
1. A hypocritically pious person
2. A hypocrite.

frosk see *frask*

---

a as in father; aw as in law; ai as in aisle; ei as in neighbor; e as in bet; i as in vaccine; ih as in tin; o as in solar; oi as in void; oo as in food; u as in put; uh as in but; ch as in chutzpa; zh as in Zhivago.

frucht see *froocht*

frum see *froom*

frumak see *froomak*

fuhnfn
>   Also spelled *funfen*.
>   1. To speak with a twang.
>   2. To mimic.
>   3. To mock.

fuhnfr see *fawnfr*

fun destvegen see *foon destveign*

funfen see *fuhnfn*

fun vanen see *foon vanen*

fus see *foos*

fussnogge
>   A jellied soup, usually garlic-flavored.

---

a as in father; aw as in law; ai as in aisle; ei as in neighbor; e as in bet; i as in vaccine; ih as in tin; o as in solar; oi as in void; oo as in food; u as in put; uh as in but; ch as in chutzpa; zh as in Zhivago.

G

ga-bai
> Also spelled *gabbai*.
> 1. A synagogue trustee or treasurer.
> 2. The fiscal head of a Jewish community.
> 3. A manager for Chassidic rabbis.
> 4. Originally, a dues collector.

Ga-lihtz-i-a-ner
> Also spelled *Glitzianer*.
> A Jew of Galician origin, as opposed to a *Litvak,* a Jew of Lithuanian origin. *Glitz* and *Glihtz* are short forms.

galoot see *gawlus*

galuptze see *holishkes*

galut see *gawluhs*

gam a-tem
> 1. Literally, "you too."
> 2. The same to you! A response to one who has been wished well.

gam zoo l'to-va*
> Also *gam zu le-to-vaw*.
> 1. Literally, "This also is for the best."
> 2. An expression addressed to one who has had an unpleasant experience.

ganef
> A distorted form of *ganuhv*. See *ganuhv*.

Gan Ei-den
> Also spelled *Gan Eden*.
> 1. Literally, "Garden of Eden."
> 2. Heaven, paradise.

(a) gang
> 1. Walk, gait.
> 2. An errand
> 3. A walkway, a path.

---

a as in father; aw as in law; ai as in aisle; ei as in neighbor; e as in bet; i as in vaccine; ih as in tin; o as in solar; oi as in void; oo as in food; u as in put; uh as in but; ch as in chutzpa; zh as in Zhivago.

gantz
> Entire, whole, all, complete.

(a) gantz-e ge-shihch-te
> 1. Literally, "a whole story."
> 2. A long, involved tale.
> 3. The entire matter.

(a) gantz-e mai-se
> Also spelled *gantze meiseh.*
> The entire story.

(a) gantz-e me-gih-luh
> Also spelled *a gantze megilla.*
> 1. Literally, "an entire scroll."
> 2. A whole, long story.

(a) gantz-er knakr
> 1. Literally, "a whole knocker."
> 2. A bigshot.

gantz-er mach-er
> 1. Literally, "a whole maker."
> 2. A bigshot.

gantz gut
> Quite good.

ga-nuhv
> Also *ga-nav,** *ga-nawv, ga-nef.*
> Also spelled *gonef, gonif.*
> 1. A thief.
> 2. A swindler.
> 3. A burglar.

ganz
> Goose.

ga-on see *gawon*

gartl
> Also spelled *gartel.*
> A silk waistband or sash worn by *Chasidim,* particularly during prayertime.

gas
> 1. A street.
> 2. A thoroughfare in the Jewish section of an East European town.

---

a as in father: aw as in law; ai as in aisle; ei as in neighbor; e as in bet: i as in vaccine: ih as in tin: o as in solar; oi as in void; oo as in food; u as in put; uh as in but; ch as in chutzpa; zh as in Zhivago.

gat-kes
> Also spelled *gotkes, gotkis.*
> Underwear.

gawld-e-ne
> Also spelled *goldene.*
> Golden.

gawld-e-ne cha-se-ne
> Also spelled *goldene chasseneh.*
> 1. Literally, "golden wedding."
> 2. Fiftieth wedding anniversary.

gawld-e-ne me-di-ne
> Also spelled *goldene medina, goldeneh medineh.*
> 1. Literally, "golden country."
> 2. The United States.

gawld-e-ne yawr-en
> 1. Literally, "golden years."
> 2. Old age.

gaw-luhs
> Also ga-lut*, ga-loot, gaw-loos.
> Also spelled *galus.*
> 1. Literally, "expulsion, dispersion."
> 2. The exile, the Diaspora.

gawl-yas
> 1. The Philistine giant slain by David (I Samuel 17:48-51).
> 2. A strong man.

gaw-on
> Also *ga-on.**
> 1. The head of an academy of higher learning in Babylonia in the post-Talmudic period.
> 2. An exceptionally erudite scholar.
> 3. A genius.
> *Geonim* is the plural form.

gawrgl
> Also spelled *gawrgel, gorgel.*
> 1. Throat, Adam's apple.
> 2. The neck of a chicken or other fowl.

---

a as in father; aw as in law; ai as in aisle; ei as in neighbor; e as in bet; i as in vaccine; ih as in tin; o as in solar; oi as in void; oo as in food; u as in put; uh as in but; ch as in chutzpa; zh as in Zhivago.

gawr-nihsht

Also spelled *gornisht*.
Nothing, nil.

gawr-niht

Also spelled *gornit*.
A variant form of *gawrnihsht*.
1. Nothing.
2. Absolutely nothing.

Gawt

Also spelled *Gott*.
God.

Gawt-en-yoo

Also spelled *Gottenyu*.
1. Oh God!
2. Dear God!

Gawt hiht up di na-a-raw-nihm

God watches out for fools.

Gawt ihn hihml

Also spelled *Gott in himmel*.
1. Literally, "God in heaven."
2. My God!

Gawt tsoo dankn

Also spelled *Gott tsu danken*.
Thank God!

Gawt veist

Also spelled *Gott vaist*.
1. Literally, "God knows."
2. God only knows!

Gawt vet shtrawfn

Also spelled *Gott vet shtrofen*.
God will punish!

Gawt zai dank

1. Literally, "God be thanked!"
2. God bless!

Gawt zawl up-hihtn

Also spelled *Gott zol uphiten*.
1. Literally, "God should protect!"

2. May God prevent!
3. God forbid!

gazln
Also *gaz-lawn, gaz-lan.***
Also spelled *gazlin, gazlen.*
A robber, crook, bandit.

ge-beks
Also *ge-baks.*
1. Something baked.
2. Pastry.

geben see *gebn*

ge-bensht
Blessed.

ge-bentsht miht kind-er
Literally, "blessed with children."

ge-bentsh-ter
A blessed person.

gebn
Also spelled *geben.*
Give.

gebn a klap
1. Literally, "to give a blow."
2. To hit someone or something.

gebn an ain haw-re
Also *gebn an ein haw-ruh.*
1. Literally, "to give an evil eye."
2. To nix someone by superfluous praise.

gebn shoi-ched
To bribe.

gebrattens see *gebrawtens*

ge-brawch-en-er Eing-lihsh
Also spelled *gebrochener English.*
1. Literally, "broken English."
2. English spoken with an accent.

ge-brawks
Also spelled *gebroks.*
A mixture of *matza* or *matza* meal and a liquid.

---

a as in father; aw as in law; ai as in aisle; ei as in neighbor; e as in bet; i as in vaccine; ih as in tin; o as in solar; oi as in void; oo as in food; u as in put; uh as in but; ch as in chutzpa; zh as in Zhivago.

ge-brawt-ens
> Also spelled *gebrottens, gebrattens.*
> Roasted meat.

ge-bren-te tzaw-res
> Also *ge-bren-te tzaw-ruhs.*
> 1. Literally, "incinerated troubles."
> 2. Utter misery.

gebroks see *gebrawks*

gebrottens see *gebrawtens*

ge-chrawp-et
> Also spelled *gechropet.*
> Snored.

ge-dacht
> 1. Thought.
> 2. Contemplated.
> 3. Imagined.

ge-dank
> A thought.

ge-dempt-e fleish
> Also *ge-demf-te flaish.*
> Also spelled *gedempte flaishe.*
> Stewed meat.

ge-denkn
> Also spelled *gedenken.*
> Remember.

gedihle see *gedule*

gedoold see *geduld*

ge-duld
> Also spelled *gedoold.*
> 1. Patience.
> 2. Temper.

ge-du-le
> Also *ge-dihle.*
> Also spelled *geduluh, geduleh.*
> 1. A great thing.
> 2. Something to exult about.
> 3. (Sarcastically) a big deal.

---

a as in father; **aw** as in law; **ai** as in aisle; **ei** as in neighbor; **e** as in bet; **i** as in vaccine; **ih** as in tin; **o** as in solar; **oi** as in void; **oo** as in food; **u** as in put; **uh** as in but; **ch** as in chutzpa; **zh** as in Zhivago.

ge-feln

Also spelled *gefelen*.
1. To suit, satisfy.
2. To appeal to, please.

ge-felt

Past tense of *gefelen,* as in *es gefelt mihr nit,* "I'm not satisfied."

(es) ge-felt mihr

It satisfies me. It pleases me.

ge-fer-lech

Also *ge-fer-lihch*.
Terrible, dangerous.

ge-fihlte fihsh

Also spelled *gefilte fish, gefulte fish*.
1. Literally, "stuffed fish."
2. A mixture of several varieties of fish chopped together and seasoned. Originally the mixture was stuffed into the head or the skin of the fish.

ge-fihlte helzl

Also spelled *gefilte helzel*.
1. Literally, "stuffed neck."
2. Stuffed derma.

ge-hak-te

1. Chopped.
2. Minced.

ge-hak-te Einglihsh

"Chopped" (broken) English.

ge-hak-te herring

Chopped herring.

ge-hak-te lebr

Also *ge-hak-te leibr*.
Also spelled *gehakter leber*.
Chopped liver.

ge-hak-te tzaw-res

Also *ge-hak-te tzaw-ruhs*.
Also spelled *gehakte tzores*.
1. Literally, "chopped troubles."

---

a as in father; aw as in law; ai as in aisle; ei as in neighbor; e as in bet; i as in vaccine; ih as in tin; o as in solar; oi as in void; oo as in food; u as in put; uh as in but; ch as in chutzpa; zh as in Zhivago.

2. Terrible troubles.
3. Utter misery.

ge-harg-et zawlst doo ver-en
1. Literally, "You should get killed!"
2. Drop dead!

ge-hargn
Also spelled *gehargen*.
Killed. *Derhargnen* is a variant form.

Ge-he-na
Also *Ge-hih-nom.**
Also spelled *Gehenna*.
1. Literally, "the Valley of Hinnom" (near Jerusalem).
2. Hell, inferno.

Gehihnom see *Gehena*

gei a-rois
Go out! Leave!

gei-en
Also *gein*.
1. Go.
2. Walk.
3. Function.

gei ge-zoont-er-heit
1. Literally, "Go in good health!"
2. Goodbye.

gei ihn drerd
1. Literally, "Go into the earth!"
2. Go to hell!

gein tzoo kihnd
Also spelled *gei-en tzu kind*.
1. Literally,"going to child."
2. Going into labor to give birth.

geit
The present tense of *geien,* as in *es geit mihr goot,* "things are going well."

geit es niht
1. Literally, "It doesn't go."
2. It doesn't work well.

ge-klih-be-ne verk
>1. Selected writings.
>2. Anthology.

ge-klihbn
>Also spelled *gekliben*.
>1. Selected, chosen.
>2. Gathered.

gel
>Yellow.

gelaimt see *geleimt*

ge-lasn
>Also spelled *gelassen*.
>1. Tender.
>2. Compassionate.
>*Gelashn* is a distorted form.

ge-lechtr
>Also spelled *gelechter*.
>Laughter.

ge-leimt
>Also spelled *gelaimt*.
>1. Numb.
>2. Paralyzed.

ge-lihb-te
>Also spelled *gelibte*.
>1. Sweetheart (feminine).
>2. Lover.

gelila see *gliluh*

ge-loint
>1. Worth it.
>2. Appropriate, suitable.

gelt
>Money, funds.

ge-malt
>Circumcised.

gemar tov see *gmar tov*

Gemara see *Gemawruh*

ge-mat-ria see *gihmatriyaw*

Ge-maw-ruh
> Also *Ge-ma-ra,** *Ge-maw-raw.*
> Also spelled *Gemarah.*
> 1. Literally, "completion."
> 2. The second part of the Talmud, that which is a commentary on the Mishna, the first part of the Talmud.
> 3. A designation for the whole of the Talmud.

ge-mihsh
> Also spelled *gemish.*
> Mixture.

ge-miht-lech
> Also spelled *gemitlech.*
> 1. Cozy.
> 2. Unhurried.

ge-mi-las che-sed
> Also *ge-mi-lat che-sed.**
> 1. Literally, "an act of kindness."
> 2. A good deed.
> 3. Jewish Free Loan society.

gemish see *gemihsh*

gemitlech see *gemihtlech*

ge-mut-shet
> 1. Suffering.
> 2. Tortured, tormented.
> 3. Inconvenienced.

ge-nawsn
> Also spelled *genawsen, genossen.*
> To sneeze, sneezed.

geneiva see *gneivuh*

geneivas daas see *gneivas daas*

geneivishe shtik see *gneivihshe shtihk*

geniza*
> Also *ge-ni-zaw.*
> 1. Literally, "hidden, stored away."
> 2. A storage place for sacred books and religious articles.
> 3. The Cairo Geniza, most famous of such deposito-

---

ries, was located (1896) in the Ben Ezra Synagogue in Fustat (Old Cairo) in Egypt.

genossen see *genawsn*

ge-nug
Enough, sufficient.

ge-nug shoin!
1. Literally, "Enough already!"
2. All right already!

geonim Plural of *gaon*. See *gaon*.

ge-oo-luh
Also *ge-oo-la*.*
Also spelled *geula*.
1. Redemption.
2. The arrival of the Messiah.

ger
1. A stranger.
2. A convert to Judaism.

ge-recht
1. Correct, right.
2. Fair, just.

ger tze-dek
1. Literally, "righteous stranger."
2. A sincere proselyte.

ge-rut
Conversion to Judaism.

ge-sel see *gesl*

ge-shat
1. Affected.
2. Damaged.

ge-sheft
Business

Ge-shem
A prayer for rain recited on Shemini Atzeret.

ge-shihch-te
Also spelled *geshichte*.
1. History.

2. A story.
3. A long narrative.

ge-shmak
Delicious, tasty.

ge-shmak-e
A very tasty dish.

geshrai see *geshrei*

ʒe-shrei
Also spelled *geshrai*.
A scream, yell, shout.

ge-shtank
Foul odor, stench.

ge-shtawr-ben
Also spelled *geshtorben*.
Deceased.

ge-shtroft
Cursed, punished.

ge-shvawln
Also spelled *geshvollen*.
1. Swollen, puffed up.
2. Haughty.

ge-shvoondn
Also spelled *geshvunden*.
Fainted.

gesl
Also *gas-el*
A diminutive form of *gas*.
1. A short street.
2. An alley.

gesundheit see *gezunthait*

get
A Jewish religious bill of divorcement.

geula see *geooluh*

gevald
A variant form of *gevalt*. See *gevalt*.

ge-vald-ihg
Terrible, awful. *Gevaldihk* is a variant form.

a as in father; aw as in law; ai as in aisle; ei as in neighbor; e as in bet; i as in vaccine; ih as in tin; o as in solar; oi as in void; oo as in food; u as in put; uh as in but; ch as in chutzpa; zh as in Zhivago.

ge-vald-ihg
> Terrible, awful.
> *Gevaldihk* is a variant form.

gevalt
> A cry of frustration, dismay, horror.
> *Gevald* is a variant form.

gevir see *gvihr*

gezl
> Also spelled *gezel.*
> Thievery, stolen merchandise.

ge-zunt
> Also spelled *gezoont, gesund, gesunt, gezund.*
> 1. Health.
> 2. Healthy.

(a) ge-zunt dirh ihn pu-pihk
> 1. Literally, "Good health to your belly button!"
> 2. Thanks for nothing!

(a) ge-zunte
> 1. A healthy person.
> 2. A strong person.

ge-zunt-er-heit
> Also spelled *gezunterhait.*
> Let it happen (or do it) in good health!

ge-zunt-hait
> Also spelled *gesundhait, gesundheit.*
> 1. Literally, "Good health to you!
> 2. God bless you!
> An expression used when one sneezes, originally to ward off evil spirits.

ge-zunt oif dain kawp
> 1. Literally, "Good health upon your head!"
> 2. More power to you!

ge-zunt vi a ferd
> 1. Healthy as a horse.
> 2. Strong as a horse.

gich see *gihch*

---

a as in father; aw as in law; ai as in aisle; ei as in neighbor; e as in bet; i as in vaccine; ih as in tin; o as in solar; oi as in void; oo as in food; u as in put; uh as in but; ch as in chutzpa; zh as in Zhivago.

gihb sihch a rihr
> 1. Literally, "Give yourself a move!"
> 2. Get a move on you!

gihb zihch a shawkl
> Also spelled *gib zich a shokl.*
> 1. Literally, "Give yourself a shake!"
> 2. Get a move on you!
> 3. Hurry up!

gihch
> Also spelled *gich.*
> Soon, fast, speedy, quick.

gihl-gul
> Also spelled *gilgul.*
> 1. Literally, "rolling, revolving."
> 2. A human being or animal into whom the soul of a deceased person may enter to atone for past sins.

gih-mat-ri-yaw
> Also *gih-mat-ri-ya.* *
> Also spelled *gimatriya, gematria.*
> From the Greek meaning "measurement."
> A form of cryptograph in which a word derives its meaning from the numerical value of its Hebrew letters. Widely employed by devotees of Kabbala.

gihml
> Also spelled *gimmel.*
> The third letter of the Hebrew alphabet.

gihtz see *gutz*

gilgul see *gihlgul*

gil-gul ne-sha-mot*
> Also *gil-gool ne-shaw-mos.*
> The reincarnation of souls.

gimatriya see *gihmatriyaw*

gimmel see *gihml*

gi-o-ret*
> Also *gi-o-res.*
> A female convert to Judaism.

---

a as in father; aw as in law; ai as in aisle; ei as in neighbor; e as in bet; i as in vaccine; ih as in tin; o as in solar; oi as in void; oo as in food; u as in put; uh as in but; ch as in chutzpa; zh as in Zhivago.

gi-tihn
>Also spelled *gittin, gitin.*
>1. The plural of *get.*
>2. A tractate of the Talmud.

glaich
>Also spelled *gleich.*
>1. Equal to.
>2. Like.
>3. Straight.

glaich-tzait-ihk
>Also spelled *gleichtseitik*
>Simultaneously.

glaich-vawrt
>Also spelled *gleichvort.*
>Witticism, wisecrack.

glaich-vertl
>Also spelled *gleichvertel.*
>A *bon mot,* a clever remark.

glat kawshr
>Also *glat ka-sher.*
>Also spelled *glatt kosher.*
>1. Literally, "smooth kosher," referring to an animal that has perfectly smooth lungs, as opposed to one that has lungs containing scar tissue. The latter is unacceptable to very Orthodox Jews.
>2. Used in recent years to indicate the highest degree of *kashrut.* See *kashrut.*

glawz
>Also spelled *gloz.*
>1. Glass.
>2. A drinking glass.

gleich see *glaich*

gleichtseitik see *glaichtzaitihk*

gleichvertel see *glaichvertl*

gleichvort see *glaichvawrt*

glez
>A glass.

---

a as in father; aw as in law; ai as in aisle; ei as in neighbor; e as in bet; i as in vaccine; ih as in tin; o as in solar; oi as in void; oo as in food; u as in put; uh as in but; ch as in chutzpa; zh as in Zhivago.

(a) glez-e-le tei
> A small glass of tea.

(a) gle-ze-le var-ems
> 1. Literally, "a glass of warmth."
> 2. Tea.

(a) glez tei
> A glass of tea.

glihk
> Also spelled *glick*.
> Good luck, good fortune.

(a) glihk hawt dihr ge-trawf-en
> Also spelled *(a) glick hot dir getrofen*.
> 1. Literally, "a bit of luck met up with you."
> 2. (Sarcastically) Big deal!

glihtsh-ihk
> Also spelled *glitshik*.
> Slippery.

Glihtz see *Galihtzianer*

gli-luh
> Also *gli-la,** *gli-law*.
> Also spelled *geliluh, gelila*.
> 1. Literally, "rolling up."
> 2. The final Torah honor, in which the recipient rolls the Torah scroll together, ties it with a special band, and then drapes the Torah mantle over it.

glitshik see *glihtshihk*

Glitzianer see *Galihtzianer*

gloib mihr
> Also spelled *gloib mir*.
> Believe me.

gloibn
> Also spelled *gloiben*.
> 1. Belief.
> 2. Conviction.
> 3. Faith.

gloz see *glawz*

---

a as in father; aw as in law; ai as in aisle; ei as in neighbor; e as in bet; i as in vaccine; ih as in tin; o as in solar; oi as in void; oo as in food; u as in put; uh as in but; ch as in chutzpa; zh as in Zhivago.

glustn
>Also spelled *glusten.*
>1. To lust.
>2. To desire, covet.

gmar tov
>Also spelled *gemar tov.*
>1. Literally "a happy conclusion."
>2. Yom Kippur holiday greeting (at the conclusion of the Days of Awe).

gnawsn
>Also spelled *genawsen, gnossen.*
>Sneezed.

gnawsn oifn e-mes
>1. Literally, "sneezed upon (about) the truth."
>2. Agreement or confirmation of a statement made.

gneiva see *gneivuh*

gnei-vas da-as
>Also *ge-nei-vat da-at.**
>1. Literally, "robbing the mind."
>2. Deception.

gnei-vih-she shtihk
>Also spelled *geneivishe shtik.*
>1. Literally, "thieving ways."
>2. Dirty tricks.
>3. Crooked activities.

gnei-vuh
>Also *gnei-vaw, gnei-va.**
>Also spelled *geneivuh.*
>Theft, robbery.

gnossen see *gnawsn*

goi
>Also spelled *goy.*
>1. Literally, "a nation."
>2. A non-Jewish person.

goi-ihsh
>Also spelled *goyish.*
>1. Non-Jewish.
>2. Gentile in attitude, appearance, or actions.

goi-im
> Also spelled *goyim*.
> Plural of *goi*. See *goi*.

goi-lem
> Also *go-lem*.*
> 1. Automaton.
> 2. An artificial man of legend created by magical means in Prague in the sixteenth century.
> 3. A clumsy person.

goi-seis
> Also *go-seis*.*
> A dying person.

goldene see *gawldene*

golem see *goilem*

Go-mel
> A prayer of thanksgiving recited in the synagogue for having been saved from a precarious situation or on the safe return from a hazardous trip.

gonif
> A distorted form of *ganuhv*. See *ganuhv*.

good Shabbos see *gut Shabes*

(a) gootn tawg
> Also spelled *(a) guten tag*.
> 1. Literally, "a good day."
> 2. Have a good day!

gorgel see *gargl*

gornisht see *gawrnihsht*

gornit see *gawrniht*

gotkes see *gatkes*

Gott see *Gawt*

Gottenyu see *Gawtenyoo*

goy see *goi*

goyim see *goiim*

goyish see *goiihsh*

gragr
> Also spelled *grager, grogger*.

---

a as in father; aw as in law; ai as in aisle; ei as in neighbor; e as in bet; i as in vaccine; ih as in tin; o as in solar; oi as in void; oo as in food; u as in put; uh as in but; ch as in chutzpa; zh as in Zhivago.

A noisemaker used in the synagogue on the Purim holiday during the reading of the Megilla, to denigrate the name of Haman whenever it is mentioned.

(a) greener see *(a) grihner*

greptz
A belch, burp.

gribenes see *grihbenes*

grieben
A variant form of *grivn*. See *grivn*.

grih-be-nes
Also spelled *gribenes*.
A variant form of *grivn*. See *grivn*.

grihn
Also *grin*.
Green.

(a) grihn-er
Also spelled *(a) greener*.
1. Literally, "a green person."
2. A newly-arrived immigrant.

grihns
Also spelled *grins*.
1. Green vegetables.
2. Green plants.

grihs
Also *grus*.
Also spelled *gris*.
1. Greetings.
2. Regards.

grihzh-ih-dihk-er
Also spelled *grizhidiker*.
1. One who gnaws away.
2. A nag.

grihzhn
Also spelled *grizhen*.
1. To gnaw at, nibble.
2. Grind.
3. Annoy.

a as in father; aw as in law; ai as in aisle; ei as in neighbor; e as in bet; i as in vaccine; ih as in tin; o as in solar; oi as in void; oo as in food; u as in put; uh as in but; ch as in chutzpa; zh as in Zhivago.

grihzhn miht di tsein
>Also spelled *grizhen mit di tsain*.
>Grind one's teeth.

grins see *grihns*

gris see *grihs*

grivn
>Also *grihbn*.
>Also spelled *grieven, griven*.
>Crisp, fried pieces of poultry fat or skin after rendering.

grizhen see *grihzhn*

grizhidiker see *grihzhihdihker*

gro
>Also *groi*.
>Gray.

grob see *gruhb*

grobber finger see *gruhber fingr*

grobber yung see *gruhber yoong*

grogger see *gragr*

groi see *gro*

grois
>Large, big, great, grand.

(a) grois-e ge-du-le
>1. Literally, "great glory."
>2. Big deal!

(a) grois-e me-tzi-e
>Also spelled *(a) groise metzia*.
>1. A great find.
>2. A big bargain.

grois-haltr
>Also spelled *groishalter*.
>1. Literally, "one who holds himself big."
>2. Conceited, boastful.

(a) groisr far-dihn-er
>Also spelled *groiser fardihner*.
>1. Literally, "big wage earner!"
>2. (Sarcastically) A great breadwinner.

(a) groisr gawr-nihsht
>Also spelled *groiser gornisht.*
>A big nothing.

(a) groisr knakr
>Also spelled *groiser knaker.*
>1. Literally, "big knocker."
>2. A big shot.

groisr shihsr
>Also spelled *groiser shisser.*
>1. Literally, "big shot."
>2. A big talker, a braggart.

grois vi a barg
>As big as a mountain.

groschen see *gruhshn*

gruhb
>Also spelled *grob.*
>1. Fat.
>2. Uncouth.
>3. Rude, coarse.
>4. Obscene.

gruh-ber fingr
>Also spelled *grobber finger.*
>1. Literally, "thick (fat) finger."
>2. Thumb.

gruhb-er yoong
>Also spelled *grobber yung.*
>1. Literally, "an uncouth young man."
>2. A boorish, coarse, rude person.

gruhb-yan
>A boor. A contraction of *gruhber yoong.*

gruhshn
>Also spelled *groschen.*
>A small coin having the value of a penny.

grus see *grihs*

(a) grus fun der heim
>1. Literally, "a greeting from home."
>2. Regards from home.

a as in father; aw as in law; ai as in aisle; ei as in neighbor; e as in bet; i as in vaccine; ih as in tin; o as in solar; oi as in void; oo as in food; u as in put; uh as in but; ch as in chutzpa; zh as in Zhivago.

gut
>   1. Good.
>   2. Well.

gut awvnt
>   Also spelled *gut ovent.*
>   Popularly expressed as *a gutn awvnt.*
>   Good evening!

(a) gut-e nacht
>   Good night!

gut far ihm
>   1. Good for him!
>   2. Serves him right!

gut ge-nug
>   Good enough!

gut ge-zawgt
>   Also spelled *gut gezogt.*
>   Well said! Well stated!

gut mawrgen
>   Also spelled *gut morgen.*
>   Popularly expressed as *a gutn mawrgen.*
>   Good morning!

(a) gutn tawg
>   Also spelled *a guten tag.*
>   Also expressed as *a guter tawg.*
>   1. Literally, "a good day."
>   2. A greeting.

gut Sha-bes
>   Also *gut Sha-buhs.*
>   Also spelled *good Shabbos.*
>   Popularly expressed as *a gutn Shabbes.*
>   Literally, "good Sabbath," a greeting equivalent to
>   *Shabbat shalom,** used in Israel and elsewhere.

gut vawch
>   Also spelled *gut voch.*
>   1. Literally, "good week."
>   2. A Saturday night, end-of-Sabbath greeting.

---

a as in father; aw as in law; ai as in aisle; ei as in neighbor; e as in bet; i as in vaccine; ih as in tin; o as in solar; oi as in void; oo as in food; u as in put; uh as in but; ch as in chutzpa; zh as in Zhivago.

(a) gut yawr
Also expressed as *a gutn yawr*.
1. Literally, "a good year."
2. A New Year (Rosh Hashana) greeting.

gut yon tov
Popularly expressed as *a gutn yontif (yawntif)*.
1. Literally, "a good holiday."
2. A holiday greeting.

gutz
Also *gihtz*.
1. Good things.
2. Goodies, sweets.
3. Good news.

(a) gvihr
Also spelled *gvier, gevir*.
A wealthy person.

---

a as in father; aw as in law; ai as in aisle: ei as in neighbor; e as in bet; i as in vaccine; ih as in tin; o as in solar; oi as in void; oo as in food; u as in put; uh as in but; ch as in chutzpa; zh as in Zhivago.

H

ha-ba-chur ha-cha-tan*

Also *ha-baw-chur ha-chaw-sawn.*

1. Literally, "the young bridegroom."
2. A phrase used to call up a bridegroom to the Torah for an *aliya* on the Sabbath before his wedding.

Habad see *Chabad*

haben see *hawbn*

hach-naw-sas or-chihm

Also *hach-na-sat or-chim.**

1. Literally, "taking in, receiving travelers."
2. Granting hospitality to wayfarers.
3. The hospitality committee set up in Jewish communities to attend to needs of visitors.

hach-sha-ra*

Also *hach-shaw-raw.*

1. Literally, "preparation."
2. Agricultural training of pioneer settlers in preparation for their settlement in Israel.

ha-das

Myrtle, one of the species used with the *lulav* on the Sukkot festival. *Hadasim* is the plural form.

Ha-da-sa*

Also *Ha-da-saw.*

Also spelled *Hadassah.*

1. A myrtle.
2. Jewish women's organization supporting medical services in Israel, founded in the United States by Henrietta Szold on Purim, 1912.
3. Hebrew name of Esther, the heroine of Purim story as recorded in the biblical Scroll of Esther.

ha-da-sihm*

Also spelled *hadasim.*

---

a as in father; aw as in law; ai as in aisle; ei as in neighbor; e as in bet; i as in vaccine; ih as in tin; o as in solar; oi as in void; oo as in food; u as in put; uh as in but; ch as in chutzpa; zh as in Zhivago.

Plural of *hadas*. Myrtle branches held with the *lulav* on Sukkot.

Hadassah see *Hadasa*

Haf-to-raw
Also *Haf-ta-ra.**
Also spelled *Haftorah, Haftarah.*
1. A selection from the books of the Hebrew Prophets which follows the reading of the Pentateuch in synagogues on the Sabbath and holidays.
2. The prophetic portion read by *Bar Mitzva* boys and *Bat Mitzva* girls.

hag see *chag*

Hagada see *Hagawdaw*

Ha-ga-na
Also *Ha-gaw-naw.*
1. Literally, "protection."
2. A Jewish self-defense underground in Palestine under the British Mandate which evolved into the army of the State of Israel.

Ha-gaw-daw
Also *Ha-ga-da**.
Also spelled *Haggada, Haggadah.*
1. Literally, "the telling, narration."
2. The Passover Seder prayerbook, in which the story of the Exodus is told. Used at the family celebrations on the first two nights of Passover.
3. A synonym for *Agada*. See *Agada*.

hag-baw
Also *hag-ba.**
The honor bestowed upon one called to lift up the Torah scroll so it can be bound before restoring it to the Ark.

Haggada see *Hagawdaw*

haham see *chacham*

hailn zihch
Also spelled *hailen zich.*
To hurry.

---

a as in father; aw as in law; ai as in aisle; ei as in neighbor; e as in bet; i as in vaccine; ih as in tin; o as in solar; oi as in void; oo as in food; u as in put; uh as in but; ch as in chutzpa; zh as in Zhivago.

hailt zihch see *ailt zihch*

haim see *heim*

haimihsh see *heimihsh*

haint
> Also spelled *heint*.
> Today.

haint ihz Purim
> Also spelled *heint iz Purim*.
> Literally,. "today is (the holiday of) Purim."

hais see *heis*

haisen see *heisn*

haise vanne see *heise vane*

haisr
> Also spelled *haizer*.
> Houses. Plural of *hoiz*.

haizer see *haisr*

hakafa see *hakawfe*

ha-kaw-fe
> Also *ha-kaw-faw, ha-ka-fa.**
> 1. Literally, "to encircle."
> 2. The procession of congregants inside the syn-
>   agogue on Sukkot, each holding a *lulav,* and on
>   Simchat Torah, each holding a Torah scroll.

hak-fleish
> Also spelled *hakflaish*.
> Chopped meat, hash.

hak mesr
> Also spelled *hak messer*.
> A chopping knife, used with a wooden bowl.

hak mihr niht ihn kawp
> Also spelled *hak mir nit in kop*.
> 1. Literally, "Stop chopping on my head!"
> 2. Stop annoying me!

hak mihr niht kain tchai-nihk
> Also *hak mihr niht kein tchai-nihk*.
> 1. Literally, "Don't bang me on a kettle!"
> 2. Don't bother me!

---

hakn
> Also spelled *haken*.
> To chop, hew.

hakn a chai-nihk
> 1. Literally, "to chop (bang) on a tea kettle."
> 2. To drivel, babble.

hak un pak
> 1. Literally, "kit and caboodle."
> 2. Everything, the whole lot.

halacha*
> Also *ha-law-chaw*.
> Also spelled *halakhah, halachah*.
> 1. Rabbinic law.
> 2. Those parts of the Talmud devoted to legal matters as contrasted with *agada* (historical and folkloristic subjects).

ha-la-chot*
> Also *ha-law-chos*.
> Plural form of *halacha*.

haldzvetik see *haltzveitihk*

Ha-leil
> Also spelled *Hallel*.
> 1. Literally, "praise."
> 2. Psalms of thanksgiving, part of the holiday liturgy.

haleva see *haluhva*

ha-le-vai
> Often pronounced *a-le-vai*.
> Also spelled *halevei*.
> 1. Perhaps.
> 2. May it only happen!

Halitza see *Chalitzuh*

halke
> Grated potato dumpling.

Hallel see *Haleil*

haltz
> Also spelled *halz*.
> Neck, throat.

---

a as in father; aw as in law; ai as in aisle; ei as in neighbor; e as in bet; i as in vaccine; ih as in tin; o as in solar; oi as in void; oo as in food; u as in put; uh as in but; ch as in chutzpa; zh as in Zhivago.

haltz-vei-tihk
  Also spelled *haldzvetik.*
  1. Literally, "throat pain."
  2. A sore throat.

ha-luh-va
  Also spelled *haleva, halva, halvah.*
  A confection made with ground sesame seeds.

halutz see *chalootz*

halva see *haluhva*

hal-vaw-yas ha-meis-ihm
  Also *hal-va-yat ha-mei-tihm.**
  1. Literally, "escorting the dead."
  2. A funeral procession, often referred to as a
  leva'ye.

haltz
  Also spelled *halz.*
  Neck, throat.

hamantash see *hawmentash*

hamantashen
  Plural of *hawmentash.* See *hawmentash.*

hametz see *chawmetz*

ha-mon
  1. The masses.
  2. Common people.

Ha-mo-tzi
  1. Literally, "He (God) who brings forth."
  2. The blessing recited before eating bread.
  3. Grace Before the Meal.

ha-na-a*
  Also *ha-nuh-uh, ha-naw-aw.*
  1. Pleasure, enjoyment.
  2. Fun.

handln
  Also spelled *handlen.*
  1. To do business, to trade.
  2. To bargain.

hanukat habayit see *chanookas habayihs*

---

a as in father; aw as in law; ai as in aisle; ei as in neighbor; e as in bet; i as in vaccine; ih as in tin; o as in solar; oi as in void; oo as in food; u as in put; uh as in but; ch as in chutzpa; zh as in Zhivago.

hanukia see *chanookiyaw*

Hanukkah see *Chanookuh*

hargn
> Murder, kill.

haroset see *charoses*

hartz
> Heart.

hartz-en-yoo
> Also spelled *hartzenyu.*
> Sweetheart, darling.

hartz-ihg
> 1. Hearty.
> 2. Sincere.
> 3. Cordial.

hartz-vei-tihk
> Also spelled *hartzvaitik.*
> Heartache.

ha-saw-gas ge-vool
> Also *ha-sa-gat ge-vul.**
> 1. Literally, "encroachment upon (a neighbor's) boundary (land)."
> 2. Unfair competition in business.

ha-Sheim
> Also *ha-Shem.**
> 1. Literally, "the (Divine) Name."
> 2. God, used as a substitute for Adonai.

hash-ga-cha*
> Also *hash-gaw-chaw.*
> Religious supervision, particularly in the preparation of food.

Hash-ka-ba*
> Memorial prayer recited in Sephardic congregations.

hasid see *chuhsihd*

hasidei Ashkenaz see *chasidei Ashkenaz*

hasidism see *chasihdihzm*

---

a as in father; aw as in law; ai as in aisle; ei as in neighbor; e as in bet; i as in vaccine; ih as in tin; o as in solar; oi as in void; oo as in food; u as in put; uh as in but; ch as in chutzpa; zh as in Zhivago.

Has-kaw-law
>Also *Has-ka-la.***
>1. Literally, "enlightenment."
>2. A movement that flourished from 1750 to 1880 to disseminate European culture among Jews.

Ha-tihk-va*
>Also *Ha-tihk-vaw.*
>Also spelled *Hatikva* and *Hatikvah.*
>1. Literally, "the hope."
>2. The anthem of the Zionist movement and State of Israel, with lyrics composed in 1878 by Naphtali Herz Imber and music based on a Moldavian-Rumanian folk song.

Hatzi Kaddish see *Chatzi Kadihsh*

Hava Nagila see *hawvaw nawgilaw*

Hav-duh-luh
>Also *Hav-daw-law, Hav-da-la.***
>Also spelled *Havdalah, Habdalah.*
>1. Literally, "separation."
>2. The ceremony that marks the conclusion of the Sabbath.

ha-veil ha-vaw-lihm
>Also *hav-eil ha-va-lihm.***
>1. Literally, "vanity of vanities."
>2. The second verse of the Book of Ecclesiastes.

haver see *chawvr*

havera see *chaveira*

havura see *chavoora*

haw-ben far-drus
>Also *haw-ben far-dris.*
>1. To harbor resentment.
>2. To be angry.
>3. To be distressed.

haw-ben tzoo zingn oon tzoo zawgn
>Also spelled *hoben tzu zingen un tzu zogen.*
>1. Literally, "to have what to sing and what to talk about."
>2. To have no end of trouble.

hawbn
>Also *haw-ben.*
>Also spelled *hoben, haben.*
>To have.

hawbn de-rech e-retz
>1. To have good manners.
>2. To be respectful.

hawl-ep-tches
>Also spelled *holeptzes, holopches.*
>Stuffed cabbage.

hawltz
>Wood.

haw-men-tash
>Also *ha-man-tash.*
>Also spelled *homentash, hamantash.*
>A triangular pastry filled with poppy seeds, prunes, or cheese and eaten on Purim; named after Haman, the Purim villain. *Hamantashen* is the plural form.

hawn
>A rooster.

haw-nihg
>Also *haw-nihk.*
>Also spelled *honik.*
>Honey.

hawst doo bai mihr an av-luh
>Also spelled *host du bei mir an avla.*
>1. Literally, "So you have a grievance against me!"
>2. So I made a mistake, so what!

hawt niht kain dai-ges
>Also *hawt niht kein deiges.*
>Don't be concerned! Don't worry!

hawt niht kain fa-rihbl oif mihr
>Also *hawt niht kein fa-ribl oif mihr.*
>Don't be angry with me!

hawt niht kain zawrg
>Also *hawt niht kein zawrg.*
>Don't worry!

---

a as in father; aw as in law; ai as in aisle; ei as in neighbor; e as in bet; i as in vaccine; ih as in tin; o as in solar; oi as in void; oo as in food; u as in put; uh as in but; ch as in chutzpa; zh as in Zhivago.

hawtz-en-plawtz
>Also spelled *hotzenplotz*.
>1. A faraway town in Central Europe.
>2. Way out in the "sticks."

hawtz mihch oon zatz mihch
>You should live and be well!

Haw-vaw Naw-gi-law
>Also *Ha-va Na-gi-la.**
>1. Literally, "Come, let's be joyous."
>2. A popular Hebrew song.

hayim see *chayihm*

Hazarat Hashatz see *Chazawras Hashatz*

Haz-kaw-ras Ne-shaw-mos
>Also *Haz-ka-rat Ne-sha-mot.**
>1. Literally, "remembrance of souls."
>2. The memorial service held on the Day of Atonement and on the final days of Pesach, Shavuot, and Sukkot.
>Also called *Yizkor*.

hazzan see *chazn*

he see *hei*

hechshr
>Also *hech-sher.**
>1. Literally, "certification."
>2. Rabbinical approval or validation, especially of *kosher* food.

heder see *cheidr*

hei
>Also spelled *he*.
>1. The fifth letter of the Hebrew alphabet.
>2. A Hebrew letter used as a neck charm because of its association with the name of God.

Hei-chal Shlo-mo
>1. Literally, "palace of Solomon."
>2. Seat of Israel's Chief Rabbinate in Jerusalem.

heiln zihch
>Also spelled *hailen zich*.
>To care for oneself, to heal oneself.

---

a as in father: aw as in law; ai as in aisle; ei as in neighbor; e as in bet; i as in vaccine; ih as in tin; o as in solar; oi as in void; oo as in food; u as in put; uh as in but; ch as in chutzpa; zh as in Zhivago.

heim
>Also *haim.*
>1. Home.
>2. Native land, as in *in der alter heim,* "in the old country."

heim-ihsh
>Also *haim-ihsh.*
>1. Homey, cozy, intimate, snug.
>2. Informal.

heim-ihsh paw-nihm
>Also *haim-ihsh paw-nihm.*
>1. Literally, "a homey face."
>2. A familiar face.

heint see *haint*

heis
>Also spelled *hais.*
>1. Hot, torrid.
>2. Fervent, devoted.

hei-se va-ne
>Also spelled *haise vanne.*
>A hot bath.

heisn
>Also spelled *haisen.*
>1. To tell.
>2. To order.
>3. To direct, command.

heizl
>Also spelled *heizel.*
>1. Literally, "a small house."
>2. House of ill repute.

heizr gei-er
>Also spelled *heizer gaier.*
>1. Literally, "house-goer."
>2. Beggar.

hek-deish
>Also *hek-desh.**
>1. A forsaken place or thing.
>2. A slum.

---

a as in father; aw as in law; ai as in aisle; ei as in neighbor; e as in bet; i as in vaccine; ih as in tin; o as in solar; oi as in void; oo as in food; u as in put; uh as in but; ch as in chutzpa; zh as in Zhivago.

3. A poorhouse.
4. A mess.

held
>1. A hero
>2. A protagonist.

helfn
>Help.

helfn vi a toitn bank-es
>1. Literally, "It will be of as much help as perform-
>ing cupping (to draw blood) on a corpse."
>2. It's of no use.
>See also *bankes*.

helzl
>Also *held-zel*.
>Also spelled *helzel*.
>1. Neck.
>2. Stuffed neck of a fowl, usually chicken.

hemd
>A shirt.

her
>1. Hear.
>2. Listen.

herem see *cheirem*

hern
>Also spelled *heren*.
>1. To hear.
>2. To listen.
>3. To obey.

hern a rei-ach
>1. Literally, "to hear an odor."
>2. To give off an odor.

herr
>German for "sir, mister, gentleman." Used by
>German-speaking Jews.

hert oif
>1. Stop!
>2. Cease!
>3. Cut it out!

---

a as in father; aw as in law; ai as in aisle; ei as in neighbor; e as in bet; i as in vaccine; ih as in tin; o as in solar; oi as in void; oo as in food; u as in put; uh as in but; ch as in chutzpa; zh as in Zhivago.

hert ois
>Literally, "hear out," hear me out.

hert zihch ain
>1. Listen attentively!
>2. Listen (to me) carefully!

hert zihch tzoo
>Listen carefully.

hesdr
>Also spelled *hesder.*
>Orthodox *yeshiva* students in Israel serving in the army and carrying on their studies.

hesed see *chesed*

hes-peid
>Also *he-sped.**
>1. A funeral eulogy.
>2. An obituary.

het see *cheit*

hetzn
>Also *hihtzn.*
>Also spelled *hetzen.*
>Incite.

hetzn oon-ter
>1. Bait, heckle.
>2. To incite.

hetzn zihch
>Also spelled *hetzen zich.*
>1. Bounce.
>2. Shake.
>3. Dance with joy.

he-vel
>1. A breath.
>2. Vanity.
>3. Nonsense.

Hevra Kaddisha see *Chevruh Kadishuh*

(a) hihbsh bisl
>Also spelled *a hibsh bissel.*
>1. A considerable amount.
>2. A large quantity.

---

a as in father; aw as in law; ai as in aisle; ei as in neighbor; e as in bet; i as in vaccine; ih as in tin; o as in solar; oi as in void; oo as in food; u as in put; uh as in but; ch as in chutzpa; zh as in Zhivago.

hihml
> Also spelled *himmel.*
> 1. Heaven.
> 2. Sky.

hihnkedihk
> One who limps, a lame person.

hihnkn
> Also spelled *hinken.*
> To limp.

hihntehn see *hinten*

hihntn
> Also spelled *hinten.*
> 1. Buttock, the behind.
> 2. Below.
> 3. In back of.

hihpsh
> Also spelled *hipsh.*
> 1. Substantial.
> 2. Sizeable.
> 3. Considerable.

hihp-sher bisl
> Also spelled *hipsher bisl.*
> An extremely large amount.

hihs-la-ha-vus
> Also *hit-la-ha-vut.**
> 1. Enthusiasm, excitement.
> 2. Fervor.
> 3. Inspiration.

Hihs-tad-rus
> Also *Hihs-tad-rut.**
> Also spelled *Histadrut.*
> 1. Literally, "an association, organization."
> 2. The Federation of Labor in Israel.

hihtl
> Also spelled *hitel.*
> A cap, hat.

hiht zihch
> Also spelled *hit zich.*

---

a as in father; aw as in law; ai as in aisle; ei as in neighbor; e as in bet; i as in vaccine; ih as in tin; o as in solar; oi as in void; oo as in food; u as in put; uh as in but; ch as in chutzpa; zh as in Zhivago.

1. Watch it! Look out!
2. Be careful!

hihtz-kuhp
Also spelled *hitzkop*.
A hothead, an excitable person.

hihtzn see *hetzn*

hilul ha-Shem see *chilool ha-Sheim*

hi-lu-la*
Also *hi-loo-law*.
1. Rejoicing.
2. A day of singing praises *(Hallel)*.
3. A day commemorating the death of a parent or a famous man (in the Sephardic tradition).

hilul Shabbat see *chilool Shabes*

himmel see *hihml*

hin-dig
Turkey.

hinken see *hihnkn*

hinten see *hihntn*

hipsh see *hihpsh*

hipsher bisel see *hihpshĕr bihsl*

Histadrut see *Hihstadrus*

hitel see *hihtl*

hitlahavut see *hihslahavus*

hitn
Also spelled *hitten*.
1. To protect oneself.
2. To guard, watch.

hit zich see *hiht zihch*

hitzkop see *hihtzkuhp*

hoben see *hawbn*

hock-messr
A chopping knife, used with a wooden bowl.

hodesh see *chodesh*

---

a as in father; aw as in law; ai as in aisle; ei as in neighbor; e as in bet; i as in vaccine; ih as in tin; o as in solar; oi as in void; oo as in food; u as in put; uh as in but; ch as in chutzpa; zh as in Zhivago.

hoi-cher drung
>Also *hoich-er drong*.
>1. Literally, "high pole."
>2. A tall person.

hoit
>Skin.

hoiz
>House.

hokhma see *chawchme*

hold-up-nihk
>A Yiddish form of "holdup-man," that is, a robber.

holeptzes see *hawleptches*

Hol Hamoed see *Chol Hamoeid*

holishkes
>Chopped meat rolled in cabbage or grape leaves.
>Also known as *galuptze* or *prokes*.

Holocaust see *Shoa*

holopches see *hawleptches*

homentash see *hawmentash*

honik see *hawnihg*

hoo-ha
>An expression of surprise, astonishment, admiration.

hoon-ger-ihk
>Also spelled *hungerik*.
>Hungry.

ho-raw
>Also *ho-ra*.*
>An Israeli circle folk-dance of Balkan origin.

Ho-sha-na Ra-ba*
>Also *Ho-shaw-naw Ra-baw*.
>Also spelled *Hoshana Rabba*.
>1. Literally, "Great Hosanna."
>2. The seventh day of the Sukkot festival.

Ho-sha-not*
>Also *Ho-sha-nos*.

---

a as in father; aw as in law; ai as in aisle; ei as in neighbor; e as in bet; i as in vaccine; ih as in tin; o as in solar; oi as in void; oo as in food; u as in put; uh as in but; ch as in chutzpa; zh as in Zhivago.

Hymns sung during the *hakafot* on Hoshana Rabba.

Ho-shi-a-na
Hymn sung during the *hakafot* of Simchat Torah.

host du bei mir an avla see *hawst doo bai mihr an avluh*

hotzenplotz
See *hawtzenplawtz*.
1. A faraway town in Central Europe.
2. Way out in the "sticks."

hotz-mach
1. Good-natured.
2. A good-natured peddler in a Yiddish play by Abraham Goldfaden.

huhbn chei-shek tzoo
Also spelled *hoben chaishek tzu*.
Have a desire for.

hul-ya-kes
Also spelled *huliakes*.
Roisterers.

hul-yen
Frolic, revel, carouse.

hul-ye-ven
A form of *hulyen*. See *hulyen*.

Humash see *Chumuhsh*

hun
A hen.

hungerik see *hoongerihk*

huppa see *chupuh*

hurban see *choorbn*

hutzpa see *chootzpuh*

---

a as in father; aw as in law; ai as in aisle; ei as in neighbor; e as in bet; i as in vaccine; ih as in tin; o as in solar; oi as in void; oo as in food; u as in put; uh as in but; ch as in chutzpa; zh as in Zhivago.

I

iberchazeren see *ihberhazren*

ibersetzen see *ihberzetzn*

Ibershter see *Eibershter*

ich see *ihch*

ihber-chazern
> Also spelled *iberchazeren*.
> 1 To repeat.
> 2. To review by repetition.

ih-ber-zetzn
> Also spelled *iberzetzen*.
> 1. To translate.
> 2. To transpose.

ihch
> Also spelled *ich*.
> I, me.

ihch bihn
> Also spelled *ich bin*.
> I am.

ihch bihn dihr niht me-ka-ne
> I don't envy you.

ihch darf es
> Also spelled *ich darf es*.
> I need it.

ihch faif oif dihr
> Also spelled *ich feif oif dir*.
> 1. Literally, "I whistle upon you."
> 2. I despise you!

ihch fihl zihch uhp-ge-nart
> Also spelled *ich fil zich opgenart*.
> 1. Literally, "I feel like I have been made to look like a fool."
> 2. I was tricked, deceived.

---

a as in father; **aw** as in law; **ai** as in aisle; **ei** as in neighbor; **e** as in bet; **i** as in vaccine; **ih** as in tin; **o** as in solar; **oi** as in void; **oo** as in food; **u** as in put; **uh** as in but; **ch** as in chutzpa; **zh** as in Zhivago.

ihch hail zihch niht
>Also *ich eil zich nit.*
>1 I'm in no hurry.
>2. Don't rush me!

ihch heis
>Also spelled *ich hais.*
>1. Literally, "I am called."
>2. My name is.

ihch huhb dihr faint
>Also spelled *ich hob dir feint.*
>I hate you!

ihch huhb dihr ihn buhd
>Also spelled *ich hob dir in bod.*
>1. Literally, "I have you in the bath (bathhouse)."
>2. I despise you!

ihch huhb dihr ihn drerd
>Also spelled *ich huhb dir in drerd.*
>1. Literally, "I have you in the ground."
>2. Go to hell!

ihch huhb dihr ihn tuh-ches
>Also spelled *ich hob dir in toches.*
>1. Literally, "I have you in my buttocks."
>2. I have no use for you!

ihch huhb zihch ge-mutsh-et
>Also spelled *ich hob zich gemutshet.*
>1. I tortured (troubled) myself.
>2. I agonized, suffered.

ihch veis
>Also spelled *ich vais.*
>1. I know.
>2. I am aware.

ihch veis niht
>Also spelled *ich vais nit.*
>I don't know.

ihch vel dihr gebn ka-daw-ches
>Also spelled *ich vell dir geben kadoches.*
>1. Literally, "I'll give you a fever, the chills."
>2. I'll give you nothing.

ihch yawg zihch
Also spelled *ich yog zich.*
1. Literally, "I'm chasing myself."
2. I'm rushing.

ihch yawg zihch niht
Also spelled *ich yog zich nit.*
1. Literally, "I'm not chasing myself."
2. I'm not rushing.
3. I'm in no hurry.

ihch zawl a-zoi vihsn foon tsaw-res
Also spelled *ich zol azoi vissen fun tsores.*
1. Literally, "I should know as little about trouble
(as I know about what you are asking me)."
2. I'm totally ignorant of the matter.

ihm-be-shri-en
Also *oom-be-shri-en.*
1. Literally, "unbewitched."
2. God forbid!
3. It shouldn't happen!
Sometimes said when praising a child, to ward off
evil.

ihm yihr-tse ha-Shem*
Also spelled *im yirtse ha-Shem.*
1. Literally, "If the (Divine) Name wills it!"
2. God willing!
Contracted to *mirtzishem* and *mihrtzeshem.*

ihn a nuh-ve-ne
Also *ihn a naw-vih-ne.*
Also spelled *in a noveneh.*
1. Literally, "in time for something new."
2. For a change.
3. Once in a blue moon.

ihn buhd
Also spelled *in bod.*
1. In the bath.
2. In the bathhouse.

ihn der erd
Also *ihn drerd.*

---

1. Literally, "in the earth."
2. Of no value.

ihn di al-te gut-e tzaitn
> Also spelled *in di alte gute tzeiten.*
> In the good old days.

ihn di al-te yawr-en
> Also spelled *in di alte yoren.*
> 1. Literally, "in the elderly years."
> 2. In (one's) old age.

ihndihg
> Also *hihndihk.*
> A turkey.

ihn drerd see *ihn der erd*

ihn drerd a-rain
> 1. Literally, "into the earth with you."
> 2. Go to hell!

ihn drerd main gelt
> Also *drerd mein gelt.*
> 1. Literally, "My money is in the earth (in hell)."
> 2. My money went down the drain.

ihn droisn ihz a glihtsh
> Also spelled *in droisen iz a glitsh.*
> It's slippery outside.

ihn es-ihg oon ihn haw-nihg
> Also *ihn es-ihk oon ihn haw-nihk.*
> 1. Literally, "in vinegar and in honey."
> 2. Dressed in finery.

ihn ka-as oif
> To be angry with.

ihn mihtn der-ihn-en
> Also spelled *in mitten derinin.*
> 1. In the midst of.
> 2. Suddenly.

ihn miht-she der-ihn-en
> A variant form of *ihn mihtn derihnen.* See above.

ihn-yen
> Also *ihn-yan.**

---

1. A subject.
2. A concern.
3. A theme (in Talmudic study).

ihp-uhsh
Also *ihp-esh*.
Also spelled *ipush*.
1. Stench.
2. Mold.

ihr ge-felt mihr
Also spelled *ir gefelt mir*.
You please me.

ihr ge-felt mihr zeir
Also spelled *ir gefelt mir zaier*.
You please me greatly.

Ihr-gun*
Short for *Ihr-gun Tsva-i Le-oo-mi.**
Also spelled *Irgun Z'vai Leumi, Irgun*.
"National Military Organization." The name of the underground Jewish military group in Palestine, founded in 1931. From 1937 to 1948 it engaged in attacks against Arabs and British mandatory officials.

ihtst
Also *yetzt*.
Also spelled *itzt*.
Now, presently.

Ihv-ri
Also spelled *Ivri*.
1. Literally, "one from across (the Euphrates River)."
2. A member of a Semitic people that traces its origins to the patriarchs Abraham, Isaac, and Jacob.
3. A Hebrew.

Ihv-rihs
Also *Ihv-riht,** *Iv-rit*.
Hebrew, the Hebrew language.

---

a as in father; aw as in law; ai as in aisle; ei as in neighbor; e as in bet; i as in vaccine; ih as in tin; o as in solar; oi as in void; oo as in food; u as in put; uh as in but; ch as in chutzpa; zh as in Zhivago.

ihz nihsht ge-fer-lach
> Also spelled *iz nisht geferlach.*
> It's not so terrible!

i-kuhr
> Also spelled *i-kar.**
> 1. Essence
> 2. Principle.
> 3. Fundamental tenet.

i-looy
> Also spelled *ilui.*
> 1. A genius.
> 2. A Talmudic prodigy.

im yirtse ha-Shem see *ihm yihrtze ha-Sheim*

in a noveneh see *ihn a nuhvene*

in bod see *ihn buhd*

in di alte gute tzeiten see *ihn di alte gute tzaitn*

in di alte yoren see *ihn di alte yawren*

in esik un in honik see *ihn esihk oon ihn hawnihk*

ing-ber
> Ginger.

ing-ber lei-kach
> Also *ing-ber le-kach.*
> Gingerbread.

ing-ber vasr
> Ginger water, ginger ale.

in mitten derinin see *ihn mihtn derihnen*

ipush see *ihpuhsh*

ir gefelt mir see *ihr gefelt mihr*

Irgun Z'vai Leumi see *Ihrgun*

Israel
> English for *Yihsraweil.* See *Yihsraweil.*
> 1. Literally, "contender with God."
> 2. The Holy Land.
> 3. The Jewish people.
> 4. The name assigned to Jacob after he contended with a divine emissary (Genesis 32:39).

---

a as in father; aw as in law; ai as in aisle· ei as in neighbor; e as in bet; i as in vaccine; ih as in tin; o as in solar; oi as in void; oo as in food; u as in put; uh as in but; ch as in chutzpa; zh as in Zhivago.

itzt see *ihtst*

Ivri see *Ihvri*

Ivrit see *Ihvrihs*

I-yar*
> Also *I-yawr.*
> Also spelled *Iyyar.*
> The second month of the Jewish religious calendar, eighth of the Civil calendar, corresponding to April-May.

I-ze-vel
> Also spelled *Jezebel.*
> 1. Wife of King Ahab of Israel (I Kings 16:31).
> 2. A shameless, wicked woman.

iz nisht geferlach see *ihz nihsht gerferlach*

---

a as in father; aw as in law; ai as in aisle; ei as in neighbor; e as in bet; i as in vaccine; ih as in tin; o as in solar; oi as in void; oo as in food; u as in put; uh as in but; ch as in chutzpa; zh as in Zhivago.

J

jahrzeit see *yartzait*

Jehovah
   1. God.
   2. The English form of YHVH.

Jezebel see *Izevel*

Judenrat
   German for the "Jewish Council" ordered by Nazis
   to carry out their orders.

Judeo-German
   Yiddish

Judeo-Spanish
   Ladino.

Judezmo
   Also spelled *Judesmo*.
   The Ladino word for Judeo-Spanish.

K

kaas see *kas*

Ka-ba-la*
> Also *Ka-baw-law.*
> Also spelled *Kabbalah, Cabala, Cabbala.*
> 1. Literally, "receipt, receiving."
> 2. Jewish mysticism.
> 3. A document certifying a *shochet* to slaughter animals.

ka-ba-lat mihtz-vot*
> Also *ka-baw-las mihtz-vos.*
> Acceptance of the commandments, a necessary prelude to conversion to Judaism.

Ka-baw-las Sha-buhs
> Also *Ka-ba-lat Sha-bat,* *Ka-baw-las Sha-bes.*
> The Friday evening prayer service ushering in the Sabbath.

kab-tzaw-nihm
> Plural of *kabtzn.* See below.

kabtzn
> Also *kab-tzan.**
> Also spelled *kabtzen, kabtzin, kobtzen, koptzen, koptzin.*
> 1. A pauper.
> 2. A mendicant, a beggar.

ka-daw-ches see *kaduhches*

Ka-dihsh
> Also spelled *kaddish.*
> 1. Literally, "sanctification."
> 2. Doxology.
> 3. Mourner's Prayer.
> 4. An orphan, often referred to as a *kadihshl.*
> 5. A person hired to say the Mourner's Prayer.

---

a as in father; aw as in law; ai as in aisle; ei as in neighbor; e as in bet; i as in vaccine; ih as in tin; o as in solar; oi as in void; oo as in food; u as in put; uh as in but; ch as in chutzpa; zh as in Zhivago.

ka-dihshl
> A young orphan. See also *Kadihsh.*

Ka-dihsh Tihs-ka-beil
> Also *Ka-dihsh Tiht-ka-bel**
> The full Kaddish, which includes the petition beginning with *Tihtkabel:* "May the prayers of the House of Israel be accepted."

kadosh see *kawdosh*

ka-duh-ches
> Also *ka-da-chat.**
> Also spelled *kadoches, kadawches.*
> 1. Fever, ague, malaria.
> 2. A bad situation.

ka-duh-ches miht kuh-sher-e fuh-dem
> 1. Literally, "a fever with *kosher* thread."
> 2. Absolutely nothing.
> 3. Of no value.

kaf*
> Also *kawf.*
> 1. A spoon, a ladle.
> 2. The eleventh letter of the Hebrew alphabet.

kaf-tan*
> Also *kaf-tuhn.*
> The long, black overgarment worn by observant Jewish men in Eastern Europe. Also called *kapawtuh.*

kahal see *kawhawl*

kailihke see *kalihke*

kain see *kein*

kainainhore see *kein ayihn huruh*

kain ayin hore see *kein ayihn huhruh*

kain mal see *kein muhl*

kai oon shpai
> Literally, "chew and spit."

kairuh see *ke'ara*

ka-la see *kale*

---

a as in father; aw as in law; ai as in aisle; ei as in neighbor; e as in bet; i as in vaccine; ih as in tin; o as in solar; oi as in void; oo as in food; u as in put; uh as in but; ch as in chutzpa; zh as in Zhivago.

kalb fleish
Veal meat.

ka-le
Also *ka-la,** *ka-law.*
Also spelled *kalle.*
Bride.

ka-lih-ke
Also *kai-lih-ke, kal-yih-ke.*
A handicapped person.

kam see *kum*

kam-puht
Also *kam-pot, kam-put.*
Also spelled *kampote, campote.*
Stewed fruit.

kamtzn
Also *kam-tzawn, kam-tzan.**
1. A skinflint.
2. A miser.

ka-nuh
Also spelled *kaneh.*
An enema.

kapara see *kapawruh.*

ka-pa-rot*
Also *ka-paw-res.*
1. Literally, "atonements."
2. Hens and roosters used as symbols of atonement
   before Yom Kippur.
Kapara is the singular form.

ka-paw-ruh
Also *ka-pa-ra,** *ka-paw-raw.*
Also spelled *kapora, kapore.*
1. Literally, "atonement."
2. A fowl used for atonement.
3. A scapegoat.

ka-paw-tuh
Also spelled *caputa, kapote.*
1. A robe.
2. A long, black overgarment.

---

a as in father; aw as in law; ai as in aisle; ei as in neighbor; e as in bet; i as in vaccine; ih as in tin; o as in solar; oi as in void; oo as in food; u as in put; uh as in but; ch as in chutzpa; zh as in Zhivago.

ka-pe-le
>A small skullcap. See also *kapl*.

kapl
>Also spelled *kappel, koppel*.
>A skullcap.

ka-poi-e
>Also *ka-poir*.
>1. Reverse.
>2. Inside out.
>3. Backwards.
>4. One who is contrary.

kapora see *kapawruh*

kapote see *kapawtuh*

kappel see *kapl*

Karaim see *Karaite*

Karaite
>A member of a Jewish settlement founded in the eighth century. These Jews, known as *Karaim* in Hebrew, rejected the Oral Law (Talmud) and followed the Written Law (Bible) literally.

kargr
>Also spelled *karger*.
>1. A miser.
>2. Cheapskate, tightwad.

kar-kuh
>Also *kar-ka*.*
>Earth, ground, soil, land.

karnatzlach
>Hamburgers in the shape of frankfurters.

karov see *kawrov*

kar-pas
>A green vegetable eaten at the Passover *Seder*.

kar-tawfl
>Also spelled *kartofel, kartoffel*.
>Potato.

kas
>Also *ka-as*.*

---

1. Anger, wrath, ire.
2. Sorrow, vexation.

kasha see *kashuh*

kashe varnihshkaz see *kashuh varnihshkez*

kasher see *kosher*

kashering see *koshering*

kash-rus
Also *kash-rut.**
Also spelled *kashruth.*
The state or condition of being kosher, in accordance with Jewish dietary laws as specified in Leviticus 11 and elaborated upon in the Talmud and later codes.

kashrut see *kashrus*

ka-shuh
Also spelled *kasha, kashe.*
1. Buckwheat kernels, cereal, porridge.
2. A mess, a mix-up.

ka-shuh var-nihsh-kez
Also *ka-she var-nihsh-kaz.*
Buckwheat groats with pasta.

ka-suh-ke
Also spelled *kasoke.*
Cross-eyed.

katch-ke
Duck.

katz-ih-sher kawp
Also spelled *katzisher kop.*
1. Literally, "cat-head."
2. Forgetful.
3. Lame-brain.

kaufen see *koifn*

kavana see *kavuhne*

ka-ve
Coffee.

kavod see *kuhved*

---

ka-vuh-ne
>Also *ka-va-na,* ka-vaw-naw.*
>Also spelled *kavanah.*
>1. Intention.
>2. Concentration.
>3. In Jewish mysticism, "to turn oneself" toward God in prayer.

kawch-a-lein
>Also spelled *kochalain, kochalayn.*
>1. Literally, "to cook alone."
>2. A boarding house with cooking privileges.

kawch-lefl
>Also spelled *kochleffel.*
>1. Literally, "cooking ladle."
>2. Busybody, meddler.

kawchn
>Also spelled *kawchen, kochen.*
>1. Cook, boil, seethe.
>2. Cooked food.

kaw-dosh
>Also *ka-dosh.**
>Holy, sacred. See also *kodesh.*

kawf see *kaf*

kaw-hawl
>Also *ka-hal.**
>Congregation.

kawl-boi-nihk
>Also *kolbonik.*
>1. A religious leader who can perform many religious functions.
>2. A know-it-all.
>3. A jack-of-all-trades.

(ihm) kawl ha-ne-aw-rihm
>Also *(ihm) kal ha-n'a-rihm.**
>1. Literally, "with all the lads."
>2. A collective *aliya* on Simchat Torah for boys under age thirteen.

kawp see *kuhp*

---

a as in father; aw as in law; ai as in aisle; ei as in neighbor; e as in bet; i as in vaccine; ih as in tin; o as in solar; oi as in void; oo as in food; u as in put; uh as in but; ch as in chutzpa; zh as in Zhivago.

k'awraw see *ke'ara*

kaw-rov
Also *ka-rov.**
1. Near, nearby.
2. A relative.

kawrt
1. A card.
2. A playing card.
Kawrtn is the plural form.

kawvod see *kuhved*

kayn see *kein*

k'dei-shuh
Also spelled *kedeisha,** *kedeishaw*.
1. A prostitute
2. A priestess.

K'doo-shas Ha-yom
Also *Ke-doo-shat Ha-yom.**
1. Literally, "the holiness of the day."
2. A blessing recited during the *Amida* on Sabbaths and holidays.

K'du-shuh
Also *Ke-du-shaw, Ke-du-sha.**
1. Holiness.
2. A portion of the liturgy consisting of verses praising God.

ke-a-ra*
Also *kai-ruh, k'aw-raw*.
A special plate used for the Passover *Seder*.

kefar see *k'far*

ke-hi-luh
Also *ke-hi-la,** *ke-hi-law*.
Also spelled *kehilla.**
1. A Jewish congregation.
2. An organized Jewish community.

kei-lihtsh
Also spelled *keylitch*.
A large *chalah* used on special occasions.

a as in father; aw as in law; ai as in aisle; ei as in neighbor; e as in bet; i as in vaccine; ih as in tin; o as in solar; oi as in void; oo as in food; u as in put; uh as in but; ch as in chutzpa; zh as in Zhivago.

kein
>Also *kain, kayn.*
>1. No, none.
>2. Nobody.

kein a-yihn huh-ruh
>Also spelled *kainainhore, kine-ahora, kain ayin hore. Kaineinhora* and *kenahora* are contracted forms.
>1. Literally, "no evil eye."
>2. May no evil befall you!

kein muhl
>Also *kain mal.*
>At no time, never.

keivr
>Also *ke-ver.**
>A grave.

kelipa see *klipaw*

kelipot see *klipot*

kelnr
>Also spelled *kelner.*
>A waiter.

kempfr
>Also spelled *kempfer.*
>1. A fighter.
>2. One who battles for a cause.

ken*
>Also *kein.*
>1. Yes.
>2. Correct.

kenahora see *kein ayihn huhruh*

kenen see *kenuhn*

ken ge-moolt zain
>It's imaginable. It's conceivable.

ken-uhn
>Also *ken-en.*
>1. To know how.
>2. To recognize.
>3. To be able.

ken zain
> Could be, maybe.

ke-puh-le
> A small head. A diminutive form of *kuhp*.

ker-en ih-ber di velt
> 1. Literally, "to turn the world upside down."
> 2. To perform the impossible.
> 3. To carry on joyfully.

Ke-ren Ka-ye-met L'Yis-ra-el*
> Also *Ke-ren Ka-ye-mes L'Yis-raw-eil*.
> Jewish National Fund, the tree planting and afforestation agency for Israel.

keria see *kriuh*

kerias haTorah see *k'rias haToraw*

kerias Shema see *k'rias Shema*

ke-ro-va*
> Also *ke-ro-vaw*.
> Also spelled *kerovah*.
> 1. Literally, "nearness (to God)."
> 2. A prayer-poem.

kerovim see *kroivihm*

kerovot*
> The plural of *kerovah*.

kertl
> Also spelled *kertel*.
> A playing card.

kesubah see *k'subuh*

ke-too-vihm*
> Also *ke-su-vim*.
> Also spelled *ketubim*.
> 1. Literally, "writings."
> 2. The third part of the Hebrew Bible, called "Sacred Writings."

ketuba see *k'subuh*

ketuva see *k'subuh*

ketuvim see *ketoovihm*

---

kever see *keivr*

ke-vod ha-be-ri-yot
Respect for human beings.

ke-vod ha-meis
Also *ke-vod ha-met.**
Respect for the dead.

ke-voo-ra*
Also spelled *k'vura*.
1. Burial.
2. Grave.

ke-voo-tza*
Also spelled *kevutza, kvutza*.
A cooperative farming settlement in Israel.

keylitch see *keilihtsh*

kezayit see *k'zayiht*

k'far
Also spelled *kefar*.
A village, especially in Israel.

Khazars
A Tatar people who allegedly converted to Judaism
in the ninth century.

kibbetz see *kihbetz*

kibbutz see *kibutz*

ki-bood*
Also *ki-bud*.
1. Honor, respect.
2. A ritual honor, such as being called to Torah in
synagogue.

ki-bood awv
Also spelled *kibud av.**
Honoring one's father.

ki-bood eim
Also spelled *kibud aym*.
Honoring one's mother.

ki-butz
Also spelled *kibbutz*.

---

a as in father; aw as in law; ai as in aisle; ei as in neighbor; e as in bet; i as in vaccine; ih as in tin; o as in
solar; oi as in void; oo as in food; u as in put; uh as in but; ch as in chutzpa; zh as in Zhivago.

A commune in Israel.
Kibbutzihm is the plural form.

ki-butz ga-loo-yot*
Also *ki-bootz gaw-loo-yos*.
Also spelled *kibbutz galuyot*.
1. Literally, "ingathering of the exiles."
2. Return of Jews from the Diaspora to Israel.

kibutznik
A member of a *kibutz*.

kichl see *kihchl*

kichlach see *kihchlach*

kiddush see *kihdoosh*

kiddushin see *kihdooshihn*

kih-betz
Also spelled *kibbetz, kibutz*.
1. To joke, kid around.
2. Tease.
3. To offer unsolicited advice as a spectator.

kih-betzr
Also spelled *kibbetzer, kibbitzer*.
1. One who offers unsolicited advice.
2. A meddlesome spectator.
3. One who teases.
4. A buttinsky.
5. One who annoys others.

kihchl
Also spelled *kichl*.
A cookie, wafer.

kihch-lach
Also spelled *kichlach*.
Light, airy cookies.

Kih-doosh*
Also *Ki-doosh*.
Also spelled *Kiddush*.
1. Literally, "sanctification."
2. The blessing recited over wine on the Sabbath and holidays.

---

a as in father; aw as in law; ai as in aisle; ei as in neighbor; e as in bet; i as in vaccine; ih as in tin; o as in solar; oi as in void; oo as in food; u as in put; uh as in but; ch as in chutzpa; zh as in Zhivago.

kih-doosh ha-Shem*
Also *ki-doosh ha-Shem.*
Also spelled *kiddush haShem, kiddush haShaym.*
1. Literally, "sanctification of the Name (of God)."
2. An act of Jewish martyrdom.

Kih-doo-shihn*
Also *Ki-doo-shihn.*
Also spelled *Kiddushin.*
1. Marriage.
2. A tractate of the Talmud dealing with matrimony.

kih-doosh Le-vuh-nuh
Also *ki-doosh Levawnaw, ki-doosh Le-va-na.**
Also spelled *kiddush Levana.*
Blessing of the New Moon, said between the third and sixteenth days of the Jewish month.

kihm miht tzuris
Also *kum mit tzores.*
1. Literally, "barely with trouble."
2. Barely made it.

kihm-puht
Also *kim-pet.*
1. A woman in labor.
2. Childbirth.
3. Confinement.

kihm-puht tzetl
Also spelled *kimpet tzetel.*
Childbirth amulet or charm containing Psalm 121 and names of angels and patriarchs.

kih-nas chi-nawm
Also *kihn-at chi-nam.**
Also spelled *kinas chinawm.*
Unwarranted jealousy.

kihnd
Also spelled *kind.*
A child, youngster.

kihn-der-lach
Also spelled *kinderlach.*
Little children.

---

a as in father; aw as in law; ai as in aisle: ei as in neighbor; e as in bet; i as in vaccine; ih as in tin; o as in solar; oi as in void; oo as in food; u as in put; uh as in but; ch as in chutzpa; zh as in Zhivago.

kihnd-oon-keit
>Also spelled *kind-un-keit.*
>Kith and kin; kit and caboodle.

kihndr
>Also spelled *kinder.*
>Children.

kih-ne
>Also *ki-naw, ki-na.**
>1. Jealousy, envy.
>2. A lamentation.

kihn-yan*
>Also *kihn-yuhn.*
>Also spelled *kinyan.*
>1. A purchase.
>2. The finalizing of an agreement whereby both parties grasp a garment at the same time.
>3. Consideration, as in a contract.

kih-shef
>Also *ki-shoof.**
>Also spelled *kishuf.*
>Magic.

kih-shef ma-cher-ihn
>1. A witch.
>2. Title of a play by Abraham Goldfaden (1840-1908), the father of Yiddish theater.

kih-shef machr
>Also spelled *kishef macher.*
>1. Literally, "magic maker."
>2. A male magician.

kihsh-kih
>Also spelled *kishka, kishke.*
>1. Intestines, guts.
>2. Stuffed derma.

Kihs-lev
>Also *Kihs-leiv.*
>Also spelled *Kislev, Kislayv.*
>Ninth month of the Jewish religious calendar, third of the Civil calendar, corresponding to No-

---

a as in father; aw as in law; ai as in aisle; ei as in neighbor; e as in bet; i as in vaccine; ih as in tin; o as in solar; oi as in void; oo as in food; u as in put; uh as in but; ch as in chutzpa; zh as in Zhivago.

vember-December, the month in which Chanukah falls.

kihtl
> Also spelled *kittel.*
> The white linen robe worn by Jewish men at High Holiday services and often also by the leader at the Passover *Seder.*

kiht-ni-ot*
> Also *kiht-ni-os.*
> Also spelled *kitniot, kitnios.*
> The lesser grains—such as rice, beans, and maize—forbidden to Ashkenazim on Passover but permitted to most Sephardim.

kihtzl
> Also spelled *kitzel.*
> To tickle.

kike
> An epithet for "Jew," much like the usage of "wop" or "dago" for Italians and "spik" for Spaniards. The origin is unknown but may be related to the Yiddish word *kaikel (kikel),* meaning "a circle." Not willing to sign their names with a cross (or an "X," which is similar to a cross), some Jews used a circle (a *kaikel*) instead.

kimpet see *kihmpuht*

kina see *kihne*

kind see *kihnd*

kinder see *kihndr*

kindunkeit see *kihndoonkeit*

kine-ahora see *kein ayihn huruh*

ki-not*
> Also *ki-nos.*
> Also spelled *kinoth, kinnot.*
> 1. Lamentations.
> 2. The biblical book Lamentations, recited on Tisha b'Av.

ki-nui
> 1. Appellation.

2. The name by which a Jew is known in non-Jewish life, not his "Jewish" name.

kinyan see *kihnyan*

kipa*

Also *ki-paw.*
A skullcap.

ki-sei shel Ei-li-yaw-hoo ha-naw-vi

Also *ki-se shel E-li-a-hoo ha-na-vi.**
Also spelled *kise shel Eliyahu hanavi.*
Literally, "the chair of the Prophet Elijah," on which a baby boy is placed before his circumcision.

kishef macher see *kihshef machr*

kishke see *kihshkuh*

Kislev see *Kihslev*

kitniot see *kihtniot*

kittel see *kihtl*

kitzel see *kihtzl*

klai zemer see *klei zemr*

klaid see *kleid*

klain see *klein*

(a) klainer gornisht see *(a) kleiner gawrnihsht*

klainikeit see *kleinihkait*

klal Yihs-raw-ayl

Also *klal Yis-ra-el.**
1. Literally, "the totality of the Jewish people."
2. The Jewish community.

klap

Also spelled *klop.*
Slap, hit, rap.

klap zihch kawp ihn vant

1. Literally, "Bang your head against the wall!"
2. Don't bother me!

klas

1. Class, classroom.
2. Grade in school.

klaus see *kloiz*

klawg
>   Also *kluhg, klug.*
>   Also spelled *klog.*
>   1. A curse.
>   2. A lament.

(a) klawg ihz mihr
>   Also *a klug iz mir.*
>   1. Literally, "A curse is (on) me!"
>   2. Woe is me!

klawgn
>   Also spelled *klogen.*
>   Complain, wail, lament.

(a) klawg tzoo Columbus
>   Also spelled *a klog tzu Columbus.*
>   1. Literally, "A curse on Columbus!"
>   2. Damn Columbus! Spoken by Jewish immigrants
>   from Eastern Europe around the turn of the
>   twentieth century when they found that the
>   streets of the New World were not "paved with
>   gold."

(a) klawg tzoo main-e saw-nihm
>   Also spelled *(a) klog tzu meine sonim.*
>   A curse on my enemies!

klawtz
>   Also spelled *kluhtz, klotz.*
>   1. Foolish.
>   2. Clumsy, awkward.
>   3. A bungler.

klawtz ka-she
>   Also spelled *klotz kashe.*
>   1. A foolish question.
>   2. A question intended to annoy someone.

kleid
>   Also spelled *klaid.*
>   Dress, apparel, clothing.

klein
>   Also *klain.*
>   Small, short.

---

a as in father; aw as in law; ai as in aisle; ei as in neighbor; e as in bet; i as in vaccine; ih as in tin; o as in
solar; oi as in void; oo as in food; u as in put; uh as in but; ch as in chutzpa; zh as in Zhivago.

(a) klein-er gawr-nihsht
Also spelled *(a) klainer gornisht.*
1. Literally, "a little nothing."
2. A nobody, a nonentity.

klein-ih-kait
Also spelled *klainikeit.*
Trifle.

kleis
A *matza*-meal dumpling. Synonymous with *kneidl (knaidel).*

klei zemr
Also spelled *klai zemer.*
1. Literally, "musical instruments."
2. Musicians.
3. A band, combo.

klekn
Also spelled *kleken.*
To suffice.

klepn tzoo
To adhere, to stick to.

(es) klept zihch vi arbes ihn vant
1. Literally, "It sticks (applies) like peas to a wall."
2. Irrelevant.
3. Incoherent.

klez-muhr
Also *klez-mihr, klez-mer.*
1. Derived from *klei zemr,* "musical instruments."
2. Musicians.
3. Itinerant musicians in Europe.

kli-paw
Also *kli-pa,* klih-puh.*
Also spelled *kelipa.*
1. Literally, "husk"
2. Used in Jewish mysticism to denote the forces of evil.
3. A shrew.
4. A gabby woman.
5. A female demon.
Klipot and *kelipot* are plural forms.

---

a as in father; aw as in law; ai as in aisle; ei as in neighbor; e as in bet; i as in vaccine; ih as in tin; o as in solar; oi as in void; oo as in food; u as in put; uh as in but; ch as in chutzpa; zh as in Zhivago.

kli-pot*
>   Also *ke-li-pot.*
>   Plural of *klipaw.*

klogen see *klawgn*

kloi-mersht
>   1. Ostensibly.
>   2. As it were.

kloiz
>   Also *klowz, klaus.*
>   1. A club, group.
>   2. A meeting place.
>   3. A small synagogue.

kloog
>   Also *kluhg, klug.*
>   Smart, clever.

klop see *klap*

klotz see *klawtz*

klowz see *kloiz*

klug see *klawg*

klupr
>   Also spelled *klupper.*
>   1. A slow worker.
>   2. A slow thinker.

klutz see *klawtz*

knaidel see *kneidl*

knakr
>   Also spelled *knaker, knocker.*
>   1. Literally, "one who snaps (his fingers, the whip)."
>   2. Big shot, showoff, big wheel.

kneidl
>   Also spelled *knaydl, knaidel, knaidle, knaidl, kneidl.*
>   A dumpling, usually made with *matza* meal, eggs, water, and chicken fat. Served in chicken soup, most often on Passover.
>   Kneidlach and *knaidlach* are plural forms.

---

a as in father; aw as in law; ai as in aisle ei as in neighbor; e as in bet; i as in vaccine; ih as in tin; o as in solar; oi as in void; oo as in food; u as in put; uh as in but; ch as in chutzpa; zh as in Zhivago.

kneppel see *knihpl*

Kne-set*
Also *Knes-es.*
Also spelled *Knesset.*
1. Literally, "an assembly."
2. Unicameral parliament of the State of Israel.

knihp
Also spelled *knip.*
To nip, pinch.

knihpl
Also spelled *knipl, knippel, kneppel.*
1. Button.
2. Knot.
3. Savings, a nest egg, because women often placed money in a handkerchief and tied it into a knot.

knihsh
Also spelled *knish.*
Crisp dough filled with potatoes, meat, or buckwheat, served hot.

knihsh-es
Also spelled *knishes.*
Plural of *knihsh.*

knip see *knihp*

knoble
Garlic.

knocker see *knakr*

kobtzen see *kabtzn*

kochalain see *kawchalein*

kochedik see *kuhchedihk*

kochen see *kawchn*

kochleffel see *kawchlefl*

ko-desh*
Also *koi-desh.*
1. Literally, "holy."
2. Holy objects.

kodoches see *kaduhches*

---

a as in father; aw as in law; ai as in aisle; ei as in neighbor; e as in bet; i as in vaccine; ih as in tin; o as in solar; oi as in void; oo as in food; u as in put; uh as in but; ch as in chutzpa; zh as in Zhivago.

Ko-hein*
>Also *ko-han, Ko-hen.*
>Also spelled *Kohayn.*
>1. A priest.
>2. A descendant of a priestly family.

koifn
>Also spelled *koifen, kaufen.*
>To buy, purchase.

koileil see *koleil*

koim see *kum*

kolbonik see *kawlboinihk*

ko-leil
>Also *koi-leil.*
>Also spelled *kolel.*
>1. An assembly, a gathering.
>2. An institution for or group engaged in advanced
>Torah study.

Kol Nihd-rei
>Also spelled *Kol Nidre.*
>1. Literally, "all vows."
>2. The opening prayer of the Yom Kippur Eve ser-
>vice, which ushers in the Day of Atonement.

koo
>Also *ki.*
>A cow.

koof
>The nineteenth letter of the Hebrew alphabet,
>sounded "k."

koogel see *kugl*

kook ihm uhn see *kuk ihm awn*

koomt a-her
>Also spelled *kumt aher.*
>Come here.

koomt a-rain
>Also spelled *kumt arein.*
>Come in.

---

a as in father; aw as in law; ai as in aisle; ei as in neighbor; e as in bet; i as in vaccine; ih as in tin; o as in solar; oi as in void; oo as in food; u as in put; uh as in but; ch as in chutzpa; zh as in Zhivago.

koomt tzoo-rihk
Also spelled *kumt tzurik.*
Come back.

koo-ni leml
Also spelled *kuni lemel.* Probably related to the
German *lummel,* meaning "bumpkin."
1. A naive person.
2. A nincompoop.
3. A simpleton in a satiric comedy (1880) by Abraham Goldfaden.

koontz
Also spelled *kuntz.*
1. Trick.
2. Trickery.

koontzn
Also spelled *koontzen, kuntzen.*
Plural of *koontz.* See above.

koontzn machr
1. Magician.
2. Trickster.

kop see *kuhp*

kopdraienish see *kuhpdreienihsh*

koppel see *kapl*

koptzen see *kabtzn*

kopvaitik see *kuhpveitig*

ko-sel
Also *ko-tel.**
A wall.

Kosel Maarawvi see *Kotel Maaravi*

kosher
Also *ka-sher,** *kuhshr, ka-sheir.*
1. Literally, "fit, proper."
2. Descriptive of a ritual article or food item that is
fit for use in accordance with Jewish law.
3. To make an article kosher. See *koshering.*
4. (Vernacular) good, all right.

koshering
Also *ka-sher-ing*.
1. An Anglicized form for the process of making kosher meats permissible for cooking by first soaking and salting in accordance with the laws of *kashrus*. See *kashrus*.
2. The process whereby certain utensils used during the year for cooking and eating are rendered permissible for use on Passover. This process involves glowing or soaking. Non-kosher utensils are also rendered kosher by this process.

ko-sher l'Pe-sach
Also *ka-sher l'Pe-sach*.*
Kosher for Passover use.

kotel see *kosel*

Ko-tel Ma-a-ra-vi*
Also *Ko-sel Ma-a-raw-vi*.
1. Literally, "Western Wall" of the Temple destroyed in 70 C.E.
2. The Wailing Wall.

koved see *kuhved*

kovid see *kuhved*

kraftihg see *kreftihg*

krank
To be sick, ill.

krank-hait
Also spelled *krankeit, cronkite*.
Sickness, illness.

kra-sa-vih-tze
Also spelled *krasavitse*.
Beautiful woman.

kratz
To scratch.

krechtz
To groan, moan.

kref-tihg
Also *kraf-tihg, kref-tihk*.

---

a as in father; aw as in law; ai as in aisle; ei as in neighbor; e as in bet; i as in vaccine; ih as in tin; o as in solar; oi as in void; oo as in food; u as in put; uh as in but; ch as in chutzpa; zh as in Zhivago.

1. Robust, sturdy, strong, husky.
2. Full-bodied.
3. Valid.

(a) kreink

Also spelled *krenk*.
A sickness, illness, disease.

kreml

A store, a shop.

krenk see *(a) kreink*

krenkn

Also spelled *krenken*.
1. To be sick (for a time).
2. To suffer.

kre-pi-ren

To die.

krepl

Also spelled *krepel*
A dumpling, filled with meat or cheese, then boiled or fried.

krep-lach

Also *krep-lech*.
Plural of *krepl*. See *krepl*.

kriah see *kriuh*

k'ri-as ha-To-raw

Also *k'ri-at ha-To-ra.**
Also spelled *kerias haTorah*.
Literally, "the reading of the Torah," performed publicly on Monday, Thursday, Saturday, and on all holiday mornings.

k'ri-as She-ma

Also *k'ri-at She-ma.**
Also spelled *kerias Sh'ma*.
1. Literally, "the reading of the Shema."
2. A prayer from the Bible (Deuteronomy 6:4-9) recited at most prayer services and at bedtime.

k'rias She-ma al ha-mi-taw

Also *k'ri-at She-ma al ha-mi-ta.**
Literally, "the recital of the *Shema* at bedtime."

---

a as in father; aw as in law; ai as in aisle; ei as in neighbor; e as in bet; i as in vaccine; ih as in tin; o as in solar; oi as in void; oo as in food; u as in put; uh as in but; ch as in chutzpa; zh as in Zhivago.

krihchn
Also spelled *krichen.*
Crawl, creep.

krihchn a-rein ihn di bein-er
1. Literally, "to creep into the bones."
2. To annoy, to irritate.

krihchn ihn di hoi-che fen-ster
1. Literally, "crawl into high windows."
2. Aspire to high position and status.
3. A social climber.

krihchn oif di glai-che vent
1. Literally, "climb up straight walls."
2. A trouble-maker
3. One who mixes in unduly.

krihch vi a vantz
1. Literally, "creep like a bedbug."
2. Slow-moving.

Kristallnacht
German for "night of broken glass," so named because of what happened in Germany on November 9-10, 1938 when Nazis broke windows of synagogues and Jewish shops.

k'ri-uh
Also *kri-a,* kri-aw.*
Also spelled *keria.*
1. Literally, "tearing."
2. Tearing of one's garment at the graveside or in the chapel as an act of mourning.

kroi-vihm
Also *kro-vihm.**
Also spelled *krovim, kerovim.*
Plural of *kawrov.* See *kawrov.*

kruhm
Also spelled *krom.*
Store, shop.

krup-nihk
Also spelled *krupnick.*
Barley soup.

k'su-buh
Also *k'tu-va,* k'su-ba, k'su-baw.*
Also spelled *ketuba, ketubah, ketuva, ketuvah.*
A Jewish marriage contract, written in Aramaic and read at the wedding ceremony.

k'tuva see *ksubuh*

kugl
Also spelled *kugel, koo-gel.*
A pudding, sweet or savory, usually made with noodles or potatoes.

kuh-che-dihk
Also spelled *kochedik.*
1. Boiling, seething.
2. Excitable.

kuhm
Barely.

kuhm der-lebt
Also *kum der-leibt.*
Literally, "barely alive to see (or enjoy) it."

kuhm vaws er krihcht
Also *kum vos er kricht.*
1. Barely able to creep.
2. A slowpoke.

kuhm vaws er leibt
Also *kum vaws er lebt.*
He's barely alive.

kuhp
Also spelled *kawp, kop, kopf.*
1. Head.
2. Brains, intelligence.

kuhp-drei-en-ihsh
Also spelled *kawpdreienihsh, kopdrayenish, kopdraienish.*
1. Literally, "head-turning."
2. A troublesome matter.
3. Bother, worry.

kuhp ihn drerd
Literally, "head in the earth." Usually used as a

curse, as in *zawl er vaksn vi a tzihbele mitn kawp in drerd,* "May he grow like an onion, with his head in the ground!"

(a) kuhp oif di plei-tzes
>Also spelled *(a) kop oif di plaitzes.*
>1. Literally, "a head on the shoulders."
>2. Level-headed.
>3. Good sense, common sense.

kuhp-vei-tig
>Also *kuhp-vei-tik.*
>Also spelled *kopvaitik.*
>Headache.

kuhpveitik see *kuhpveitig*

kuhshr v'yuhshr
>1. Literally, "kosher and straight."
>2. Fair and square.
>3. Legitimate.

kuhved
>Also *ka-vod,* kaw-vod.*
>Also spelled *koved, kovid.*
>1. Honor.
>2. Respect.
>3. Glory.
>4. Dignity.

kuk ihm awn
>Also spelled *kook ihm uhn.*
>Look at him!

kukn
>Also spelled *kuken.*
>To look, view.

kum
>Also *kam, koim.*
>Hardly, barely.

kum derleibt see *kuhm derlebt*

kumen
>Come, arrive.

kum ihch niht haint, kim ihch mawr-gen
>Also spelled *kum ich nit heint, kum ich morgen.*

---

a as in father; aw as in law; ai as in aisle; ei as in neighbor; e as in bet; i as in vaccine; ih as in tin; o as in solar; oi as in void; oo as in food; u as in put; uh as in but; ch as in chutzpa; zh as in Zhivago.

1. Literally, "If I don't come today, I'll come tomorrow."
2. A procrastinator.

kum mit tzores see *kihm miht tzuris*

kum vos er kricht see *kuhm vaws er krihcht*

kumn tzoo gast
Also spelled *kumen tzu gast*.
1. Literally, "come to be a guest."
2. Come to visit.

kumn tzu Gawt bawr-ves
Also spelled *kumen tsu Gawt bawrves*.
1. Literally, "come before God barefoot."
2. Be humble.

kumsitz see *kumzihtz*

kumt aher see *koomt aher*

kumt arein see *koomt arain*

kumt tzurik see *koomt tzoorihk*

kum-zihtz
Also spelled *kumsitz*.
1. Literally, "come sit."
2. An informal get-together.
3. A social hour.

kuni lemel see *kooni leml*

kuntz see *koontz*

kuntzen see *koontzn*

kur-vuh
Also spelled *kurve, kurveh*.
A prostitute.

kvat-er
Also spelled *kvatter*.
The man who brings the child to the *sondek* at the time of circumcision.

kvat-er-ihn
Also spelled *kvatterin*.
Feminine of *kvater*. See above.

kvel
1. To derive pleasure.
2. To swell with pride.

kvetsh
1. To complain, whine.
2. One who complains a great deal, also called *a kvetsher*.

kvetsh-er-ke
Feminine of *kvetsh*.

kvitl
Also spelled *kvitel, kvitle*.
1. A slip.
2. A ticket.
3. A receipt.
4. A prescription.
5. A note slipped into the cracks of the Western Wall on which a petition or prayer has been inscribed.

kvitsh
To scream, shriek, screech.

kvura see *kevoorah*

k'za-yiht*
Also *ke-za-yihs*.
Also spelled *kezayit*.
1. Literally, "like an olive."
2. A piece (usually of food) the size of an olive, the minimum required for certain blessings.

L

lachn
>Also spelled *lachen*.
>To laugh.

Ladino
>A mixture of Spanish and Hebrew, written in Hebrew characters and spoken by Sephardic Jews of Turkey, Iberia, and the Middle East.

Lag Ba-o-mer*
>Also *Lag Boi-mer, Lag Baw-o-mer*.
>Also spelled *Lag B'Omer*.
>Literally, "the thirty-third day of the *Omer*," a semi-holiday between Passover and Shavuot, occuring on the thirty-third day after the second day of Passover.

laid
>Also spelled *leid*.
>Pain, anguish.

laidik see *leidihg*

laidik geher see *leidihk geier*

laidn
>Also spelled *leiden*.
>1. To suffer.
>2. To endure.

laigen zich shlofen see *leign zihch shlawfn*

laing see *lang*

lamdn
>Also *lam-dan.**
>1. A Talmudic scholar.
>2. One who is erudite.

la-muhd
>Also *la-med.**

---

a as in father; aw as in law; ai as in aisle; ei as in neighbor; e as in bet; i as in vaccine; ih as in tin; o as in solar; oi as in void; oo as in food; u as in put; uh as in but; ch as in chutzpa; zh as in Zhivago.

The twelfth letter of the Hebrew alphabet, corresponding to "l."

la-muhd vawv-nihk
Also spelled *lamed vawvnihk, lamed vovnick.*
See *lamuhd vawv tzadikim.*

la-muhd vawv tza-di-kim
Also *la-med vav tza-di-kihm.**
Literally, "thirty-six saintly people."
According to a tradition, the world continues to exist because of the merit of thirty-six righteous persons whose identity is not known. Each such individual is referred to as a *lamed vovnick.* (The numerical value of the Hebrew letters *lamed* and *vawv* is thirty-six.)

lands-leit
Plural of *landsman.* See *landsman.*

lang
Also *laing.*
Long, referring to time and distance.

lang leibn zawlt ihr
Also spelled *lang leben zolt ir.*
Long may you live!

lashon see *luhshn*

lashon hakodesh see *l'shon hakodesh*

lashon hara see *luhshn hawruh*

lashon kodesh see *luhshn koidesh*

latke see *latkuh*

lat-kes
Pancakes. Plural of *latkuh.*

lat-kuh
Also *lat-ke, lat-ka.*
Potato pancakes, traditionally associated with Chanukah. *Latkes* is the plural form.

lawch see *luhch*

lawshon see *luhshn*

lawshon hawraw see *luhshn hawruh*

---

a as in father; aw as in law; ai as in aisle; ei as in neighbor; e as in bet; i as in vaccine; ih as in tin; o as in solar; oi as in void; oo as in food; u as in put; uh as in but; ch as in chutzpa; zh as in Zhivago.

lawz mihr tzoo roo
>Also spelled *loz mir tzu ru.*
>1. Literally, "Let me be in peace."
>2. Leave me alone! Let me be!

laytz see *letz*

l'cha-yihm
>Also spelled *l'chaim, l'chayim, lechayim.*
>1. Literally, "to life."
>2. A toast offered before drinking liquor or wine.

(a) le-be-dih-ke velt
>A lively world, a spirited world.

lebedik see *leibedihk*

leber
>Liver.

lebn
>Also spelled *leben.*
>1. Living.
>2. To live.

lebn a cha-zihr-she tawg
>Also spelled *leben a chazershen tog.*
>1. Literally, "living a pig's day."
>2. Living high off the hog.
>3. Uninhibited pleasure.

lebn a-zoi vi Gawt ihn Aw-des
>Also spelled *leben azi vi Gott in Odess.*
>1. Literally, "living like God in Odessa."
>2. Living like a king.

(a) lebn oif dain kawp
>Also spelled a *leben oif dein kop.*
>1. Literally, "a life upon your head."
>2. Live and be well!
>3. Well said!
>4. Well done!

le-chat-chi-law
>Also *l'chat-chi-la.**
>1. From the outset.
>2. A priori.
>See also *bihd'eved.*

Le-chi
Also spelled *LeHi*.
An acronym for Lochamei Cherut Yisrael ("Figh-ters for the Freedom of Israel"), the anti-British underground in pre-Israel Palestine, formerly part of the Irgun.

lef-e-le
A small spoon.

lefl
Also spelled *lefel*.
A teaspoon.

le-hach-ihs
Also spelled *l'hachis*.
To annoy, anger, irritate, provoke.

lehavdil see *l'havdihl*

LeHi see *Lechi*

lehveiyeh see *levaya*

lei-be-dihk
Also spelled *lebedik*.
1. Lively, alive.
2. Sprightly.

leid see *laid*

leiden see *laidn*

lei-dihg
Also *lei-dihk*.
Also spelled *laidik*.
1. Empty.
2. Vacant.

lei-dihk gei-er
Also spelled *laidik geher*.
1. Literally, "idle goer."
2. Idler.
3. Vagabond.

leign t'fihlihn
Also spelled *legen tefilin*.
To don phylacteries.

---

a as in father; aw as in law; ai as in aisle: ei as in neighbor; e as in bet; i as in vaccine; ih as in tin; o as in solar; oi as in void; oo as in food; u as in put; uh as in but; ch as in chutzpa; zh as in Zhivago.

leign zihch shlawfn
>Also spelled *laigen zich shlofen.*
>1. Literally, "to lay oneself (down) to sleep."
>2. To go to bed.

lei-kuhch
>Also *lei-kech, lei-kach.*
>Also spelled *lekach, lekech.*
>A sweet cake, usually honey cake.

lei-kuhch-el
>A cookie. A diminutive form of *leikuhch.*

lei-men-er goi-lem
>1. Literally, "clumsy robot."
>2. A clumsy person.

lekach see *leikuhch*

lekn
>Also spelled *leken.*
>To lick.

(a) lek oon a shmek
>1. A lick and a sniff.
>2. A little bit.

lekr
>Also spelled *leker.*
>Literally, "one who licks."

lemech
>Plural of *leml.*

le-mihsh-ke
>Also spelled *lemishke.*
>1. Literally, "porridge."
>2. A naive, wishy-washy person.

leml
>Also spelled *lemel.*
>1. Literally, "a lamb."
>2. Meek, mild.
>3. A nincompoop.

leshon hakodesh see *l'shon hakodesh*

le-shon tar-gum*
>Also *law-shon tar-goom.*

---

a as in father: aw as in law; ai as in aisle; ei as in neighbor; e as in bet; i as in vaccine: ih as in tin: o as in solar; oi as in void; oo as in food; u as in put; uh as in but; ch as in chutzpa: zh as in Zhivago.

1. Aramaic language.
2. Aramaic translation.

letz*

Also *laytz*.
1. A prankster, jester, wag, buffoon, clown.
2. A mocker, scorner, scoffer.

le-va-yuh

Also *le-va-ya**
Also spelled *levaiye, levahyah, leveiyeh*.
1. Literally, "accompaniment."
2. A funeral procession, cortege.

le-va-yat ha-met*

Also *le-vaw-yas ha-meis*.
Literally, "accompanying the deceased" (in the funeral cortege).

Le-vi*

Also *Lei-vi*.
1. A descendant of the tribe of Levi, who were assistants to the priests in Temple times.
2. A Torah honor bestowed upon the non-priestly members of the tribe of Levi.

Levirate marriage

A biblical law requiring the brother of a childless widow either to marry her or to submit to the ritual *chalitza*. See *chalitza*.

Levite

A descendant of the tribe of Levi, including both priests and Levites. See *Levi*.

l'hachis see *lehachihs*

l'hav-dihl*

Also spelled *lehavdil*.
1. To differentiate, distinguish.
2. To establish a distinction between the sacred and profane, between the Sabbath and week-days, between the living and the dead.
See also *havdala*.

li-al-ke

Doll.

lib hawben see *lihb huhbn*

libe see *lihbe*

libn
>Also spelled *liben*.
>To love.

licht see *lihcht*

liebe see *lihbe*

lieb hoben see *lihb huhbn*

ligen see *lihgn*

ligner see *lihgner*

lihb huhbn
>Also spelled *lieb hoben, lib hawben*.
>1. To love.
>2. To be fond of.
>3. To care for.

lih-be
>Also spelled *libe, liebe*.
>1. Love.
>2. Beloved.
>3. A romance, a love affair.

lihcht
>Also spelled *licht*.
>Candle, light.

lihcht benshen
>Also spelled *licht bentshen*.
>1. Candle blessing.
>2. Candlelighting ceremony conducted to usher in Sabbaths and holidays.

lihcht-ihg
>Also spelled *lichtig*.
>Bright, lighted.

lihgn
>Also spelled *ligen*.
>1. Lay down.
>2. Be situated.

lihgnen
>To lie, to prevaricate.

---

a as in father; aw as in law; ai as in aisle; ei as in neighbor; e as in bet; i as in vaccine; ih as in tin; o as in solar; oi as in void; oo as in food; u as in put; uh as in but; ch as in chutzpa; zh as in Zhivago.

lihg-ner
>Also spelled *ligner.*
>Liar, prevaricator.

lihgn ihn zih-nen
>1. Literally, "to lay on one's mind."
>2. To be concerned with, to think of.

lih-liht
>Also *li-liht.*
>Also spelled *Lilith.*
>1. Literally, "of the night."
>2. In Semitic folklore, a female demon.
>3. A magazine published by and for Jewish women *(Lilith).*

Liht-vak
>Also spelled *Litvak.*
>1. A Jewish native of Lithuania.
>2. A descendant of Lithuanian Jews.

Lilith see *lihliht*

Litvak see *Lihtvak*

lo a-lei-chem
>1. Literally, "not upon you."
>2. May it not happen to you!

loch see *luhch*

loch in kop see *lawch ihn kawp*

loifn
>To run.

loksh see *luhksh*

lokshn see *luhkshen*

loo-ach
>Also spelled *luach* and *luah.*
>1. Calendar.
>2. Tablet.
>3. Timetable.

loo-chos
>Also *loo-chot,* lu-chot.*
>Plural of *looach.* See *looach.*

---

a as in father; aw as in law; ai as in aisle; ei as in neighbor; e as in bet; i as in vaccine; ih as in tin; o as in solar; oi as in void; oo as in food; u as in put; uh as in but; ch as in chutzpa; zh as in Zhivago.

loo-luhv
Also *loo-lav.* *
Also spelled *lulav.*
1. A palm branch.
2. One of the four species of plants used in the ritual of the Sukkot festival.

loong
Also spelled *lung.*
Lung.

(a) loong oon le-ber oif der nawz
Also spelled *(a) lung un leber oif der noz.*
1. Literally, "a lung and a liver on your nose."
2. Stop being a hypochondriac!
3. Stop imagining things!

lox
Pronounced *laks.*
Smoked salmon, usually eaten on a bagel with cream cheese. From the German *Lachs,* "salmon."

loz mir tzu ru see *lawz mihr tzoo roo*

l'shaw-naw to-vaw
Also *l'sha-na to-va.* *
Literally, "a good year." An abbreviated form of the salutation *l'shana tova tikateivu.*

l'shaw-naw to-vaw ti-chaw-sei-moo
Also *l'sha-na to-va ti-cha-tei-mu.* *
1. Literally, "May you be sealed in the Book of Life!"
2. A Yom Kippur greeting.

l'shaw-naw to-vaw ti-kaw-sei-voo
Also *l'sha-na to-va ti-ka-tei-vu.* *
1. Literally, "May you be inscribed for a good year!"
2. A Jewish New Year greeting, often abbreviated to *l'shuhnuh toivuh* or *l'shana tova.* *

l'shon ha-ko-desh
Also *la-shon ha-ko-desh.* *
Also spelled *leshon hakodesh.*
1. Literally, "holy tongue."
2. Hebrew language.

---

a as in father; aw as in law; ai as in aisle; ei as in neighbor; e as in bet; i as in vaccine; ih as in tin; o as in solar; oi as in void; oo as in food; u as in put; uh as in but; ch as in chutzpa; zh as in Zhivago.

l'shon hawraw see *luhshuhn hawruh*

luach see *looach*

luchot see *loochos*

luft
> Air, atmosphere.

luft-mensh
> 1. Literally, "air man."
> 2. A person without an occupation or income, improvising for a livelihood.
> 3. A dreamer.

luhch
> Also *lawch*.
> Also spelled *loch*.
> 1. Hole, aperture.
> 2. Cavity.

luhch ihn kawp
> Also spelled *loch in kop*.
> 1. Literally, "a hole in the head."
> 2. A person whose mental faculties are not in tact.
> 3. Something unwanted.

luhksh
> Also spelled *loksh*.
> 1. Noodle.
> 2. (Slang) a tall, thin person.

luhk-shen
> Also spelled *lokshn, lokshen, luhkshn*.
> Noodles. Plural of *luhksh*.

luhkshn kugl
> Also spelled *lukshen kugel*.
> Noodle pudding.

luhshn
> Also *law-shon, la-shon.**
> Also spelled *luhshen*.
> 1. Language.
> 2. Tongue.
> 3. Speech.

luhshn haw-ruh
> Also *lawshn haw-ruh, l'shon haw-raw,*

and *la-shon ha-ra.**
1. Literally, "evil tongue."
2. Gossip, slander.
3. Bad-mouthing.

luhshn koi-desh
Also *law-shon ko-desh, la-shon ko-desh.**
1. Literally, "holy language."
2. Hebrew.

lukshen kugel see *luhkshn kugl*

lulav see *looluhv*

lump
A scoundrel.

lung see *loong*

(a) lung un leber oif der noz see *(a) loong oon leber oif der nawz*

M

maachal see *maichl*

maala see *mailuh*

maalos
>Also *ma-a-lot.**
>Steps.

Maariv see *Marihv*

maase see *maisuh*

maaser see *maisr*

ma-ba-ra*
>Also *ma-baw-raw.*
>A transit camp for immigrants to Israel, following statehood in 1948.

ma-ba-rot*
>Also *ma-baw-ros.*
>Plural of *mabara.* See above.

ma-cha-shei-fuh
>Also *ma-cha-shei-fa.**
>1. A witch.
>2. A sorceress.
>*Mechasheif* is the masculine form.

machateinihste see *mechuteneste*

machen see *machn*

macher see *machr*

mach-er-ai-ke
>Also spelled *machereike.*
>A gimmick, contraption.

mach es kail-ech-dihk oon shpihtz-ihk
>Also spelled *mach es keilechdik un shpitzik.*
>1. Literally, "Make it round and pointed."
>2. Come to the point! Stop beating around the bush!

mach es shnel
>Make it quick! Hurry up!

---

a as in father; aw as in law; ai as in aisle; ei as in neighbor; e as in bet; i as in vaccine; ih as in tin; o as in solar; oi as in void; oo as in food; u as in put; uh as in but; ch as in chutzpa; zh as in Zhivago.

machn
> Also spelled *machen*.
> 1. To make.
> 2. To do.
> 3. To feel.

machn a ge-vald
> Also spelled *machen a gevald*.
> 1. To shout, make an outcry.
> 2. To call for help.

machn a lebn
> Also spelled *machen a leben*.
> To make a living.

machn a tsih-mes
> Also spelled *ma-chen a tzimmes*.
> 1. Literally, "to make a stew".
> 2. To make a fuss.
> See also *tzihmes*.

machn bluh-te foon
> Also spelled *machen blote fun*.
> 1. To make a mess of.
> 2. To take someone apart.
> 3. To vilify.
> 4. To reprimand.

mach niht kein tsih-mes fun dem
> Also spelled *mach nit kain tzimmes fun dem*.
> 1. Literally, "Don't get into a stew over this."
> 2. Don't make a big fuss over this!

machn ois
> Also spelled *ma-chen ois*.
> Literally, "to make out," used in the negative sense:
> *es macht mihr niht ois*, "It doesn't matter to me."

machn Shabuhs far zihch
> 1. Literally, "to make (prepare) Sabbath for oneself."
> 2. To do something one's own way.

machn zihch ba-kvem
> Also spelled *machen zich bakvem*.
> To make oneself comfortable.

---

a as in father; aw as in law; ai as in aisle; ei as in neighbor; e as in bet; i as in vaccine; ih as in tin; o as in solar; oi as in void; oo as in food; u as in put; uh as in but; ch as in chutzpa; zh as in Zhivago.

machn zihch niht vihs-en-dihk
> Also spelled *machen zich nit visendik.*
> To pretend not to know (about a matter).

machr
> Also spelled *macher.*
> 1. Literally, "a maker," one who makes things happen.
> 2. A wheeler-dealer.

machzor see *machzuhr*

Mach-zuhr
> Also *Mach-zor.**
> Also spelled *Mahzor.*
> 1. Literally, "cycle."
> 2. The Jewish prayerbook containing the holiday and festival liturgies, as contrasted with the *Siddur,* which contains the daily and Sabbath prayers.

maf-tir
> Also spelled *maphtir.*
> 1. Literally, "conclusion."
> 2. The concluding portion of the Torah reading on Sabbaths and holidays.
> 3. The person who receives the final Torah reading honor *(aliya)* on Sabbaths and holidays.

(a) ma-gei-fuh zawl dihch trefn
> Also spelled *a magaife zol dich trefen.*
> 1. Literally, "A pestilence should befall you!"
> 2. May you enjoy bad luck!

Magen David see *Muhgn Duhvihd*

ma-gihd
> Also spelled *magid, maggid.*
> 1. An itinerant preacher.
> 2. An orator.

mahyofisnik see *mayawfihsnihk*

Mahzor see *Machzuhr*

maichl
> Also *ma-a-chal.**
> Also spelled *meichel.*

---

a as in father; aw as in law; ai as in aisle; ei as in neighbor; e as in bet; i as in vaccine; ih as in tin; o as in solar; oi as in void; oo as in food; u as in put; uh as in but; ch as in chutzpa; zh as in Zhivago.

1. Food, delicacy.
2. A gourmet delight.

maidel see *meidl*

mai-luh
Also *ma-a-law, ma-a-la.**
Also spelled *meileh.*
1. Virtue, good quality.
2. Merit.
3. An asset.

Mai-mu-na
A feast held by Moroccan Jews celebrating the end of Passover

main baw-buhz tam
Also spelled *mein bobe's tam.*
1. Literally, "my grandma's taste."
2. Bad taste, tacky.

mainen see *meinen*

mai-ne suh-nihm zawl-en a-zoi lebn
Also *meine sonim zolen azoi leben.*
1. Literally, "My enemies should live so."
2. It will never happen!

mainung see *meinung*

Mairihv see *Marihv*

mais see *meis*

maise see *maisuh*

maisr
Also *ma-a-ser.**
Also spelled *maiser.*
The taking of a tithe or a tenth of the farmer's first fruits (of the field and livestock) for the upkeep of the Temple and for the support of the Levites.

mai-suh
Also *mai-se, ma-a-se*.*
Also spelled *meiseh.*
1. A story.
2. An episode.

mai-suh she-haw-yaw
An old story.

mait mitzvah see *meis mihtsvuh*

maivin see *meivihn*

ma-kes
Plural of *makuh*.

ma-kuh
Also *ma-ka.**
1. A pestilence.
2. A plague.
3. A scourge.
4. A wound.

(a) ma-kuh un-ter yen-emz uhr-em ihz niht shver tzoo trawgn
1. Literally, "an abscess under another's arm is not hard to bear."
2. Someone else's afflication is easy to endure.

malach see *maluhch*

Malach Hamavet see *Maluhch Hamawves*

Mal-choo-yos
Also *Mal-choo-yot.**
Also spelled *Malchuyos, Malkhuyot, Malchuyot.*
1. Literally, "Sovereignty."
2. Part of the *Musaf* prayer of the Rosh Hashana service.

mal-shi-noos
Also *mal-shi-nes, mal-shi-nut.**
1. Slander.
2. Calumny.
3. Libel.

mal-uhch
Also *mal-awch, mal-ach**
Angel.

Mal-uhch Ha-maw-ves
Also *Mal-ach ha-Ma-vet.**
Angel of Death.

mamalige see *mamelihge*

---

a as in father; aw as in law; ai as in aisle; ei as in neighbor; e as in bet; i as in vaccine; ih as in tin; o as in solar; oi as in void; oo as in food; u as in put; uh as in but; ch as in chutzpa; zh as in Zhivago.

mama loshen see *mame lawshn*

mamash see *mamuhsh*

ma-maw-shus
>Also *ma-ma-shut.**
>1. Literally "substance."
>2. Reality, concreteness.

ma-me lawshn
>Also spelled *mama loshen, mameh loshen.*
>1. Literally, "mother tongue" (of East European Jews and their descendants).
>2. Yiddish.

ma-me-lih-ge
>Also spelled *mamalige, mamelige.*
>Cornmeal pudding, of Rumanian origin.

ma-men-yoo
>Also spelled *mamenyu.*
>A pet form of *mamuh.* See below.

ma-muh
>Also *ma-me.*
>Mother, mama, mom.

ma-muhsh
>Also *ma-mash.**
>1. Actually.
>2. The way it happened.
>3. Truly.
>4. Absolutely.

mam-zei-rus
>Also *mam-zei-rut**
>Also spelled *mamzerus.*
>Bastardy, the state of being a *mamzr.*

mamzr
>Also *mam-zer.**
>Bastard.

man
>1. Man.
>2. Husband.

mandel see *mandl*

---

a as in father; aw as in law; ai as in aisle; ei as in neighbor; e as in bet; i as in vaccine; ih as in tin; o as in solar; oi as in void; oo as in food; u as in put; uh as in but; ch as in chutzpa; zh as in Zhivago.

man-del-brot

Sweet, almond-flavored pastry, baked in long strips, cut into thin slices, then usually toasted in the oven.

mandl

Also spelled *mandel.*
Almond.

mand-len

Also *mand-lin, mandln.*
Plural of *mandl.* See above.

ma nihsh-ta-naw

Also *ma nihsh-ta-na.**
1. Literally, "What is the difference?"
2. The opening words of the "Four Questions" in the Haggada, asked by the youngest child at the Passover *Seder.*

mantl

Also spelled *mantel.*
1. Covering (garment).
2. Cloak.
3. Torah covering.

maot chitihm see *mawos chitihm*

ma-paw

Also *ma-pa.**
Also spelled *mapah, mappah.*
1. Literally, "a tablecloth."
2. The name of a commentary on the *Shulchan Aruch.*

(a) ma-paw-luh

Also *a ma-paw-law, a ma-puh-le.*
1. A downfall.
2. A catastrophe.
3. A miscarriage.

mappah see *mapaw*

mapuhle see *mapawluh*

Mar Chesh-van*

Also *Mar Chesh-von.*
Also spelled *Mar Heshvan.*

---

a as in father; aw as in law; ai as in aisle; ei as in neighbor; e as in bet; i as in vaccine; ih as in tin; o as in solar; oi as in void; oo as in food; u as in put; uh as in but; ch as in chutzpa; zh as in Zhivago.

1. Literally, "bitter (sad) Cheshvan," a month in which there are no Jewish holidays.
2. A synonym for the Hebrew month Cheshvan, which follows Tishri, a month filled with holidays.

Ma-rihv
Also *Ma-a-rihv,* Mai-rihv.*
Also spelled *Maariv.*
1. The daily evening prayer service.
2. An Israeli afternoon newspaper.

maror see *mawror*

Marrano
1. From the Spanish meaning "pig."
2. In fifteenth-century Spain and Portugal, a contemptuous designation for Jewish converts to Christianity who clandestinely practised Judaism.
3. A secret Jew.

masechta see *mesihchtuh*

ma-ser*
Also spelled *masser.*
1. Literally, "to hand over."
2. To betray.
3. To denounce to the authorities.
4. To tattle.

mash-gi-ach
1. Watchman, observer.
2. *Kashrut* inspector, an overseer who attests to the kosher status of the food that is prepared and served.

mashiach see *meshiach*

mash-ke
1. Any alcoholic liquor.
2. In modern Hebrew, any beverage.

mas-kihl
Also spelled *maskil.*
1. A serious student.
2. An enlightened person.

---

a as in father; aw as in law; ai as in aisle; ei as in neighbor; e as in bet; i as in vaccine; ih as in tin; o as in solar; oi as in void; oo as in food; u as in put; uh as in but; ch as in chutzpa; zh as in Zhivago.

mas-ki-lihm
> Also spelled *maskilim*.
> Plural of *maskil*.

mas-mihd
> Also *mat-mihd*.*
> Also spelled *masmid, matmid*.
> 1. Diligent, zealous.
> 2. An industrious student.

ma-so-ruh
> Also *ma-so-raw, me-so-ra, ma-so-ra,* * *me-so-ruh*.
> 1. Tradition.
> 2. The accumulation of tradition concerning the correct Hebrew text of the Bible.

massekhet
> A variant form of *mesihchtuh*. See *mesihchtuh*.

masser see *maser*

matmid see *masmihd*

mat-ri-ach
> 1. To burden.
> 2. To impose upon.
> 3. To trouble.

mat-ri-ach zain
> Also spelled *matriach zein*.
> 1. To trouble oneself, burden oneself.
> 2. To take pains.
> 3. To be so good as to.
> 4. To take the trouble to.

matseivah see *matzeivuh*

matza see *matzuh*

ma-tza she-mu-ra*
> Also *ma-tzuh shmoo-ruh*.
> Literally, "guarded *matza*," made under specially rigorous supervision in which moisture is kept off the grain from the time of reaping until the time of baking. See also *matzuh (matza)*.

ma-tzei-vuh
> Also *ma-tzei-va,* * *ma-tzei-vaw*.
> Also spelled *matseiva*.

1. Pillar.
2. Tombstone.

ma-tzot*
Also *ma-tzuhs, ma-tzos.*
Also spelled *matzas.*
Plural of *matzuh.* See *matzuh.*

ma-tzot shel mihtz-va*
Also *ma-tzos shel mihtz-vaw.*
Three symbolic *matzot* used at the *Seder.*

ma-tzuh
Also *ma-tzaw, ma-tza**
Also spelled *matzo, matsa, matzah.*
Unleavened bread eaten particularly during
Passover.

ma-tzuh balls
Dumplings made with *matza* meal.

maven see *meivihn*

mawd-ne
Also spelled *modne.*
Odd, strange.

mawd-ne draw-chihm
Odd ways, peculiar habits.

Mawgein Dawvihd see *Muhgn Duhvihd*

mawgn kugl
Also spelled *mogen kugel.*
1. Literally, "stuffed pudding."
2. Another term for stuffed derma, also referred to
as *kishke.*

mawl-en ge-mawl-ene mel
1. Literally, "to grind ground flour."
2. To repeat, rehash things.

maw-os chi-tihm
Also *ma-ot chi-tihm.**
Also spelled *maos chitim.*
Literally, "wheat money," collected before Pass-
over and distributed to the poor so that they can
buy *matza* and other articles for the holiday.

---

a as in father; aw as in law; ai as in aisle; ei as in neighbor; e as in bet; i as in vaccine; ih as in tin; o as in solar; oi as in void; oo as in food; u as in put; uh as in but; ch as in chutzpa; zh as in Zhivago.

mawrgn
>Also spelled *mawrgen, morgen.*
>1. Morning.
>2. Tomorrow.

maw-ror
>Also *ma-ror.**
>Also spelled *moror.*
>Bitter herbs, primarily horseradish, eaten at the
>Passover *Seder.*

mawshiach see *meshiach*

ma yaw-fihs-nihk
>Also spelled *mah yofisnik.*
>1. Literally, "a how-beautiful, how-lovely one."
>2. A cringing, servile Jew who plays up to non-
>   Jews by telling them how wonderful they are.
>3. A pollyana.

ma-yihm
>Also spelled *mayim.*
>Water.

ma-yihm ach-ro-nihm
>Also spelled *mayim acharonim.*
>1. Literally, "final water."
>2. Water used at the end of a meal to rinse the
>   fingers before reciting Grace After Meals.

mazal see *mazl*

mazal tov see *mazl tuhv*

ma-zihk
>Also spelled *mazik.*
>One who is destructive mischievous, especially a
>child.

mazl
>Also *ma-zawl, ma-zal.**
>Also spelled *mazel.*
>1. Literally, "a star, planet."
>2. Luck.
>3. Destiny.

mazl tuhv
>Also *ma-zawl tov, ma-zal tov.**

---

a as in father; aw as in law; ai as in aisle; ei as in neighbor; e as in bet; i as in vaccine; ih as in tin; o as in
solar; oi as in void; oo as in food; u as in put; uh as in but; ch as in chutzpa; zh as in Zhivago.

Also spelled *mazel tov, mazzeltov.*
1. A good star.
2. Good fortune.
3. Good luck!
4. Congratulations!

m'cha-leil Sha-buhs
Also *me-cha-leil Sha-baws, me-cha-lel Sha-bat.* *
1. One who desecrates the Sabbath.
2. A violator of Sabbath law.

m'cha-ye
Also spelled *mechaye* and *mechaieh.*
1. Literally, "to revive, to bring back to life."
2. A pleasure, delight.

m'cha-ye ha-mei-sihm
Also *m'cha-ye ha-me-tihm.* *
Literally, "He (God) revives the dead."

m'darf hawb-en mazl
Also spelled *men darf hoben mazel.*
One has to have luck.

m'darf niht zain shein; m'darf hoben chein
Also spelled *men darf nit zein shain; men darf hoben chain.*
One doesn't have to be pretty; one needs (only) to have charm.

mead see *med*

Mea Shearim
1. Literally, "One Hundred Measures," commonly translated "One Hundred Gates." Based on the verse, "And Isaac sowed the land and it yielded him in that same year a hundredfold *(mea shearim),* for the Lord blessed him" (Genesis 26:12).
2. The ultra-Orthodox quarter of Jerusalem.

mechalel Shabat see *m'chaleil Shabuhs*

me-cha-sheif
1. A sorcerer.
2. A wizard.

---

3. A magician.
Machasheifa is the feminine form.

mechaye see *m'chaye*

me-chih-tzuh
Also *me-chi-tza,* * *me-chi-tzaw.*
A panel or curtain separating men from women,
particularly in the synagogue.

me-chi-luh
Also *me-chi-law, me-chi-la.* *
Forgiveness, pardon.

me-choo-ta-nihm
Also spelled *mechutanim.*
Plural of *me-chu-tuhn.*

me-chu-luh
Also spelled *mechule.*
1. Sick.
2. Spoiled.
3. Crazy.
4. Wild.
5. Bankrupt.

m-chu-tan-ihm
Also spelled *mechutanim.*
Plural of *mechutan.*

me-chu-ten-es-te
Also *ma-cha-tei-nihs-te.*
1. A female relative.
2. A relative through marriage (mother of a son-in-
   law or daughter-in-law).

me-chu-tuhn
Also *me-chu-tan,* * *me-chu-tawn.*
1. Related.
2. A relative through marriage (the father of a son-
   in-law or daughter-in-law).

med
A fermented beverage made of honey, water, and
hops.

me-dih-ne
Also *me-di-naw, me-di-na.* *

Also spelled *medine.*
1. Land.
2. Country.

medruhsh see *mihdruhsh*

me-gih-luh
Also *me-gih-le, me-gi-law, me-gi-la.**
Also spelled *megilla.*
1. Literally, "scroll."
2. A generic name of five biblical books: Esther, Ecclesiastes, Song of Songs, Ruth, and Lamentations.
3. "The *Megilla*" is the Book of Esther, read on Purim.
3. Any long, involved, or boring narrative.

Megillat Ester see *M'gilas Ester*

mehren see *merihn*

meichel see *maichl*

meidl
Also spelled *maidel.*
1. A girl.
2. A young, unmarried woman.

meileh see *mailuh*

mein bobe's tam see *main bawbuhz tam*

mein cha-yes geit ois
Also spelled *mein chaies gait ois.*
1. Literally, "My life is ebbing."
2. I'm dying (for it).
3. A yearning.

mei-nen
Also spelled *mainen.*
1. To mean, intend.
2. To believe.
3. To indicate.

meine sonim zolen azoi leben see *maine suhnihm zawlen azoi lebn*

mein-ung
Also spelled *mainung.*

---

a as in father; aw as in law; ai as in aisle; ei as in neighbor; e as in bet; i as in vaccine; ih as in tin; o as in solar; oi as in void; oo as in food; u as in put; uh as in but; ch as in chutzpa; zh as in Zhivago.

1. Meaning.
2. Idea.
3. View, opinion.

meir see *mer*

meirihn see *merihn*

meis
> Also *met,* mes.*
> Also spelled *mais.*
> 1. A deceased person.
> 2. A corpse.

meiseh see *maisuh*

meis mihtz-vuh
> Also *met mihtz-va.**
> Also spelled *mais mitzvah.*
> 1. A good deed honoring the dead.
> 2. An "abandoned" corpse. When no one else is available to care for the deceased, the obligation falls upon the first Jew who finds it to arrange for the burial.

mei-vihn
> Also spelled *maven, maivin.*
> 1. Expert.
> 2. Authority.
> 3. Connoisseur.

me-ka-ne*
> Also *me-ka-nei.*
> Jealous, envious.

mek-ler-ke
> The feminine form of *meklr.*

meklr
> Also spelled *mekler.*
> 1. A broker.
> 2. A go-between.

me-la-muhd
> Also *me-la-med.**
> 1. A teacher.
> 2. A teacher in a *cheder.* See *cheder.*

---

a as in father; aw as in law; ai as in aisle; ei as in neighbor; e as in bet; i as in vaccine; ih as in tin; o as in solar; oi as in void; oo as in food; u as in put; uh as in but; ch as in chutzpa; zh as in Zhivago.

me-la-ve mal-kuh
> Also *me-la-ve mal-ka,** *me-la-ve mal-kaw.*
> Also spelled *melaveh malkah.*
> 1 Literally, "to accompany the queen."
> 2. To usher out the Sabbath Queen.
> 3. A repast get-together at the end of the Sabbath.

mel-da-do
> A Ladino word describing a get-together of Sephardic Jews at which there are readings from religious literature.

melech* see *meluhch*

Me-lech Mal-chei Ha-me-law-chihm
> Literally, "the King of Kings (God)," a phrase used often in the liturgy.

me-lech Sobieski's yawr-en
> Also spelled *melech Sobieski's yoren.*
> 1. Literally, "King (John) Sobieski's years." Sobieski was a seventeenth-century Polish monarch.
> 2. The good old days.

me-li-tza*
> Also *me-li-tzaw.*
> Also spelled *melitsa, melizah.*
> 1. A parable.
> 2. An elegant, florid style in Hebrew prose writing.

mellah
> 1. A ghetto.
> 2. The Jewish quarter in North African cities.

mel-uhch
> Also *me-lach, me-lech.**
> King, sovereign.

mem
> The thirteenth letter of the Hebrew alphabet, corresponding in sound to "m."

men
> One (person). Often used as a prefix in the form *m'———* or *me———*.

---

a as in father: aw as in law: ai as in aisle: ei as in neighbor; e as in bet: i as in vaccine: ih as in tin: o as in solar: oi as in void: oo as in food; u as in put; uh as in but; ch as in chutzpa: zh as in Zhivago.

me-na-cheim aw-vel zain
>   Also spelled *menachem avel zein.*
>   1. Literally, "to comfort the mourner."
>   2. Paying a condolence call.

mench see *mentsh*

men darf hoben mazel see *m'darf hawben mazl*

men darf nit zein shain; men darf hoben chain
>   see *m'darf niht zain shein; m'darf hoben chein*

men hawt a-lein uhn-ge-kawcht
>   Also spelled *men hot alain ungekocht*
>   1. Literally, "you cooked it yourself."
>   2. You did it yourself!
>   3. Don't blame anyone but yourself!

men ken brech-en
>   1. Literally, "One can vomit (from it)."
>   2. It's disgusting!

men ken d'harg-et ver-en
>   1. Literally, "One can get killed" (sarcasm).
>   2. It's dangerous!

men ken es ihn moil niht ne-men
>   1. Literally, "One can't take it in his/her mouth."
>   2. It's unpalatable!

men ken leck-en di fing-ers
>   1. Literally, "One can lick his/her fingers."
>   2. It's delicious!

men ken me-shu-ge ver-en
>   1. Literally, "One can go crazy (over it)."
>   2. It's terrific!

men ken niht puh-ter ver-en
>   1. Literally, "One can't get rid of it (him/her)."
>   2. It's an insoluble problem.

men ken niht tansn oif tzvei cha-se-nez miht ein mawl
>   1. Literally, "One can't dance at two weddings at the same time"
>   2. We can do only one thing at a time.

men ken tse-zetst ve-ren
>   Literally, "One can burst."

---

a as in father; aw as in law; ai as in aisle; ei as in neighbor; e as in bet; i as in vaccine; ih as in tin; o as in solar; oi as in void; oo as in food; u as in put; uh as in but; ch as in chutzpa; zh as in Zhivago.

men ken zihch ba-lekn di fing-ers
Also spelled *men ken baleken di fingers.*
1. Literally, "One can lick the fingers."
2. It's delicious!

men lawzt niht leibn
1. Literally, "They (people) don't let one live."
2. People don't stop pestering one.

me-noo-vuhl
Also *me-nu-vawl, me-nu-val.**
Ugly, corrupt, contemptible person.

menorah see *menoruh*

me-no-ruh
Also *me-no-raw, me-no-ra.**
1. A candelabrum with two or more branches used on the Sabbath and holidays in the home and the synagogue.
2. An eight-branched candelabrum used on Chanuka.

men ret oon ret
They keep on talking and talking (and say nothing).

men ret zihch ois daws hartz
One talks his/her heart out.

men shush-kiht zihch
Also spelled *men shushkit zich.*
They whisper to each other.

mentsh
Also spelled *mench, mensh.*
1. A man.
2. A real person of worth and dignity.

(a) mentsh awn glihk ihz a toi-ter mentsh
A person without luck is a dead person.

menuval see *menoovuhl*

men zugt see *m'zuhgt*

mer
Also *meir.*
Carrot.

---

a as in father; aw as in law; ai as in aisle; ei as in neighbor; e as in bet; i as in vaccine; ih as in tin; o as in solar; oi as in void; oo as in food; u as in put; uh as in but; ch as in chutzpa; zh as in Zhivago.

mer-ihn
　　Also *mei-rihn, me-ren.*
　　Also spelled *meiren, merin, mehren.*
　　Plural of *mer.* See *mer.*

me-rihn tzih-muhs
　　Also spelled *mehren tzimmes.*
　　A sweet dish made with carrots and occasionally
　　with a combination of other ingredients: sweet po-
　　tatoes, prunes, meat, etc.

mer-ka-va*
　　Also *mer-kaw-vaw.*
　　Also spelled *merkavah.*
　　Literally, "chariot." Associated in Jewish mysti-
　　cism with the prophet Ezekiel's vision of the Divine
　　throne-chariot.

merkavah see *merkava*

mes see *meis*

mesader gitin see *m'sadeir gitihn*

mesader kiddushin see *m'sadeir kidooshihn*

me-shi-ach
　　Also *maw-shi-ach, ma-shi-ach.**
　　1. The anointed one.
　　2. The Messiah.

meshigaas see *meshugaas*

meshigene see *meshugenuh*

me-shih-gas-ihm
　　Also spelled *mishigasim.*
　　1. Crazy actions.
　　2. Foolish deeds.

me-shu-ga-as
　　Also *me-shu-ga-at.**
　　Also spelled *mishegaas, meshigaas, m'shugaas.*
　　Craziness, madness.

me-shu-ga-ner
　　A variant form of *meshugenuh.*

me-shu-ge
　　Also *me-shu-guh, me-shu-ga.**

---

a as in father; aw as in law; ai as in aisle; ei as in neighbor; e as in bet; i as in vaccine; ih as in tin; o as in
solar; oi as in void; oo as in food; u as in put; uh as in but; ch as in chutzpa; zh as in Zhivago.

1. Insane.
2. Mad.
3. Crazy.

me-shu-ge bihst du?
Are you crazy?

me-shu-ge bihst du, tzoo chaw-seir dei-uh?
Also spelled *meshuga bistu tzu chasser daie?*
Are you crazy or just of diminished mental capacity?

me-shu-ge-ne genz, me-shu-ge-ne grih-be-nes
Also spelled *meshugane genz, meshugane gribenes.*
1. Literally, "crazy geese, crazy pieces of rendered fat."
2. Like parents, like children.

me-shu-ge-ner
Also spelled *meshuganer.*
Crazy person (masculine).

me-shu-ge-ner mam-zer
Crazy bastard.

(a) me-shu-ge-ne velt
Also spelled *(a) meshugane velt.*
1. A crazy world.
2. A mad world.

me-shu-ge-nuh
Also spelled *meshugane, meshigine, meshigina.*
1. A crazy person.
2. A madman.

me-shu-ge oif toit
Also *me-shu-ge tzum toit.*
Also spelled *meshuga oif toit.*
1. Literally, "dead crazy."
2. Really crazy.

meshuge tzum toit see *meshuge oif toit*

meshuguh see *meshuge*

me-shu-luhch
Also *me-shu-lach.**

---

a as in father; aw as in law; ai as in aisle; ei as in neighbor; e as in bet; i as in vaccine; ih as in tin; o as in solar; oi as in void; oo as in food; u as in put; uh as in but; ch as in chutzpa; zh as in Zhivago.

1. Literally, "one who has been sent forth."
2. A courier, messenger, envoy.
3. A fund-raising emissary for charitable or academic institutions.

me-shu-muhd
Also *me-shu-med, me-shu-mad.* *
An apostate, a Jew who converted to another religion.

me-shu-nuh
Also *me-shu-ne, me-shu-na* *.
1. Different.
2. Changed.
3. Strange, queer.
4. Curious, eccentric.

me-sihch-tuh
Also *me-sihch-ta* *, ma-sech-ta, ma-sech-tuh.*
Also spelled *messekhet.*
A tractate (book) of the Talmud.

mesihvtuh
Also *me-tihv-ta,* * me-sihv-taw.*
Also spelled *metivta, mesifta.*
An academy of Jewish learning for advanced Talmudic studies.

me-soo-she-lach
1. The Hebrew name of Methuselah, the biblical character said to have lived 969 years, (Genesis 5:27).
2. An old man.

mesora see *masoruh*

mesr
Also spelled *meser.*
A knife.

met see *meis*

metihvta   see *mesihvtuh*

metivta see *mesihvtuh*

met mihtzva see *meis mihtzvuh*

metsia see *metziuh*

---

a as in father; aw as in law; ai as in aisle; ei as in neighbor; e as in bet; i as in vaccine; ih as in tin; o as in solar; oi as in void; oo as in food; u as in put; uh as in but; ch as in chutzpa; zh as in Zhivago.

me-tur-ge-man
> Literally, "translator (of the Bible)."

metzitzuh see *m'tzitza*

me-tzi-uh
> Also *me-tzi-a,* me-tzi-aw, m'tzi-uh.*
> Also spelled *metziye, metsieh, metsia.*
> 1. Literally, "a find."
> 2. A bargain.
> 3. A discovery.
> 4. A windfall.

(a) me-tzi-uh foon a ga-nef
> Also spelled *(a) metzia fun a ganav.*
> 1. Literally, "a find from a thief."
> 2. An extraordinary bargain.

me-ya-eish
> Also *me-ya-esh.**
> To be sorry.

me-ya-eish zain
> Also spelled *meyaesh zein.*
> 1. To be disappointed.
> 2. To give up hope.

me-zo-not*
> Also *me-zo-nos.*
> 1. Provisions.
> 2. Bread and breadlike products over which the *Hamotzi* prayer must be recited.

me-zumn
> Also *me-zu-muhn, me-zu-man.**
> Also spelled *m'zumen.*
> 1. Literally, "ready, prepared."
> 2. Ready cash, money.
> 3. A quorum of three or more for joining in the *Grace After Meals* prayers.

mezuza see *mezuzuh*

me-zu-zuh
> Also *me-zu-ze, me-zu-za,* mezuzaw.*
> Also spelled *mezzuza, m'zooza, mezuzah.*
> 1. Doorpost.

---

a as in father; aw as in law; ai as in aisle; ei as in neighbor; e as in bet; i as in vaccine; ih as in tin; o as in solar; oi as in void; oo as in food; u as in put; uh as in but; ch as in chutzpa; zh as in Zhivago.

2. A small parchment upon which passages from the Bible are handwritten and placed in a container which is affixed to the right doorpost (as one enters) of a Jewish home and also of each room used for living purposes.

3. A wooden or metal container which holds the parchment upon which are written words (the *Shema*) from Deuteronomy 6:9 and following.

mezzuza see *mezuzuh*

M'gi-las Es-ter
Also *M'gi-lat Es-ter.**
Also spelled *Megillat Esther.*
Literally, "the Scroll of Esther," the biblical Book of Esther.

mich shrekt men nit see *mihch shrekt men niht*

mi-das haw-ra-cha-mihm
Also *mi-dat ha-ra-cha-mim.**
1. Literally, "the quality, measure of mercy."
2. Divine justice tempered with mercy.
3. Compassion.

mi-dat ha-din*
Also *mi-das ha-dihn.*
Also spelled *middat hadin.*
The attribute of Divine justice.

mi-es
Also *mi-uhs, mi-oos.**
Also spelled *mius.*
1. Ugly.
2. Disgusting, revolting.

mi-es-kait
Also spelled *mieskeit.*
1. Ugliness.
2. An ugly thing.
3. An ugly person.

mi-esr ne-fesh
Also spelled *mieser nefesh.*
1. An ugly person.
2. A cheap person.

---

a as in father; aw as in law; ai as in aisle· ei as in neighbor; e as in bet; i as in vaccine; ih as in tin; o as in solar; oi as in void; oo as in food; u as in put; uh as in but; ch as in chutzpa; zh as in Zhivago.

mihch shrekt men niht
> Also spelled *mich shrekt men nit.*
> Me, no one scares!

mihd-ruhsh
> Also *med-ruhsh, mihd-rash,* mihd-rawsh.*
> Also spelled *midrash.*
> 1. Literally, "investigation" or "interpretation."
> 2. Commentary on and interpretation of the Bible.
> 3. A category of books in which various books of the Bible are interpreted and explained.

Mih-hag Se-far-ad
> The Spanish (Sephardic) ritual of Jews of Iberian and Middle Eastern descent.

mihk-raw
> Also *mihk-ra.**
> Also spelled *mikra.*
> 1. Literally, "reading."
> 2 The written Torah.

mihk-vuh
> Also *mihk-vaw, mihk-va.**
> Also spelled *mikva, mikvah, mikve, mikveh.*
> 1. Reservoir, body of water.
> 2. A pool of water, derived from natural springs, for use in Jewish ritual purification.

mihl-chihk
> Also *mihl-che-dihg, mihl-che-dihk.*
> Also spelled *milchik.*
> Dairy foods and utensils used specifically in the preparation and serving of such foods, in contradistinction to *fleishihg.*

mihltz
> Also spelled *miltz.*
> Spleen, milt.

mihncha see *mihnchuh*

Mihn-chuh
> Also *Mihn-cha,* Mihn-chaw.*
> Also spelled *Mincha, Minha.*
> 1. Literally, "a gift."
> 2. The name of the daily afternoon prayer service.

---

mihn-hawg
> Also *mihn-hag.**
> Also spelled *minhag.*
> 1. Custom.
> 2. Ritual practice.

mihn-hawg-ihm
> Also *mihn-ha-gihm.**
> Also spelled *minhagim.*
> Customs, practices. Plural of *minhawg.*

mihn-yuhn
> Also *mihn-yan,** *mihn-yawn.*
> Also spelled *minyan, minyon.*
> 1. Literally, "count."
> 2. A quorum of ten (traditionally male) Jews, over the age of thirteen, required for communal worship.

mihp-nei dar-kei sha-lom*
> Also spelled *mipne darkay shawlom.*
> 1. Literally, "because of the ways of peace."
> 2. In order to establish a climate of peace, for the sake of peace.

mihr
> Also spelled *mir.*
> We.

mihr-tse-shem
> Also *mihr-tsih-shem.*
> Also spelled *mirtzishem.*
> God willing! A contraction of the Hebrew words *ihm yihr-tse ha-Shem.*

mihr veln benshn
> Also spelled *mir velen bentshen.*
> 1. Literally, "We will bless."
> 2. The invitation to all present to say the *Grace After Meals.*

mihr veln ihm ba-graw-ben
> Also spelled *mir velen im bagroben.*
> We will bury him.

---

a as in father; aw as in law; ai as in aisle; ei as in neighbor; e as in bet; i as in vaccine; ih as in tin; o as in solar; oi as in void; oo as in food; u as in put; uh as in but; ch as in chutzpa; zh as in Zhivago.

mihr zawln der-lebn
Also spelled *mir zolen derleben.*
We should only live (to see it)!

mihr zawln zihch ba-geig-nen oif sihm-ches
May we meet on happy occasions!

mihsh
Also spelled *mish.*
Mix.

mihsh-mash
Also spelled *mish-mash, mish-mosh.*
1. A mix-up.
2. Mixture.
3. Mess, hodge podge.

mihsh-lo-ach maw-nos
Also *mihsh-lo-ach ma-not.**
Also spelled *mishloach manot.*
1. Literally, "to send portions."
2. Gift-giving, usually goodies, on the Purim holiday.

mihshn a-rain
Also spelled *mishen arein.*
1. To mix in (to another's affairs).
2. To butt in.

mihshn di Yoitz-res
1. Literally, "to mix up the *Yotzer* prayers" of the morning service by reciting them out of order.
2. To mix things up.

Mihsh-nuh
Also *Mihsh-ne, Mihsh-na.**
Also spelled *Mishna, Mishnah.*
1. Literally, "repetitive study."
2. The first part of the Talmud, which contains rabbinic oral interpretations of Scriptural ordinances.

mihsh-puh-che
Also *mihsh-paw-chaw, mihsh-paw-che, mihsh-pa-cha.**
Also spelled *mishpoche.*

---

a as in father; aw as in law; ai as in aisle; ei as in neighbor; e as in bet; i as in vaccine; ih as in tin: o as in solar; oi as in void; oo as in food; u as in put; uh as in but; ch as in chutzpa; zh as in Zhivago.

1. Family, relatives.
2. Clan.

mihshugaas see *meshugaas*

mihs-nag-dihm
> Also *miht-nag-dihm.**
> Also spelled *mitnagdim.*
> Plural of *mihsnageid.* See below.

mihs-na-geid
> Also *miht-na-ged.**
> Also spelled *misnaged, mitnaged.*
> 1. Literally, "opponent."
> 2. An opponent of the Chassidic movement.

miht a-le mai-les
> Also spelled *mit alle meiles.*
> 1. Literally, "with all good qualities."
> 2. A talented person.
> 3. One who is perfection.

miht ein klap
> Also spelled *mit ain klap.*
> With one stroke, with one blow.

mih-tel-muh-sih-kait
> Also spelled *mittelmosikeit.*
> Mediocrity.

mih-tel-muh-sih-ker
> Also spelled *mittelmosiker.*
> Mediocre person.

mihtn
> Also spelled *mitten.*
> The middle, center.

mihtnagdihm see *mihsnagdihm*

mihtnageid see *mihsnageid*

mihtsva see *mihtsvuh*

mihtsvos see *mihtsvuhs*

mihtsvot see *mihtsvuhs*

mihts-vuh
> Also *mihts-ve, mihts-va.**
> Also spelled *mitzva, mitzvah, mitsva, mitsvah.*

---

a as in father; aw as in law; ai as in aisle; ei as in neighbor; e as in bet; i as in vaccine; ih as in tin; o as in solar; oi as in void; oo as in food; u as in put; uh as in but; ch as in chutzpa; zh as in Zhivago.

1. A commandment.
2. A religious obligation.
3. A good deed, considerate act.

mihts-vuhs
Also *mihts-vos, mihts-vot.**
Also spelled *mitzvot, mitsvot.*
Plural of *mihts-vuh.*

mihzrach see *mihzruhch*

mihz-ra-chihm
Also spelled *mizrachim.*
Plural of *mizrach.* See *mizrach.*

Mihz-raw-chi
Also *Mihz-ra-chi.**
Also spelled *Mizrachi.*
1. Literally, "one who comes from the East."
2. A religious Zionist organization.
3. A person who belongs to the Mizrachi Zionist organization.

mihz-ruhch
Also *mihz-rech, mihz-rach.**
Also spelled *mizrach.*
1. East, eastern.
2. The direction of Jerusalem, toward which Jews in the West pray.
3. A decorative object depicting Jerusalem scenes, placed on the eastern wall of a home to indicate the direction of the holy city.

mihz-ruhch bihld
Also spelled *mizrach bild.*
A calligraphic picture hung on the eastern wall of a house.

mihz-ruhch vant
Also spelled *mizrach vant.*
The eastern wall of the synagogue, where the privileged members are usually seated. See *mizrach.*

mikva see *mihkvuh*

mila see *miluh*

milchedik see *mihlchihk*

---

a as in father; aw as in law; ai as in aisle; ei as in neighbor; e as in bet; i as in vaccine; ih as in tin; o as in solar; oi as in void; oo as in food; u as in put; uh as in but; ch as in chutzpa; zh as in Zhivago.

milchik see *mihlchihk*

miltz see *mihltz*

mi-luh
> Also *mi-la,* mi-law.*
> 1. Circumcision.
> 2. The rite of circumcision.

mi-mihsh-pa-chat*
> Also *mi-mihsh-pa-chas.*
> Literally, "from the family of."

mimona see *Noche de Mimona*

Mincha see *Mihnchuh*

minhag see *mihnhawg*

minyan see *mihnyuhn*

mioos see *mies*

mipne darkay shawlom see *mihpnei darkei shalom*

mirtzishem see *mihrtseshem*

mir velen bentshen see *mihr veln benshn*

mir velen im bagroben see *mihr veln ihm bagrawben*

mir zolen derleben see *mihr zawln derlebn*

misaw see *misuh*

mise meshunuh see *misuh meshunuh*

mish see *mihsh*

mi she-bei-rach
> Also spelled *mi sheberach.*
> 1. Literally, "May He who blessed."
> 2. The opening words and name of a prayer offered
>   in the synagogue for the well-being of an indi-
>   vidual.

mishegaas see *meshugaas*

mishen see *mishn*

mishigasim see *meshihgasihm*

mishloach manot see *mihshloach mawnos*

mish-mash see *mihsh mash*

---

a as in father; aw as in law; ai as in aisle; ei as in neighbor; e as in bet; i as in vaccine; ih as in tin; o as in solar; oi as in void; oo as in food; u as in put; uh as in but; ch as in chutzpa; zh as in Zhivago.

mishn
> Also spelled *mishen.*
> To mix.

Mishna see *Mihshnuh*

mishpoche see *mihshpuhche*

mi-suh
> Also *mi-saw* and *mi-ta.**
> Death, dying.

mi-suh m'shoo-nuh
> Also *mi-saw m'shoo-naw, mi-ta m'shoo-na.**
> Also spelled *misa m'shoone, misa meshunuh.*
> 1. Literally, "strange death."
> 2. Untimely death.
> 3. Unnatural death.
> 4. A tragic end.

mita see *misuh*

mit ain klap see *miht ein klap*

mit alle meiles see *miht ale mailes*

mitnaged see *mihsnageid*

mitsvot see *mihtsvuhs*

mittelmosikeit see *mihtelmuhsihkait*

mitten see *mihtn*

mitzva see *mihtzvuh*

mitzvoth see *mihtsvuhs*

miuhs see *mies*

mizrach see *mihzruhch*

mizrach bild see *mihzruhch bihld*

Mizrachi see *Mihzrawchi*

mizrachim see *mihzrachihm*

mizrach vant see *mihzruhch vant*

m'ken see *men* and *men ken*

mode ani see *moide ani*

modeh ani see *moide ani*

modne see *mawdne*

---

a as in father; aw as in law; ai as in aisle; ei as in neighbor; e as in bet; i as in vaccine; ih as in tin; o as in solar; oi as in void; oo as in food; u as in put; uh as in but; ch as in chutzpa; zh as in Zhivago.

mogen see *muhgn*

Mogen David see *Muhgn Duhvihd*

mogen kugel see *mawgn kugl*

mohayl see *moil*

mohel see *moil*

moichl
> Also *mo-cheil.*
> Also spelled *moichel.*
> Thanks, but no thanks! Forget it!

moichl zain
> Also spelled *moichel zein.*
> To excuse, forgive, pardon, condone.

moid
> Girl. A distorted form of *meidl.*

moi-de a-ni
> Also *mo-de a-ni.**
> Also spelled *modeh ani.*
> 1. Literally, "I render thanks."
> 2. The first words of prayer uttered by a traditional Jew upon arising in the morning.

moil
> Also *mo-hel,** mo-heil, mo-hayl.*
> Also spelled *moel.*
> 1. Mouth.
> 2. A person trained to perform circumcisions according to Jewish law.

moi-she ka-poi-er
> 1. Literally, "Moses topsy-turvy."
> 2. One who does things wrong or in reverse order.

mooktze see *muktzuh*

moo-sar*
> Also *mu-sar, mu-suhr.*
> 1. Literally, "moralization, reproaching."
> 2. A nineteenth-century ethical movement among Lithuanian Jews.

moo-suhf
> Also *Mu-saf,** Mu-sawf.*

---

a as in father; aw as in law; ai as in aisle; ei as in neighbor; e as in bet; i as in vaccine; ih as in tin; o as in solar; oi as in void; oo as in food; u as in put; uh as in but; ch as in chutzpa; zh as in Zhivago.

Also spelled *Musaph.*
1. Literally, "additional, added."
2. An additional service on Sabbath and festivals.

moo-tihk
Also spelled *mutik.*
Bold, courageous, daring, brave.

mordeven zich see *muhrdeven zihch*

Mo-re Ne-vu-chim
Guide for the Perplexed, a book written in 1190 by
Moses ben Maimon (Maimonides), the RaMBaM.

morgen see *mawrgn*

moror see *mawror*

mo-seir
Also *mo-ser.**
Also spelled *mosser.*
A stool pigeon, betrayer, informer.

mo-shav*
The earliest type of settlement in modern Israel, in
which the individual leases the land, and the farming, equipment, and sale of produce are conducted
collectively.

mo-shav ov-dim*
A workers' *moshav.*

mo-shav shi-tu-fi*
A collective in Israel.

mosser see *moseir*

mo-tsaw-ei Sha-bes
Also *Mo-tsaw-ei Sha-buhs, Mo-tsa-ei Sha-bat.**
Also spelled *Motza'ai Shabbat, Motzei Shabbat.*
1. Literally, "Sabbath's exit."
2. Saturday night.

Motzei Shabbat see *Mo-tsaw-ei Sha-bes*

motzi see *Hamotzi*

m'sadeir gi-tihn
Also spelled *mesader gitin.*
A rabbi who specializes in issuing divorces.

---

a as in father; aw as in law; ai as in aisle; ei as in neighbor; e as in bet; i as in vaccine; ih as in tin; o as in
solar; oi as in void; oo as in food; u as in put; uh as in but; ch as in chutzpa; zh as in Zhivago.

m'sa-deir ki-doo-shihn*
> Also spelled *mesader kiddushin.*
> A rabbi or any Jew qualified to perform marriages.

m'shugaat see *meshugaas*

m'shumad
> An apostate from Judaism.

m'tzi-tza*
> Also *me-tzi-tzuh, me-tzi-tzaw.*
> The drawing of blood from the wound left by circumcision.

m'tziuh see *metziuh*

muhgn
> Also spelled *muhgen, mogen.*
> Stomach.

Muhgn Duh-vihd
> Also *Maw-gein Daw-vihd, Ma-gen Da-vihd.**
> Also spelled *Magen David, Mogen David.*
> 1. Literally, "Shield of David."
> 2. Six-pointed Star of David.
> 3. Jewish star.

muhr-de-ven zihch
> Also spelled *mordeven zich.*
> 1. To overwork.
> 2. To overexert oneself.

muk-tzuh
> Also *muk-tze.*
> Also spelled *mooktsa, mooktze.*
> 1. An article that may not be touched on the Sabbath because it was not intended for Sabbath use.
> 2. An article set aside, not to be used presently.

mum-che
> An expert, a specialist.

mu-me
> Also *mi-me.*
> Aunt.

musaf see *moosuhf*

---

a as in father; aw as in law; ai as in aisle; ei as in neighbor; e as in bet; i as in vaccine; ih as in tin; o as in solar; oi as in void; oo as in food; u as in put; uh as in but; ch as in chutzpa; zh as in Zhivago.

musar see *moosar*

mutche see *mutshe*

mutik see *mootihk*

mutr
>Also *moo-tar.**
>1. Permitted, permissible.
>2. Mother.

mut-she
>Also spelled *mutche.*
>1. To nag, pester.
>2. To annoy.
>3. To torment.

mutshn zihch
>Also spelled *mutshen zich.*
>1. To overwork.
>2. To slave away.
>3. To suffer (at a job).

m'zooza see *mezuzuh*

m'zuhgt
>Also spelled *men zugt.*
>1. They say.
>2. People say.
>3. It is said.

m'zumen see *mezumn*

N

na
> 1. Here (when handing something)!
> 2. Take it!

naar see *nar*

NaCH
> An acronym from the initials of the Hebrew words *Nevi'im* (Prophets) and *Ketuvim* (Writings), the second and third parts of the Hebrew Bible.

na-cha-la*
> Death anniversary among Sephardic Jews.

nachas see *nachuhs*

nachat see *nachuhs*

nacht
> Night.

nacht falt tzu
> 1. Literally, "Night is falling."
> 2. Twilight.

na-chuhs
> Also *nach-es, nach-as, nach-at.**
> 1. Ease.
> 2. Rest.
> 3. Pride.
> 4. Satisfaction from another's achievement.

na-chuhs roo-ach
> Also *na-chat ru-ach,* na-ches roo-ach.*
> 1. Literally, "ease of spirit."
> 2. Pleasure, satisfaction.

nadn
> Also *na-dan.**
> Dowry.

nad-van*
> Also *nad-vawn.*

---

1. A philanthropist.
2. A donor, benefactor.

naf-ke
>Also *naf-ka.**
>A prostitute.

nagihd see *nawgihd*

naies see *nais*

naigel vasser see *neigl vaser*

nain see *nein*

nais
>Also *nai-es.*
>Also spelled *neies.*
>News.

nar
>Also *na-ar.**
>1. A boy (Hebrew).
>2. A fool (Yiddish).

na-raw-nihm
>Also spelled *naronim.*
>Fools, stupid people. Plural of *nar.*

(a) nar fihlt niht
>A fool feels nothing.

na-rihsh
>Also spelled *narish.*
>Foolish, stupid.

na-rihsh-kait
>Also spelled *narishkeit.*
>Nonsense.

naronim see *narawnihm*

(a) nar vaist men (or tsaigt men) kain nihsht hal-be ar-biht
>1. Literally, "One doesn't show a fool half a task."
>2. Don't reveal something half-finished to a fool.

nash
>Also spelled *nosh.*
>1. A snack.

2. A sweet.
3. An in-between-meals treat.

nashen see *nashn*

nasher see nashr

nash-er-ai
Also spelled *nasherei*.
1. Sweets, junk food.
2. A place that serves goodies.

nash-ing
Indulging in a *nash*. See *nash. nashn*
Also spelled *nashen*.
To nibble, especially on sweets.

nashr
Also spelled *nasher, nosher*.
1. A nibbler.
2. A person with a sweet-tooth.

na-si*
Also *naw-si*.
1. Leader, head.
2. Head of an academy of Jewish learning in ancient times.
3. President of the Sanhedrin in ancient times.
4. President of the State of Israel.

navi see *nawvi*

nawch
Also spelled *noch*.
1. Yet.
2. After.
3. Following.
4. Next.

nawch nihsht
Also spelled *noch nisht*.
Not yet.

nawch shlepr
Also spelled *nochshlepper*.
1. An unwanted follower.
2. A hanger-on.

---

a as in father; aw as in law; ai as in aisle; ei as in neighbor; e as in bet; i as in vaccine; ih as in tin; o as in solar; oi as in void; oo as in food; u as in put; uh as in but; ch as in chutzpa; zh as in Zhivago.

naw-gihd
> Also *na-gihd*.
> Also spelled *nogid*.
> 1. A prince.
> 2. A person of high estate.

nawmn
> Also spelled *nawmen, nomen*.
> Name.

nawr
> Merely, only, just.

nawr Gawt veist
> Also spelled *nor Gott vaist*.
> Only God knows.

naw-vi
> Also *na-vi*.*
> Prophet.

naw-zihr
> Also *na-zihr*.*
> Also spelled *nazir*.
> 1. Nazarite.
> 2. In the Bible, a person who leads an ascetic life, abstaining from wine and cutting of his hair.

Nazirite
> A person following the discipline of a *nawzihr*. See *nawzihr*.

nebech see *nebuhch*

ne-bihsh
> Also spelled *nebish*.
> 1. Ineffective, shy, dull.
> 2. An inept person.
> A variant form of *nebuhch*.

ne-buhch
> Also spelled *nebech*.
> 1. A pity, a pitiful situation.
> 2. A pitiful individual, a person to be pitied.

ne-buhchl
> Also spelled *nebechl*.
> A variant form of *nebuhch*. See above.

---

a as in father; aw as in law; ai as in aisle; ei as in neighbor; e as in bet; i as in vaccine; ih as in tin; o as in solar; oi as in void; oo as in food; u as in put; uh as in but; ch as in chutzpa; zh as in Zhivago.

ne-chaw-meh
> Also *ne-cha-ma.**
> 1. Literally, "comfort."
> 2. A feminine personal name.

(a) nech-tihger tawg
> Also spelled *(a) nechtiger tog.*
> 1. Literally, "a yesterday's day."
> 2. Nothing of the kind! Forget it! Nonsense! It never happened!

nedr see *neidr*

ne-duh-ve
> Also *ne-daw-vuh, ne-du-ve, ne-da-va.**
> 1. Literally, "an offering."
> 2. A donation.
> 3. Charity.
> 4. Almsgiving.

ne-fuhsh
> Also *ne-fesh,** *nei-fihsh.*
> Also spelled *nafish, nayfish, nefish.*
> 1. Spirit.
> 2. Soul.
> 3. Breath.

Ne-gev
> The southern region of the State of Israel.

neidr
> Also *nedr.**
> 1. A pledge, vow, promise.
> 2. Charity pledged on the Sabbath or a holiday by someone honored with an *aliya.* See *aliya.*

neies see *nais*

neifish see *nefuhsh*

neigl va-ser
> Also spelled *naigel vasser.*
> Literally, "finger water," used by Orthodox Jews upon rising in the morning.

Ne-i-luh
> Also *Ne-i-law, Ne-i-la.**
> Also spelled *Neilah.*

---

a as in father; aw as in law; ai as in aisle; ei as in neighbor; e as in bet; i as in vaccine; ih as in tin; o as in solar; oi as in void; oo as in food; u as in put; uh as in but; ch as in chutzpa; zh as in Zhivago.

1. Literally, "closing (of the gates of the Temple and forgiveness)."
2. Concluding service of Yom Kippur (Day of Atonement).

nein
Also *nain*.
No, not.

neis see *nes*

neisuhch see *nesech*

nekama see *n'kuhme*

nekeva see *n'keivuh*

nem
Take!

nemn
Also spelled *nemen*.
To take.

nemn shoi-ched
Also spelled *nemen shoichuhd*.
To take a bribe.

nem zihch a va-ne
Also spelled *nem zich a vanne*.
1. Literally, "take a bath."
2. Don't bother me!

Ner Ta-mid*
Also *Ner Taw-mihd*.
Literally, "perpetual light" or "eternal light," a designation derived from Leviticus 24:2 for the light suspended above the Holy Ark.

nes*
Also *neis*.
Miracle.

ne-sech*
Also *nei-suhch*.
1. Literally, "pouring."
2. Refers to wine poured on the altar in pagan worship.
3. Wine not usable by Jews.

---

a as in father; aw as in law; ai as in aisle; ei as in neighbor; e as in bet; i as in vaccine; ih as in tin; o as in solar; oi as in void; oo as in food; u as in put; uh as in but; ch as in chutzpa; zh as in Zhivago.

neshama see *neshuhmuh*

ne-shuh-me-le
   1. Literally, "little soul."
   2. Darling, sweetheart.

ne-shuh-muh
   Also *ne-shaw-maw, ne-sha-ma.**
   Also spelled *ne-shuh-me*.
   1. Soul.
   2. Spirit.

ne-shuh-muh y'sei-ruh
   Also *ne-shaw-maw ye-sei-raw, ne-sha-ma ye-tei-ra.**
   Literally, "an extra soul," which in Jewish tradition is awarded Jews on the Sabbath.

ne-si-at ka-pa-yihm*
   Also *ne-si-as ka-pa-yihm*.
   1. Literally, "the raising of hands."
   2. The Priestly Blessing.

Ne-tu-rei Kar-ta
   1. Literally, "Guardians of the City."
   2. A group of anti-Zionist, extreme Orthodox Jews living in Jerusalem.

ne-vi-ihm
   Also spelled *n'viim, neviim*.
   1. Prophets (plural of *navi*).
   2. The prophets of the Bible.
   3. The name of the second division of the Bible.

ni-chum a-vei-lihm
   Also spelled *nichum avelim*.
   Literally, "comforting of mourners."

nidda see *niduh*

nider see *nihdr*

nidertrechtik see *nihdertrechtihk*

ni-duh
   Also *ni-daw, ni-da.**
   Also spelled *nidda*.
   A menstruating woman.

---

a as in father; aw as in law; ai as in aisle: ei as in neighbor; e as in bet; i as in vaccine; ih as in tin; o as in solar; oi as in void; oo as in food; u as in put; uh as in but; ch as in chutzpa; zh as in Zhivago.

niftar see *nihftr*

ni-gun*
>   Also *nihgn*.
>   A wordless Chassidic melody.

(a) nihd-er-ih-ker kerl
>   An inferior, a good-for-nothing.

nih-der-trech-tihk
>   Also spelled *nidertrechtik*.
>   Outrageous, vile.

nihdr
>   Also spelled *nider*.
>   Down.

nihftr
>   Also *nihf-tar*.*
>   Also spelled *niftar*.
>   1. Literally, "one who has departed."
>   2. A deceased person.

nihftr-shmihftr, a lebn macht er?
>   Also spelled *niftar-schmifter, a leben macht er?*
>   Dead or not—what's the difference, so long as he
>   makes a living. (A play on the words *niftar*, "de-
>   ceased," and *leben*, "living.")

nihs
>   Also spelled *nis*.
>   Nuts.

nihsht duh ge-dacht
>   1. May it not happen here!
>   2. May it not happen to us!

nihsht ge-fer-lach see *nit geferlich*

nihsht gut
>   Not good! It's not good!

nihsht haint, nihsht mawrgn
>   Also spelled *nisht heint, nisht morgen*.
>   1. Literally, "neither today nor tomorrow."
>   2. It will never happen.

nihsht kaw-she
>   Also spelled *nishkoshe, nihsht kusher, nish
>   kusher*.

1. Combination of the Yiddish *nihsht* ("not") and the Hebrew *kawshe* ("difficult, hard").
2. Not bad.
3. Bearable.
Erroneously associated with *nihsht kuhsher,* meaning "not kosher."

nihsht kuh-sher
Also spelled *nish kushr.*
Not kosher. See also *nihsht kawshe.*

nihsht neitihg see *nit neitihk*

Nihsn
Also *Ni-san.**
The first month of the Jewish religious calendar, seventh of the Civil calendar, corresponding to March-April; the month in which Passover is celebrated.

niht
Also *nihsht.*
Also spelled *nit.*
1. Not.
2. Nothing.

niht a-hihn, niht a-her
Also spelled *nit ahin, nit aher.*
1. Literally, "neither here nor there."
2. Irrelevant.

niht a-zoi gihch
Also spelled *nit azoi gich.*
1. Not so fast!
2. Take it easy!

niht-duh
A contraction of *niht* ("not") and *duh* ("here").
1. Literally, "(there is) nothing here."
2. No one's here.
3. Nothing to it!

niht duh far aich
Also spelled *nit do far eich.*
May this never happen here to you!

niht duh far vaws
Also *nit do far vos.*

a as in father; aw as in law; al as in aisle; el as in neighbor; e as in bet; i as in vaccine; ih as in tin; o as in solar; oi as in void; oo as in food; u as in put; uh as in but; ch as in chutzpa; zh as in Zhivago.

1. Literally, "not here for what."
2. There's no reason at all (to do something or to be thankful).

niht far kein Yidn ge-dacht
Also spelled *nit far kain yidden gedocht.*
1. It should not befall Jews.
2. Jews don't deserve it.

niht ge-dai-giht
Also spelled *nit gedeiget.*
Not to worry! Don't worry!

niht ge-fer-lich
Also *nihsht ge-fer-lach.*
Also spelled *nit geferlech, niht geferlach.*
Not so terrible!

niht ge-fuhnf-et
Also spelled *nit gefonfet.*
1. Literally, "Don't mumble."
2. Don't use double-talk!
3. Don't hedge!

niht ge-shtoign oon niht ge-floign
Also spelled *nit geshtoigen un nit gefloigen.*
1. Literally, "doesn't stand and doesn't fly."
2. Not true whatsoever, completely false.
3. It never happened!

niht ge-trawfn
Also spelled *nit getrofen.*
1. Literally, "did not meet."
2. Did not guess right.

(a) niht gut-nihk
Also spelled *a nit gutnik.*
A no-account person.

niht-ih-kait
Also spelled *nitikeit.*
1. Nothingness.
2. Worthlessness.
3. Triviality.

---

a as in father; aw as in law; ai as in aisle; ei as in neighbor; e as in bet; i as in vaccine; ih as in tin; o as in solar; oi as in void; oo as in food; u as in put; uh as in but; ch as in chutzpa; zh as in Zhivago.

niht kein var-shlawf-en-er
   Also spelled *nit kain farshloffener.*
   1. Not a sleepyhead.
   2. A lively person.

niht nei-tihk
   Also *nihst nei-tihg.*
   Also spelled *nit naitik.*
   Unnecessary.

niht oif dihr ge-dacht
   We don't wish it on you!

niht oif unz ge-dacht
   We don't wish it on ourselves!

niht shat-uhn tsoom shih-duch
   Also spelled *nit shatten tsum shidduch.*
   1. Literally, "It won't damage the matrimonial ar-
      rangement.".
   2. It won't interfere with what is underway.

niht vihs-en-dihk
   Also spelled *nit vissendik.*
   Unknowing.

niht vihsn miht vaws est men daws
   Also spelled *nit vissen mit vos est men dos.*
   1. Literally, "not know with what one eats it."
   2. Not know how to go about doing things.

nis see *nihs*

Nisan see *Nihsn*

nisht see *nihsht*

nisht heint, nisht morgen see *nihsht haint, nihsht
   mawrgn*

nisht kosher see *nihsht kuhsher*

ni-sihm*
   Also spelled *nissim.*
   Miracles. Plural of *nes.*

ni-sihm v'nihf-law-os
   Also *ni-sihm v'nihf-la-ot.**

---

a as in father; aw as in law; ai as in aisle; ei as in neighbor; e as in bet; i as in vaccine; ih as in tin; o as in
solar; oi as in void; oo as in food; u as in put; uh as in but; ch as in chutzpa; zh as in Zhivago.

1. Literally, "miracles and wonders."
2. Something unbelievable.

ni-soo-ihn
Also spelled *nissuin*.
The Jewish marriage ceremony, also called *kidu-shin*.

nissim see *nisihm*

nissuin see *nisooihn*

nit see *niht*

n'kei-vuh
Also *n'kei-va.**
Also spelled *nekeva*.
1. Female.
2. Feminine.

n'kuh-me
Also *n'kuh-muh, ne-ka-ma.**
Revenge.

noch see *nawch*

Noche de Mimona
Moroccan Jewish feast of sweet foods, held on the last night of Passover.

nochshlepper see *nawch shlepr*

nogid see *nawgihd*

nomen see *nawmn*

noo see *nu*

nor Gott vaist see *nawr Gawt veist*

no-sei ha-mi-taw
Also *no-sei ha-mi-ta.**
Literally, "bearers of the bier," pallbearers.

nosh see *nash*

no-ta-ri-kon
Also *not-ri-kon*.
Method of abbreviating Hebrew words or phrases by writing single letters.

---

a as in father; aw as in law; ai as in aisle; ei as in neighbor; e as in bet; i as in vaccine; ih as in tin; o as in solar; oi as in void; oo as in food; u as in put; uh as in but; ch as in chutzpa; zh as in Zhivago.

nu
>Also *noo.*
>1. Well? So? So what? What about it?
>2. Let's go! Hurry up!
>3. Haven't you finished?

nud-nihk
>Also spelled *nudnik.*
>1. A pest.
>2. A bore.

nudzh
>Also *nudj.*
>1. A pest.
>2. A bore.
>3. To pester, be tedious.

nuhch Ne-i-luh
>Also spelled *nach Neila.*
>1. Literally, "after *Neila.*"
>2. Too late.

nuhch-shlepr
>Also spelled *nuchshlepper.*
>1. One who follows or hangs on to someone else.
>2. A fawner.

nun
>The fourteenth letter of the Hebrew alphabet, corresponding to the "n" sound in English.

nusach see *nusuhch*

Nu-sach Ashkenaz
>The liturgy according to the Ashkenazic tradition. See *Ashkenaz.*

Nu-sach Se-pha-rad
>The liturgy according to the Sephardic tradition. See *Sephardic.*

nu-suhch
>Also *nu-sawch, nu-sach,* nu-sech.*
>The order and style of the liturgy according to different traditions: *Nusach Ashkenaz, Nusach Sepharad,* etc.

---

a as in father; aw as in law; ai as in aisle; ei as in neighbor; e as in bet; i as in vaccine; ih as in tin; o as in solar; oi as in void; oo as in food; u as in put; uh as in but; ch as in chutzpa; zh as in Zhivago.

nu-zhe
>   To pester.

n'viim see *neviihm*

O

ober see *uhber*

och!
> Oh! Ah! or any exclamation of surprise, admiration, dismay, regret, disapproval, anxiety.

och oon vai see *awch un vei*

odem naket see *awdem naket*

oder see *uhder*

o-heiv Yihs-raw-eil
> Also *o-hev Yihs-ra-el.**
> Also spelled *ohev Yisrael.*
> 1. Literally, "lover of Israel."
> 2. Friend of the Jewish people.

oho see *uhhuh*

oi
> Also spelled *oy.*
> 1. Oh!
> 2. Ouch!
> 3. Wow!

oich
> 1. Also.
> 2. Furthermore.
> 3. Too.

oich a ba-shef-e-nihsh
> 1. Literally, "also a creature" (sarcasm).
> 2. An unimportant person.

oich mihr a lebn
> Also spelled *oich mir a leben.*
> 1. Literally, "also a living" (sarcasm).
> 2. You call this making a living?

oier see *oir*

oifen himmel a yarid see *oifn himl a yarihd*

---

a as in father; aw as in law; ai as in aisle; ei as in neighbor; e as in bet; i as in vaccine; ih as in tin; o as in solar; oi as in void; oo as in food; u as in put; uh as in but; ch as in chutzpa; zh as in Zhivago.

oif-ge-ku-men-er
1. An upstart, Johnny-come-lately.
2. A parvenu.

oif-ge-ku-men-er ge-vir a parvenu
A nouveau riche.

oif ka-paw-res
Also spelled *oif kapores*.
1. Literally, "for an atonement sacrifice."
2. Of no value.

oif mai-ne suh-nihm ge-zawgt
Also spelled *oif meine sonim gezogt*.
1. Literally, "(such a fate) should be said about my enemies."
2. May my enemies have my fate!

oif mihr ge-zawgt ge-vawr-en
Also spelled *oif mir gezogt gevoren*.
1. Literally, "May it be said about me!"
2. It should only happen to me!

oif'n ga-nef brent daws hihtl
Also spelled *oif'n ganef brent dos hitel*.
1. Literally, "Upon the thief burns his hat."
2. The wrongdoer has the guilty conscience.

oif'n himl a ya-rihd
Also spelled *oifen himmel a yarid*.
1. Literally, "a fair in the sky."
2. Much ado about nothing.

oifrifung
Also *oif-ruf*.
Literally, "a calling up," with special reference to a bridegroom called to the Torah on the Sabbath before his wedding.

oif tsaw-res
Also spelled *oif tzores*.
1. In trouble.
2. In a bad way.

oif tsuh-luh-chihs
Also spelled *oif tsulochis*.

---

a as in father; aw as in law; ai as in aisle; ei as in neighbor; e as in bet; i as in vaccine; ih as in tin; o as in solar; oi as in void; oo as in food; u as in put; uh as in but; ch as in chutzpa; zh as in Zhivago.

1. In order to anger.
2. Despite.

oig

An eye.

oi-lem

Also *oi-luhm, o-lam.**
1. The world.
2. The masses.
3. Crowd, congregation, public, audience.

oiluhm ha-baw

Also *o-lawm ha-baw, o-lam ha-ba.**
1. Literally, "the world to come."
2. The future.

oi-luhm haw-e-mes

Also *oi-lehm haw-e-mes, o-lam ha-e-met.**
1. Literally, "the true world" or "the world of truth."
2. The world (realm) of the dead.
3. A cemetery.

oi-luhm ha-ze

Also *o-lawm ha-ze, o-lam ha-ze.**
1. Literally, "this world."
2. The here and now.

oimer see *omer*

Oineg Shabes see *Oneg Shabat*

oir

Also spelled *oier.*
Ear.

oi-rei-ach

Also *o-rei-ach.**
Also spelled *oreach.*
Visitor, guest.

oi-ren

Also spelled *oieren.*
Ears. Plural of *oir.*

ois

1. Finished, ended.

2. No more.
3. All out.

ois-ge-blawz-en
1. To blow out.
2. To end up with nothing, to fizzle out, as in *oisgeblawzene eir,* "a blown-out egg."

ois-ge-dart
Skinny, thin, emaciated.

ois-ge-huhr-e-vet
Also spelled *oisgehorevet.*
Exhausted.

ois-ge-ma-tert
Weary, tired, exhausted.

ois-ge-mutsh-et
1. Exhausted.
2. Tired.

ois-ge-putzt
1. Dressed up.
2. Overdressed.
3. Overadorned, overdecorated.

ois-ge-tsats-ket
Also spelled *oisgetzatzket.*
1. Overdressed.
2. Overadorned.
3. Ostentatious.
4. Ornate.

ois-ge-tsert
Also spelled *oisgetzert.*
Emaciated.

ois-ge-zei-chent
1. Excellent.
2. Outstanding.

ois-heil-en
Also spelled *oishailen.*
To heal, be cured.

ois-hei-len far dem cha-se-ne
1. Literally, "It (the problem) will be cured before the wedding."

a as in father: aw as in law; ai as in aisle; ei as in neighbor: e as in bet: i as in vaccine: ih as in tin: o as in solar; oi as in void; oo as in food; u as in put; uh as in but; ch as in chutzpa: zh as in Zhivago.

2. Things will work out in time.

oi-sher
Also *o-sher.**
Wealth, riches.

ois-kratzn
Also spelled *ois kratzen.*
1. Literally, "to scratch out."
2. To eke out (a living).
3. To move slowly.

ois-presn
Also spelled *ois-pressen.*
1. Literally, "to press out," a term borrowed from the needle trades and garment industry.
2. To work itself out.
3. The problem will be solved.

ois-redn di hartz
1. Literally, "to talk out the heart."
2. To get things off one's chest.

ois-shih-duhch
Also spelled *ois shidduch.*
The marriage is off.

ois-shte-ler
One who flaunts, a showoff, braggart.

ois-vawrf
Also spelled *ois-vorf.*
1. A reject.
2. A scoundrel.
3. An outcast.

ois-vawrfn
Also spelled *ois-vorfen.*
To reproach, rebuke.

oitsr
Also *o-tsar,** *o-tsawr.*
1. A treasure.
2. Treasury.
3. Treasure-trove, abundance.

---

a as in father; aw as in law; ai as in aisle; ei as in neighbor; e as in bet; i as in vaccine; ih as in tin; o as in solar; oi as in void; oo as in food; u as in put; uh as in but; ch as in chutzpa; zh as in Zhivago.

oi vei
> Also spelled *oi vai.*
> Oh my! An expression of sorrow, defeat.

oi vei ihz mihr
> Also spelled *oi vais mir.*
> Oh! Woe is me!

oi-ver-buhtl
> Also spelled *oiverbotel.*
> 1. Senile.
> 2. Disoriented.
> 3. Absent-minded.

olam see *oilem*

olav hasholem see *awluhv hashawluhm*

olawm habaw see *oiluhm habaw*

olawm haze see *oiluhm haze*

omed see *uhmed*

o-mer*
> Also *oi-mer.*
> 1. A dry measure mentioned in the Bible.
> 2. First sheaf of barley harvest brought to the Temple in Bible days.
> 3. The period of forty-nine days from the second day of Passover until Shavuot.

on see *uhn*

O-neg Sha-bat*
> Also *O-neg Sha-buhs, Oi-neg Sha-bes.*
> Also spelled *Oneg Shabbat.*
> 1. Literally, "delight of the Sabbath." Based on Isaiah 58:13.
> 2. A celebration held on Friday night or Saturday afternoon to honor the Sabbath. Introduced in the 1920s by the Hebrew poet Chayyim Nachman Bialik.

o-nein
> Also *o-nen.**
> 1. Bereaved.
> 2. A mourner from the time of death until the funeral.

ongeblozen see *awngeblawzen*

ongepatshket see *awngepatshket*

ongeshtopt see *awngeshtawpt*

ongevorfen see *awngevawrfn*

on lange hakdomes see *uhn lange hakdawmes*

onshikenish see *awnshihkenihsh*

onzaltzen see *awnzaltzn*

ooduhm hurishoin see *adam harishon*

ooduhr see *Adar*

opgeflikt see *awpgeflihkt*

opgehit see *awpgehiht*

opgekrochen see *awpgekrawchen*

opgelozen see *awpgelawzn*

opgenart see *awpgenart*

ophiten see *awphihtn*

opnaren zich see *awpnaren zihch*

opnarer see *awpnarer*

optshepen see *awptshepn*

oreach see *oireiach*

orem see *awrem*

oremeleit see *awremelait*

oremkeit see *awremkait*

or-la*
>   Also *awr-la, awr-law.*
>   1. Literally, "uncircumcised."
>   2. Fruit produced by trees during their first three years of life. According to biblical law such fruit cannot be eaten.

osher see *oisher*

oto ha-ihsh*
>   Also *o-so haw-ihsh.*
>   Literally, "that man (Jesus)."

otsar see *oitsr*

ovel see *uhvl*

---

ovent see *awvent*

oy see *oi*

oz-nei Ha-man*

    Also *awz-nei Haw-mawn.*

    1. Literally, "Haman's ears."

    2. The Hebrew name for *hamantashen.*

a as in father; **aw** as in law; **ai** as in aisle; **ei** as in neighbor; **e** as in bet; **i** as in vaccine; **ih** as in tin; **o** as in solar; **oi** as in void; **oo** as in food; **u** as in put; **uh** as in but; **ch** as in chutzpa; **zh** as in Zhivago.

P

pai see *pei*

paigaren see *peigeren*

paik-ler
  Also spelled *peikler*.
  A drummer.

pai-tan*
  Also *pai-tawn*.
  Composer of a *piyut* (a poem or hymn of a religious nature). *Paitanihm** is the plural form.

Pal-mach
  An acronym for *Pelugot Machatz*,* "shock companies," the commando forces of the Hagana in pre-state Israel.

pa-me-lach
  Also *pa-me-lech*.
  1. Slowly.
  2. By degrees.
  3. Little by little.

panim see *pawnihm*

pa-pih-ruhs
  Also spelled *papiros*.
  Cigarette.

parasha see *parshuh*

parch
  1. A scab.
  2. A nasty person.

parech see *parihch*

Pardesi
  Certain light-skinned Jews of Cochin, India.

pa-rev
  Also *pa-re-ve*.

---

a as in father; aw as in law; ai as in aisle; ei as in neighbor; e as in bet; i as in vaccine; ih as in tin; o as in solar; oi as in void; oo as in food; u as in put; uh as in but; ch as in chutzpa; zh as in Zhivago.

1. Neutral.
2. Food products that are neither *milchik* (dairy) nor *flaishik* (meat), including fruit, vegetables, fish, and all meatless and synthetic products.

pa-rihch
Also spelled *parech, paruhch.*
A wig.

par-naws
Also *par-nas.**
Also spelled *parnass.*
1. A supporter.
2. The chief synagogue administrative officer in previous generations.
3. A community representative.

par-naw-saw
Also *par-na-sa.**
Also spelled *parnuse, parnuhse.*
1. Livelihood.
2. Income.

parshe see *parshuh*

par-shih-ve
Also spelled *parshive.*
1. Nasty, ugly.
2. Cheap, vile, mean.

par-shoin
1. Person, personage.
2. Beauty.

par-shuh
Also *paw-raw-shaw, pa-ra-sha.**
Also spelled *parshe.*
1. Section, division, part.
2. One of the sections of the Pentateuch.
3. Among Sephardim, the name by which the Torah reading of a particular week is called.
4. A deviation from the norm.
5. A scandal (modern Israeli usage.)

par-tatsh
A botcher, one who fouls up.

---

a as in father; aw as in law; ai as in aisle; ei as in neighbor; e as in bet; i as in vaccine; ih as in tin; o as in solar; oi as in void; oo as in food; u as in put; uh as in but; ch as in chutzpa; zh as in Zhivago.

par-tatsh-ihsh
> Sloppy, inferior, bungled (merchandise or workmanship).

paruhch see *parihch*

pas-kud-nak
> Also *pas-kud-nihk, paskudnyak.*
> A nasty person.

pas-kud-ne
> Also spelled *paskudnye.*
> Vile, nasty, dirty, filthy (referring to a person).

pas-kust-vuh
> Also spelled *paskustve.*
> Feminine form of *paskudne.* See above.

pasn
> Also spelled *pasen, passen.*
> 1. To suit someone.
> 2. Appropriate, proper, fitting.

Passover see *Peisuhch*

past niht
> Unbecoming. Also used in the form of *s'past niht,* a short form of *es past niht.*

past zihch
> Also spelled *past zich.*
> Suitable.

past zihch vi a patsh tzoo a goot Sha-bes
> 1. Literally, "as appropriate as a slap in response to a 'Good Sabbath' greeting."
> 2. An illogical and unbefitting reaction.

pa-sul*
> Also *paw-sul.*
> 1. Disqualified.
> 2. Ritually unusable, in reference to things other than food.

patch see *patsh*

pa-ter-en
> Also spelled *patern.*
> 1. To waste, ruin, spoil.
> 2. To get rid of.

---

a as in father; aw as in law; ai as in aisle; ei as in neighbor; e as in bet; i as in vaccine; ih as in tin; o as in solar; oi as in void; oo as in food; u as in put; uh as in but; ch as in chutzpa; zh as in Zhivago.

pa-ter-en tsait
>   Also spelled *pateren zeit.*
>   To waste time.

patsh
>   Also spelled *patch, potsh.*
>   Slap, smack.

patsh-ke
>   Also *patsh-ki.*
>   Also spelled *potchki.*
>   A variant form of *patshkn.* See below.

patshkn
>   Also spelled *patshken.*
>   1. Literally, "to smear, daub."
>   2. To fuss, to play around.
>   3. To be slipshod, messy.

pa-vuhl-ye
>   Also spelled *pavolye.*
>   1. Slowly.
>   2. To move with care.

paw-nihm
>   Also *pa-nihm.**
>   Also spelled *panim.*
>   1. A face.
>   2. Appearance.

pawrawshaw see *parshuh*

paw-ro-ches
>   Also *pa-ro-chet.**
>   Also spelled *parokhet.*
>   1. Literally, "curtain."
>   2. The curtain that hangs in front of the Holy Ark
>   *(Aron Hakodesh).*

pawsul see *pasul*

pay see *pei*

paya see *peia*

payess see *peies*

pei*
>   Also spelled *pe, pay, pai.*

---

a as in father; aw as in law; ai as in aisle; ei as in neighbor; e as in bet; i as in vaccine; ih as in tin; o as in solar; oi as in void; oo as in food; u as in put; uh as in but; ch as in chutzpa; zh as in Zhivago.

The seventeenth letter of the Hebrew alphabet, sounded like "p."

pei-a*
> Also *pei-aw*.
> Also spelled *peah, paya*.
> 1. Literally, "corner."
> 2. In the Bible, "corners of a field," the produce of which had to be left for the poor.

pei-es
> Also *pei-uhs, pei-os, pei-ot.**
> Also spelled *peiess, payes, payess, peot*.
> Earlocks, sideburns, worn particularly by Chasidim.

pei-ger-en
> Also spelled *paigaren*.
> To die (said of an animal).

pei-ger-en zawl er
> Also spelled *paigaren zol er*.
> 1. Literally, "He should only die."
> 2. He should drop dead unceremoniously.

peikler see *paikler*

pei nun
> Two Hebrew letters that appear on tombstones as an abbreviation for the Hebrew words *po nihkbar,* "here lies buried," or *po noach,* "here rests."

peiot see *peies*

pei-sach-dihg
> Also *pei-sach-dihk*.
> Also spelled *pesachdik, pesadik*.
> Food and utensils that are maintained in compliance with the laws of Passover.

Pei-suhch
> Also *Pe-sach.**
> Also spelled *Pesah*.
> 1. Literally, "to pass over."
> 2. Passover, the Festival of Freedom that is observed for seven days in Israel and for eight days by most Jews of the Diaspora.

---

a as in father; aw as in law; ai as in aisle; ei as in neighbor; e as in bet; i as in vaccine; ih as in tin; o as in solar; oi as in void; oo as in food; u as in put; uh as in but; ch as in chutzpa; zh as in Zhivago.

3. The Paschal Lamb, eaten on Passover in ancient times.

pe-ke-she
>A festive robe worn by Chasidim.

pekl
>Also spelled *pekel*.
>Bundle, parcel, package.

peot see *peies*

pe-rek*
>Also *per-uhk*.
>1. Chapter, section.
>2. Abbreviated reference to *Pirkei Avot* (Ethics of the Fathers), a tractate of the Talmud.

periah see *pria*

peruhk see *perek*

Pesach
>Also spelled *Pesah*. See *Peisuhch*.

pesachdik see *peisachdihg*

peshat see *p'shat*

pesichaw see *p'sichuh*

pesil t'cheiles see *p'tihl t'cheilet*

Pesukei D'zihmruh see *P'sukei D'zihmruh*

peticha see *p'sichuh*

pe-ti-ruh
>Also *pe-ti-ra*.*
>1. Literally, "freed of, rid of."
>2. Death, demise.

petshai see *p'tsha*

Pharisee
>A member of the association of scholars and laity in the first century B.C.E. and the first century C.E. that observed the Written Law, interpreted Scriptures liberally, and adhered to the Oral Law.

pihd-yon ha-ben
>Also spelled *pidyon haben*.
>Literally, "redemption of the son," a biblical cere-

---

a as in father; aw as in law; ai as in aisle; ei as in neighbor; e as in bet; i as in vaccine; ih as in tin; o as in solar; oi as in void; oo as in food; u as in put; uh as in but; ch as in chutzpa; zh as in Zhivago.

mony of redemption of the mother's firstborn son
so he will not be required to devote his life to Temple
service.

pihd-yon she-vu-yihm
Also spelled *pidyon shevuyim.*
The ransom of captives, hostages.

pihl-puhl
Also spelled *pilpul.*
1. Casuistry, dialectics.
2. A method of Talmudic debate.

pihpihk see *pupihk*

pihr-o-gen
Also *pihr-uh-gen.*
Also spelled *pirogen.*
Turnovers with meat or dairy fillings.

pihr-uhsh-ki
Also spelled *piroshki.*
Turnovers filled with meat, cheese, mashed po-
tatoes, etc.

pih-she pei-she
Also spelled *pisha payshe.*
A card game.

pihshkeh see *pushke*

pihshn
Also spelled *pish-en.*
To urinate.

pihshr
Also spelled *pisher.*
1. A person who urinates.
2. A nobody.
3. A little squirt.

pihsk
Also spelled *pisk.*
1. Mouth.
2. Snout.
3. A big mouth.

pihsk me-luh-che
Also spelled *pisk maloche.*

a as in father; aw as in law; ai as in aisle; ei as in neighbor; e as in bet; i as in vaccine; ih as in tin; o as in
solar; oi as in void; oo as in food; u as in put; uh as in but; ch as in chutzpa; zh as in Zhivago.

1. Literally, "mouth worker."
2. A big talker who achieves little.

pihtom see *pihtuhm*

pihts-e-le
>Also spelled *pitseιe*.
>A pet form of *pihtsl*. See *pihtsl*.

pihtsl
>Also spelled *pitsel*.
>Small, tiny.

pih-tuhm
>Also *pih-tom*.*
>Also spelled *pitom*.
>The button-like protuberance on the *etrog* (citron) used on Sukkot.

pihz-mon
>Also spelled *pizmon*.
>A hymn.

pihz-mon-ihm
>Also spelled *pizmonim*.
>Hymns. Plural of *pihzmon*. Refers particularly to hymns sung on Saturday nights by Sephardim.

pi-ku-ach ne-fesh
>1. Literally, "the saving of a soul."
>2. The saving of an endangered life.

pilpul see *pihlpuhl*

pipik see *pupihk*

pirogen see *pihrogen*

piroshki see *pihrushki*

pisha paysha see *pihshe peishe*

pisher see *pihshr*

pishkeh see *pushke*

pisk see *pihsk*

pitom see *pihtuhm*

pitsel see *pihtsl*

pitsele see *pihtsele*

---

a as in father; aw as in law; aι as in aisle; eι as in neighbor; e as in bet; ι as in vaccine; ih as in tin; o as in solar; oι as in void; oo as in food; u as in put; uh as in but; ch as in chutzpa; zh as in Zhivago.

pi-yut
> Also spelled *piyyut*.
> 1. A liturgical Hebrew poem.
> 2. A poem.

pi-yut-ihm
> The plural of *piyut*. See above.

pizmon see *pihzmon*

plagn
> Also spelled *plagen*.
> Torment, harass, afflict.

plagn zihch
> Also spelled *plagen zich*.
> To torment oneself.

plapln
> Also spelled *plaplen*.
> To chatter, babble.

plat-ke
> To gossip.

plat-ke machr
> Also spelled *plotke macher*.
> A gossiper.

platz
> Also spelled *plotz*.
> 1. To burst open.
> 2. A place.

platzn
> Also spelled *platzen*.
> 1. To burst.
> 2. To split.

pla-va
> A Passover sponge cake in which ground almonds replaces flour.

pletzl
> Also spelled *pletzel*.
> A flat onion roll. *Pletzlach* is the plural form.

ploshr
> Also spelled *plosher*.

1. To chat.
2. To gossip.

plotz see *platz*

plotke-macher see *platke-macher*

poi-er
> Also spelled *poyer*.
> Peasant, farmer.

poik
> A drum.

polke see *puhlke*

Poo-rihm
> Also spelled *Purim*.
> A holiday celebrated on Adar 14, marking the deliverance of the Jews of ancient Persia from Haman's plot to exterminate them, as recorded in the biblical Book (Scroll) of Esther.

Poo-rihm Shpiel
> Also spelled *Purim Shpiel*.
> A Purim masquerade play.

pootz see *puhtz*

por see *puhr*

porech see *puhrech*

poretz see *puhrihtz*

po-seik
> Also *po-sek.**
> 1. Literally, "one who decides."
> 2. A scholar who makes decisions on matters of Jewish law.

potchke see *patshke*

potsh see *patsh*

poyer see *poier*

prepln
> Also spelled *preplen*.
> To mutter, mumble.

pri-a*
> Also *pri-aw*.

---

a as in father; aw as in law; ai as in aisle; ei as in neighbor; e as in bet; i as in vaccine; ih as in tin; o as in solar; oi as in void; oo as in food; u as in put; uh as in but; ch as in chutzpa; zh as in Zhivago.

Also spelled *peria, periah*.
The uncovering of the glans penis at the time of circumcision.

prih-tse

Also spelled *pritzteh*.
1. Literally, "an aristocratic woman and a landowner's wife."
2. A proud woman, a prima donna. Feminine form of *puhrihtz*.

pritzteh see *prihtse*

prokes see *holishkes*

pruhst

Also spelled *prost*.
1. Common.
2. Vulgar.
3. Boorish.

pruhst-er

Also spelled *proster*.
1. A boor.
2. A vulgar person.

pruhst-ih-kait

Also spelled *prostikeit*.
Vulgarity.

p'shat

Also spelled *peshat*.
The plain meaning of the Torah text.

p'si-chuh

Also *pe-si-chaw, pe-ti-cha*.*
1. Literally, "opening."
2. The honor given to a person who is designated to open the Holy Ark in the synagogue.

P'su-kei D'zihm-ruh

Also *P'su-kei D'zihm-ra*.*
1. Literally, "verses of praise."
2. Psalms and other biblical passages of praise to God which form part of the introductory prayers of the morning service.

p'tihl te-chei-let*
>   Also *pe-sihl t'chei-les*.
>   Also spelled *pesil t'cheiles*.
>   The blue thread of the *tsitsit* (no longer used except by Bratzlaver *Chasidim)*.

p'tsha
>   Also *pe-tshai*.
>   Also spelled *petsha, p'tcha*.
>   Jellied calf's or beef's feet, sometimes called *sulze*.

pu
>   An exclamation of disdain.

puhl-ke
>   Also *pul-ke*.
>   Also spelled *polke*.
>   The drumstick of a fowl.

puhl-kes
>   Also *pul-kes*.
>   Chicken legs.

puhr
>   Also spelled *por*.
>   A pair, couple.

puh-rech
>   Also spelled *porech*.
>   Dust.

puh-rihtz
>   Also spelled *poretz*.
>   1. An aristocrat.
>   2. A landowner.

puhtz
>   Also spelled *pootz, putz*.
>   1. To decorate.
>   2. A fool, a stupid person.
>   3. Penis (slang).

pul-ke see *puhlke*.

pul-ta-bul-tshas
>   Cinnamon buns.

punkt far-kert
>   1. The exact opposite.

---

a as in father; aw as in law; ai as in aisle; ei as in neighbor; e as in bet; i as in vaccine; ih as in tin; o as in solar; oi as in void; oo as in food; u as in put; uh as in but; ch as in chutzpa; zh as in Zhivago.

   2. The reverse is true.

pu-pihk
   Also *pih-pihk.*
   Also spelled *pupik, pipik.*
   Navel, bellybutton.

Purim see *Poorhim*

push-ke
   Also *pihsh-ke.*
   Also spelled *pishke, pishkeh.*
   A charity box.

pust un pas
   Idle.

pust un pas-nihk
   A loafer, an idler.

putz see *puhtz*

---

a as in father; aw as in law; ai as in aisle: ei as in neighbor; e as in bet; i as in vaccine; ih as in tin; o as in solar; oi as in void; oo as in food; u as in put; uh as in but; ch as in chutzpa; zh as in Zhivago.

R

rabbi
>   1. Literally, "my master."
>   2. My teacher.
>   3. An ordained Jewish clergyman.

ra-bo-sai n'vaw-reich
>   Also *ra-bo-tai ne-va-rech.**
>   1. Literally, "Gentlemen, let us bless."
>   2. The call to say Grace After Meals when a quorum of three or more is present.

rach-muhn-es
>   Also *rach-ma-nut.**
>   Also spelled *rachmones.*
>   1. Compassion.
>   2. Pity.
>   3. Mercy.

raich
>   Also spelled *reich.*
>   Rich, wealthy.

rain see *rein*

rainiken see *reinihken*

raisn
>   Also spelled *raisen, reissen.*
>   To rip, tear.

raisn di fleish
>   Also spelled *reissen di flaish.*
>   1. Literally, "to tear off the flesh."
>   2. Take someone apart.

raisn di hoit
>   Also spelled *reissen di hoit.*
>   1. Literally, "to tear off the skin."
>   2. Skin someone alive.

---

a as in father: **aw** as in law; **ai** as in aisle; **ei** as in neighbor; **e** as in bet: **i** as in vaccine: **ih** as in tin: **o** as in solar; **oi** as in void; **oo** as in food; **u** as in put; **uh** as in but; **ch** as in chutzpa: **zh** as in Zhivago.

rai-ze
>A trip, journey.

rasha see *rawshuh*

rav see *ruhv*

raw-le
>Also spelled *role*.
>1. A part in a play.
>2. A role.

raw-shuh
>Also *raw-shaw, ra-sha**.
>Also spelled *ruhshe*.
>1. A mean, evil, malicious person.
>2. A villain.

raw-zhihn-ke
>Also spelled *rozhinke*.
>Raisin.

raw-zhihn-kes miht mandln
>Also spelled *rozhinkes mit mandln, rozhinkes mit mandlen*.
>1. Literally, "raisins with almonds."
>2. The name of a folk lullaby adapted by Abraham Goldfaden in his operetta *Shulamis* (1880).

rayach see *reiach*

reb
>1. The equivalent of *rav*, meaning "mister."
>2. A short form of *rebi (rebbe)*. See below. See also *ruhv*.

re-betzn
>Also *re-be-tsihn*.
>Also spelled *rebetsen, rebetsin, rebbetzen*.
>Rabbi's wife.

re-bi
>Also spelled *rebbe, rebbi*.
>1. Teacher.
>2. Title of a Chassidic leader.

re-chi-les
>Also *re-chi-lus, re-chi-lut**.

---

a as in father; aw as in law; ai as in aisle; ei as in neighbor; e as in bet; i as in vaccine; ih as in tin; o as in solar; oi as in void; oo as in food; u as in put; uh as in but; ch as in chutzpa; zh as in Zhivago.

1. Gossip.
2. Slander.

redn
Also spelled *reden*.
To say, talk, speak, tell.

redn ihn der velt a-rain
1. Literally, "to talk into the world."
2. To speak nonsense.

redn re-chi-les
Also spelled *reden rechiluhs*.
1. Literally, "to speak gossip."
2. To spread gossip.

redn tzoo der vant
Also spelled *reden tzu der vant*.
1. Literally, "to talk to the wall."
2. To talk in vain.

redn uhn a maws
Also spelled *reden un a moss*.
1. Literally, "to speak without a measure."
2. To be loquacious.
3. To chatter endlessly.

redn zihch ain *(a-rain)* **a kreink**
Also spelled *reden zich ein a krenk*.
1. Literally, "to talk oneself into an illness."
2. Sickness by autosuggestion.
3. Hypochondria.

redn zihch ois daws hartz
Also spelled *redn zich ois dos hartz*.
1. Literally, "talk one's heart out."
2. Get it off one's chest.

re-fu-e shlei-muh
Also *re-fu-aw shlei-maw, re-fu-a shlei-ma.**
Also spelled *refuah shlema*.
1. Literally, "a complete healing."
2. A wish for a full recovery.

refusenik see *refyuznihk*

re-fyuz-nihk
Also spelled *refusenik*.

---

a as in father; aw as in law; ai as in aisle; ei as in neighbor; e as in bet; i as in vaccine; ih as in tin; o as in solar; oi as in void; oo as in food; u as in put; uh as in but; ch as in chutzpa; zh as in Zhivago.

In the late twentieth century, a Soviet Jew seeking to emigrate who meets with official refusal, harassment, and persecution.

regn
>Also spelled *regen.*
>Rain.

rei-ach
>Also spelled *rayach.*
>1. Odor, smell.
>2. Flavor.

reich see *raich*

rein
>Also spelled *rain.*
>Clean, pure.

rei-nih-ken
>Also spelled *rainiken.*
>To clean up, purify, sanitize.

reisen di hoit see *raisn di hoit*

reish
>Also spelled *resh.*
>The twentieth letter of the Hebrew alphabet, corresponding in sound to the letter "r."

reissen see *raisn*

reitach see *rettach*

re-mez
>1. A hint, a sign.
>2. Hidden meaning in the text of the Torah.

resh see *reish*

re-shus
>Also *re-shut.**
>Permission.

Responsa
>Answers by learned rabbis to questions submitted them on Jewish law. In Hebrew, *sh'ei-lot u-t'shu-vot.**

(es) ret zich a-zoi
>1. Literally, "It speaks so."

---

a as in father; aw as in law; ai as in aisle; ei as in neighbor; e as in bet; i as in vaccine; ih as in tin; o as in solar; oi as in void; oo as in food; u as in put; uh as in but; ch as in chutzpa; zh as in Zhivago.

2. This is what's said, but I don't believe it.
3. It seems so.

rettach see *reitach*

Ri-bo-no Shel O-lawm
Also *Ri-bo-no Shel O-lam**.
1. Literally, "Master of the universe."
2. God.

rihch-tihk
Also *rihch-tihg*.
Also spelled *richtig, richtik*.
Correct, O.K., right.

rihch-tih-ker chei-fetz
Also *richtiker chaifetz*.
1. The right article.
2. The real thing.

rihr-ev-dihk
Also spelled *rirevdik*.
Vivacious, lively, agile.

rihsl bawrsht see *ruhsl*

ri-mon
Also spelled *rimmon*.
1. Literally, "a pomegranate."
2. A Torah crown that fits on one finial.

ri-mo-nihm
Also spelled *rimmonim*.
Plural of *rimon*. See above.

rirevdik see *rihrevdihk*

Roish Choidesh see *Rosh Chodesh*

roit
Also spelled *royt*.
Red.

role see *rawle*

roo see *ru*

Rosh Cho-desh*
Also *Roish Choi-desh*.
1. Literally, "the head of the month," the first day
of each Hebrew month.

2. A semi-holiday marking the beginning of the Hebrew month.

Rosh Ha-shaw-naw
Also *Rosh Ha-sha-na**
Also spelled *Rosh Hashanah, Rosh Hashona.*
1. Literally, "the head (beginning) of the year."
2. The Jewish New Year, at the beginning of the month of Tishri (September-October), observed for two days by Orthodox and Conservative Jews, for one day by Reform Jews.

rov see *ruhv*

royt see *roit*

rozhinkes see *rawzhinkes*

ru
Also spelled *roo.*
1. Rest.
2. Calm.
3. Quiet.

ru-ach
Also spelled *ruah.*
1. Spirit.
2. Wind, breath.
3. Demon, evil spirit, ghost.

Ru-ach Ha-ko-desh
1. Literally, "The Holy Spirit."
2. God.

(a) ru-ach ihn dain ta-te's ta-ten a-rain
Also spelled *a ruach in dein tate's taten arein.*
1. Literally, "A demon (evil spirit) should enter your father's father!" (to which "Amen" is sometimes appended).
2. Go to the devil!

rufn *see also* Preface.
Also spelled *rufen.*
1. To call
2. To appeal.

---

a as in father; aw as in law; ai as in aisle; ei as in neighbor; e as in bet; i as in vaccine; ih as in tin; o as in solar; oi as in void; oo as in food; u as in put; uh as in but; ch as in chutzpa; zh as in Zhivago.

ruhg-e-lach
>Also spelled *rugelach, rugelah.*
>A rolled-dough pastry filled with nuts and raisins.

ruhshe see *rawshuh*

ruhsl
>Also spelled *ruhsel, russel.*
>Fermented beet juice, also called beet sour, used to prepare borsht.

ruhsl fleish
>Also spelled *russel flaish.*
>Meat prepared with *ruhsl.* See *ruhsl.*

ruhv
>Also *rav.**
>Also spelled *rov* and *rawv.*
>1. Rabbi.
>2. Teacher.
>3. The ordained leader of a Jewish congregation.

russel see *ruhsl*

S

Sabbateans
Followers of seventeenth-century pseudo-messiah Sabbatai (Shabbetai Tzevi).

Sabbath see *Shabuhs*

sabra see *sabruh*

sab-ruh
Also *sab-ra.**
1. Literally, "a cactus."
2. A native Israeli, reputed to be like a cactus, tough on the outside, sweet on the inside.

(a) sach
A lot, many, much.

(a) sach tzoo redn
Also spelled *(a) sach tzu reden.*
Much to talk about.

(a) sach tzoo redn, vei-nihk tzoo her-en
1. Literally, "much to say, little to be heard."
2. Talk devoid of substance.

saftig see *zaftihg*

saichel see *seichl*

sa-ka-nat ne-fa-shot*
Also *sa-kaw-nas ne-faw-shos.*
Danger to life.

sa-kaw-ne
Also *sa-kaw-naw, sa-ka-na.**
Danger.

sa-lat
1. Lettuce.
2. Salad.

Samaritans see *Shomronihm*

sameiach b'chelko see *sawmeiach b'chelko*

---

a as in father; aw as in law; ai as in aisle; ei as in neighbor; e as in bet; i as in vaccine; ih as in tin; o as in solar; oi as in void; oo as in food; u as in put; uh as in but; ch as in chutzpa; zh as in Zhivago.

sa-muhch
Also *sa-mech.**
The fifteenth letter of the Hebrew alphabet, corresponding in sound to the letter "s."

Sanctification of the Name see *kihdoosh ha-Shem*

san-dek*
Also *san-duhk.*
Also spelled *sandik, sondek.*
The godfather of a boy at the time of the infant's circumcision.

San-hed-rihn
Also spelled *Sanhedrin.*
1. The Jewish Supreme Court and legislative body in Palestine before 70 C.E.
2. A tractate of the Talmud.

Satan see *Sawtawn*

sawchawr veonesh see *s'char v'onesh*

saw-mei-ach b'chel-ko
Also *sa-mei-ach b'chel-ko.**
1. Literally, "happy with his portion."
2. A contented person.

Saw-tawn
Also *Sa-tan.**
1. The devil, Satan.
2. Adversary.
3. Evil inclination.

s'chach
Branches used to cover the roof of a *suka.*

schalet see *tschawlent*

s'char v'o-nesh*
Also *saw-chawr v'o-nesh.*
Reward and punishment.

scharf see *sharf*

schav see *shav*

schlemiel see *shlemiel*

schmaltz see *shmaltz*

schnaps see *shnaps*

---

a as in father; aw as in law; ai as in aisle; ei as in neighbor; e as in bet; i as in vaccine; ih as in tin; o as in solar; oi as in void; oo as in food; u as in put; uh as in but; ch as in chutzpa; zh as in Zhivago.

schnorrer see *shnawrer*

schochet see *shochuht*

s'choi-ruh
>Also *se-cho-ra,* se-cho-raw.*
>1. Merchandise.
>2. Goods, wares.
>3. Commodity.

S'dom see *Sedom*

sechel see *seichl*

Se-da-rihm*
>Also *Se-daw-rihm.*
>Also spelled *Sedarim.*
>Plural of *Seidr.* See below.

Seder see *Seidr*

Se-dom
>Also spelled *S'dom, Sodom.*
>A biblical city destroyed, along with neighboring Gomorra, because of its sinfulness (Genesis 18-19).

sed-ruh
>Also *sihd-ra,* sihd-raw.*
>Also spelled *sidra.*
>1. Literally, "order, arrangement."
>2. One of the fifty-four sections into which the Pentateuch is divided for weekly sequential readings in the synagogue.

Se-far-dic
>Also *Se-far-di.**
>Also spelled *Sephardic, Sephardi.*
>1. Literally, "Spanish."
>2. Liturgical rites of the Spanish, Portuguese, and Oriental Jews.

Se-far-dihm
>Also spelled *Sefardim, Sephardim.*
>Iberian and Middle Eastern Jews and their descendants, so named because of their original residence in regions influenced by the hegemony or culture of Spain.

Sefer Torah see *Seifr Toruh*

sefira see *s'firuh*

Se-fi-ras Haw-o-mer
> Also *Se-fi-rat Ha-o-mer.**
> 1. Literally, "the counting of the *Omer.*
> See also *s'firuh.*

seichel see *seichl*

seichl
> Also spelled *seichel, saichel, sechel.*
> 1. Brains, common sense.
> 2. Good judgment.
> 3. Intelligence.
> 4. Reason.
> 5. Shrewdness, wits.

Seidr
> Also *Se-der.**
> 1. Literally, "order, arrangement."
> 2. Passover service and banquet during which the *Haggadah,* which recounts the exodus of the Hebrew slaves from Egyptian bondage, is read.

seifr
> Also *se-fer.**
> 1. Book.
> 2. A religious book from which one studies.

Seifr To-ruh
> Also *Sei-fer To-raw, Sei-fer To-ra, Se-fer To-ra.**
> Also spelled *Sefer Torah.*
> The text of the Pentateuch, handwritten on a parchment scroll by a scribe and read in the synagogue.

se-la*
> Also *se-law.*
> Also spelled *selah.*
> A word of uncertain meaning, possibly an ancient musical notation, appended to many Psalms and liturgical selections.

selicha see *selichuh*

Se-li-chot*
> Also *S'li-chuhs, S'li-chos.*
> Penitential prayers. Plural of *Selicha.*

---

a as in father; aw as in law; ai as in aisle; ei as in neighbor; e as in bet; i as in vaccine; ih as in tin; o as in solar; oi as in void; oo as in food; u as in put; uh as in but; ch as in chutzpa; zh as in Zhivago.

se-li-chuh
> Also *se-li-cha.**
> Also spelled *selihah.*
> 1. Forgiveness.
> 2. (Modern Hebrew) Pardon me!
> 3. A penitential prayer.
> *Selichot* is the plural form.

Semanada Buena
> The Sephardic (Ladino) Saturday night greeting expressed on the departure of the Sabbath.

semicha see *smichuh*

Sephardi see *Sefardic*

Sephardic see *Sefardic*

Sephardim see *Sefardihm*

se-u-da*
> Also *se-u-daw, su-duh, su-de.*
> A festive meal.

Se-u-da She-li-shiht*
> Also *Se-u-daw Shelishihs.*
> The third meal of the Sabbath.

Se-u-dat Mihtz-va*
> Also *Se-u-das Mihtz-vaw.*
> Also spelled *Seudat Mitzvah.*
> A feast in honor of the performance of a commandment *(mitzva).*

Sfardi see *sefardic*

Sfi-ruh
> Also *Se-fi-ra.**
> 1. Literally, "counting."
> 2. A short form of *Sefirat Haomer,** meaning "counting the *Omer,*" the period of forty-nine days between the second day of Passover and the Shavuot festival.

sha
> Be quiet! Shut up!

shaa see *shuh*

Shabat see *Shabuhs*

---

a as in father; aw as in law; ai as in aisle; ei as in neighbor; e as in bet; i as in vaccine; ih as in tin; o as in solar; oi as in void; oo as in food; u as in put; uh as in but; ch as in chutzpa; zh as in Zhivago.

Sha-bat Ha-ga-dol*
　　Also *Sha-baws Ha-gaw-dol.*
　　1. Literally, "the Great Sabbath."
　　2. The Sabbath before Passover.

Shabat Kodesh see *Shabuhs Koidesh*

Sha-bat Na-cha-moo*
　　Also *Sha-buhs Nach-moo.*
　　Also spelled *Shabbat Nachamu.*
　　1. Literally, "Sabbath of Comfort," the Sabbath
　　　immediately following Tisha B'Av, when the
　　　haftara reading is from Isaiah 40, beginning
　　　with the words, *Nachamu, nachamu ami,* mean-
　　　ing "Comfort ye, comfort ye, my people."

Sha-bat Sha-lom*
　　Also *Sha-baws Shaw-lom.*
　　1. Literally, "Sabbath peace."
　　2. A Sabbath greeting, the Yiddish equivalent of
　　　which is *Gut Shabes.*

Shabaws Hagawdol see *Shabat Hagadol*

Shabbat see *Shabuhs*

Shabbos see *Shabuhs*

Sha-bes goi
　　Also *Sha-buhs goi.*
　　Also spelled *Shabbos goy.*
　　A non-Jew employed to perform minimum mainte-
　　nance work (e.g., turning electricity on and off)
　　prohibited to a traditional Jew on the Sabbath.

Sha-buhs
　　Also *Sha-baws, Sha-bat.***
　　Also spelled *Shabbos, Shabes, Shabbes.*
　　1. Literally, "rest."
　　2. The Sabbath day, a day of rest.

Sha-buhs Koi-desh
　　Also *Sha-bat Ko-desh.***
　　Holy Sabbath.

Sha-buhs tihsh
　　Sabbath table.

---

a as in father; aw as in law; ai as in aisle; ei as in neighbor; e as in bet; i as in vaccine; ih as in tin; o as in
solar; oi as in void; oo as in food; u as in put; uh as in but; ch as in chutzpa; zh as in Zhivago.

sha-char
Dawn.

Sha-cha-riht*
Also *Sha-cha-rihs.*
Also spelled *Shaharit, Shachris.*
1. Dawn.
2. The morning prayer service.

Sha-dai*
Also spelled *Shaddai.*
Almighty God.

shadchn
Also *shad-chan,* shad-chawn, shad-chuhn.*
Also spelled *shadchen, shatchen.*
1. Matchmaker.
2. Marriage broker.

shaharit see *shachariht*

shaigetz see *sheiguhtz*

sh'ailos u'tshuvos see *she'eilos uteshuvos*

shain see *shein*

shaine kind see *sheine kihnd*

(a) shainem dank eich see *(a) sheinem dank aich*

(a) shainer gelechter see *(a) sheiner gelechter*

(a) shainer Yid see *(a) sheiner Yihd*

shainkeit see *sheinkait*

shaitel see *sheitl*

Shakuhl see *Shehakol*

Shalach Manot see *Shalachmuhnes*

shalet see *cholent*

sha-li-ach*
Also *shaw-li-ach.*
1. Emissary, messenger.
2. A representative dispatched by the State of Israel to Diaspora communities for public relations, fundraising, and educational purposes.

shaliach tsibur see *shliach tsibur*

Shal-lach-muh-nes
> Also *Shlach-maw-nes, Sha-lach Ma-not.**
> Literally, "the sending of gifts," a tradition connected with the Purim holiday. The original form of the term as found in the Book of Esther is *mishloach manot.*

sha-lom*
> Also *shaw-lom, shuh-lem.*
> 1. Literally, "peace."
> 2. Hello.
> 3. Goodbye.
> 4. Greetings!

shalom aleichem see *shawlom aleichem*

shalom bayit see *shuhlem bayihs*

shalosh regalihm see *shawlosh regawlihm*

sha-muhs
> Also *sha-mes, sha-mash.**
> Also spelled *shammes, shammos, shamus, shammus.*
> 1. Synagogue sexton or beadle.
> 2. The extra candle used to kindle the other tapers in the Chanukah *menorah.*

shana tova see *shuhnuh tovuh*

shan-de
> Also *shan-der.*
> A shame, a shameful situation, a disgrace.

(a) shan-de far di kihn-der
> Also spelled *(a) shande far di kinder.*
> 1. Literally, "a disgrace for the children."
> 2. A terrible act.

(a) shan-de oon a char-pe
> A shame and a disgrace.

shander see *shande*

shand-hoiz
> 1. Literally, "house of shame."
> 2. Brothel.

---

a as in father; aw as in law; ai as in aisle; ei as in neighbor; e as in bet; i as in vaccine; ih as in tin; o as in solar; oi as in void; oo as in food; u as in put; uh as in but; ch as in chutzpa; zh as in Zhivago.

sharf
>   Also spelled *scharf.*
>   1. Highly seasoned.
>   2. Sharp.

shas
>   Also spelled *shass.*
>   An acronym from the two Hebrew words, *shisha sedarim,* "the six sections" of the Talmud.

shatchen see *shadchn*

shatn
>   Also spelled *shaten.*
>   1. Damage.
>   2. Hurt.
>   3. Harm

shat-nez
>   Also spelled *shatnes.*
>   The biblical prohibition against mixing certain materials (Deuteronomy 22:11). A fabric that is an animal product (silk or wool, for example) may not be mixed with a fabric that is a vegetable product (cotton, for example).

shav
>   Also spelled *schav, s'shav.*
>   1. Cold spinach soup.
>   2. Sorrel (sour grass) soup.

sha-voo-a tov*
>   Also *shaw-voo-a tov.*
>   Also spelled *shavua tov.*
>   1. Literally, "good week."
>   2. A greeting used on Saturday night, after the Sabbath has ended.

shavua see *shawvoo-a*

Sha-vu-ot*
>   Also *Shvoo-es, Shaw-voo-os.*
>   Also spelled *Shevuos, Shvues, Shawvuos, Shavuoth.*
>   1. Literally, "weeks." Plural of *sha-voo-a.*
>   2. Pentecost, the Festival of Weeks, marking the receiving of the Torah by Moses on Mount Sinai.

---

a as in father; aw as in law; ai as in aisle; ei as in neighbor; e as in bet; i as in vaccine; ih as in tin; o as in solar; oi as in yoid; oo as in food; u as in put; uh as in but; ch as in chutzpa; zh as in Zhivago.

shawliach see *shaliach*

shawliach tzibur see *shliach tsibur*

shawlom see *shalom*

shaw-lom a-lei-chem
Also *sha-lom a-lei-chem,** *shuh-luhm a-lei-chem.*
Also spelled *shalom alaichem.*
1. Literally, "Peace be upon you!"
2. A salutation.
3. A pseudonym of the Yiddish writer Sholom Rabinowitz (1859-1916).

shawlom bayihs see *shuhlem bayihs*

shaw-losh re-gaw-lihm
Also *sha-losh re-ga-lihm.**
Also spelled *sholosh regolim.*
1. Literally, "three pilgrimage festivals."
2. Passover, Shavuot, and Sukkot. In Temple times these were festivals on which Jews visited the Temple in Jerusalem.

shawnaw tovaw see *shuhnuh tovuh*

shaw-voo-a
Also *sha-voo-a.**
Also spelled *shavua.*
Week.

Shawvuos see *Shavuot*

shaygetz see *sheiguhtz*

shayn see *shein*

shayner Yid see *sheiner Yihd*

shaytl see *sheitl*

Sh'chinah see *Shechinuh*

sh'chi-tuh
Also *she-chi-ta,** *she-chi-taw.*
Also spelled *sh'chite.*
The slaughter of cattle and fowl according to Jewish law.

She-chi-nuh
Also *She-chi-naw, She-chi-na.**

---

a as in father; aw as in law; ai as in aisle; ei as in neighbor; e as in bet; i as in vaccine; ih as in tin; o as in solar; oi as in void; oo as in food; u as in put; uh as in but; ch as in chutzpa; zh as in Zhivago.

Also spelled *Sh'chinah, Shekhinah, Shechina, Shechinah.*
1. Literally, "indwelling."
2. The Divine Presence (God).
3. God's immanence.

shechita see *sh'chituh*

she'eila see *sheile*

she-ei-los u-te-shu-vos
Also *sh'ei-lot u'tshu-vot.**
Also spelled *sh'ailos u'tshuvos.*
1. Literally, "questions and answers."
2. Responsa, queries and responses on matters of Jewish law.

sheeny
A disparaging name for "Jew."

shefichat dam see *shfichas duhm*

She-ha-kol*
Also *Sha-kuhl.*
1. Literally, "for all."
2. The name of the blessing said over liquids, meats, and several other types of food.

She-he-che-yaw-nu
Also *She-he-che-ya-nu.**
1. Literally, "Who has kept us in life."
2. A prayer of gratitude and celebration, recited on the eve of a holiday and on other special occasions.

shei-guhtz
Also *shei-gihtz, she-ketz.**
Also spelled *shaigetz, shaggetz.*
1. A non-Jewish male.
2. Sometimes, a Jew ignorant of Judaism.
3. An unruly lad.
Shihkse is the feminine form.

sheim
Also *shem.**
Also spelled *shaym.*

---

1. Literally, "name."
2. Shem, Noah's eldest son.

sheim tov
Also *shem tov.**
A good name.

shein
Also spelled *shain, shayn.*
Pretty, beautiful.

shein-e kihnd
Also spelled *shaine kind.*
Beautiful child.

(a) shein-em dank aich
Also spelled *(a) shainem dank eich.*
1. Literally, "a pretty thank you."
2. Thank you kindly.

(a) shein-em dank dihr ihn pupihk
Also spelled *(a) shainem dank dir in pupik.*
1. Literally, "a pretty thank-you in your bellybutton"
2. Thanks for nothing.

shein-e meidl
Also spelled *shaine maidel.*
Pretty girl.

(a) shein-e, rein-e ka-paw-re
Also spelled *(a) shaine, raine kapore.*
1. Literally, "a beautiful, pure sacrificial fowl."
2. Serves him (her) right!
3. To hell with it! It's doomed!

shei-ner-e leigt men ihn der erd (drerd)
1. Literally, "Prettier (more beautiful) ones than you are placed in the earth."
2. You are very ugly.

(a) shein-er ge-lech-ter
Also spelled *(a) shainer gelechter.*
1. Literally, "a pretty bit of laughter."
2. Some joke!
3. This is serious business.

---

a as in father; aw as in law; ai as in aisle; ei as in neighbor; e as in bet; i as in vaccine; ih as in tin; o as in solar; oi as in void; oo as in food; u as in put; uh as in but; ch as in chutzpa; zh as in Zhivago.

(a) shein-er Yihd
>Also spelled *shayner Yid, (a) shainer Yid.*
>1. Literally, "a beautiful Jew."
>2. A person of good character.

shein-kait
>Also spelled *shainkeit.*
>Beauty.

shein vi di le-vuh-ne
>1. Literally, "as beautiful as the moon."
>2. The title of a Yiddish song, the music of which
>was popularized as the "Miami Beach Rumba."

shein vi di zih-ben velt-en
>Also spelled *shain vi di zibben velten.*
>1. As pretty as seven worlds.
>2. Very beautiful.

sheitl
>Also *shaitl.*
>Also spelled *shaytl, sheitel, shaitel.*
>Wig worn by married Orthodox Jewish women.

shekel see *shekl*

sheketz see *sheiguhtz*

Shekhinah see *Shechinuh*

shekl
>Also *she-kel.**
>1. An ancient unit of weight.
>2. An ancient coin.
>3. A unit of currency in modern Israel.

she-li-chihm
>Also spelled *shlichim.*
>Plural of *shaliach.*

shem see *sheim*

she-ma
>Also spelled *sh'ma.*
>1. Literally, "hear."
>2. Short form of *Shema Yihsrael.* See below.

She-ma Yihs-ra-el*
>Also *She-ma Yihs-raw-eil.*

---

a as in father; aw as in law; ai as in aisle; ei as in neighbor; e as in bet; i as in vaccine; ih as in tin; o as in solar; oi as in void; oo as in food; u as in put; uh as in but; ch as in chutzpa; zh as in Zhivago.

Also spelled *Shema Yisrael, Shema Yisroel, Sh'ma Yisrael.*
1. Literally, "Hear, O Israel."
2. The basic declaration of Jewish faith, from Deuteronomy 6:4.

Shem Ha-me-fo-rash*
Also *Sheim Ha-me-fo-rawsh.*
1. Literally, "the explicit Name."
2. The name of God, pronounced only by the High Priest in the Temple.

She-mi-ni A-tse-ret*
Also *She-mi-ni A-tse-res.*
Also spelled *Shmini Atzeres.*
1. Literally, "the eighth day of convocation."
2. The conclusion of the Sukkot festival, based on Leviticus 23:36.

shemiras Shabbos see *shmiras Shabuhs*

shemita see *shmitaw*

shemn zihch
Also spelled *shemen zich.*
To be ashamed of oneself.

shemn zihch ihn dain vaitn haltz a-rain
1. Literally, "You should be ashamed down to the bottom of your throat!"
2. Shame on you!

Shemoneh Esreh see *Shmone Esrei*

shem tov see *sheim tov*

shenadar see *shnuhdr*

She-ol
1. Literally, "to dig."
2. The biblical dwelling place of the dead in the depths of the earth (Deuteronomy 32:22; Psalms 55:15, 86:13).
3. Hades.

shep a bihsl na-ches
Also spelled *shep a bissel nachas.*
1. To be proud.
2. Derive a bit of satisfaction.

---

a as in father; aw as in law; ai as in aisle; ei as in neighbor; e as in bet; i as in vaccine; ih as in tin; o as in solar; oi as in void; oo as in food; u as in put; uh as in but; ch as in chutzpa; zh as in Zhivago.

3. Enjoy, derive pleasure (especially from off-spring).

shepping naches
Deriving pleasure.

shepp naches
To derive joy.

shetar see *shtar*

shetar gerut see *shtar geirus*

Sheva Berachot see *Shevuh Brawches*

shevarim see *shevawrihm*

Shevat see *Shvat*

shevawrihm
Also *she-va-rihm.**
1. Literally, "broken."
2. *Shofar* blasts consisting of three staccato sounds.

She-vuh Brawch-es
Also *She-va Be-ra-chot.**
1. Literally, "seven blessings."
2. Prayers recited during the marriage ceremony.

Shevuos see *Shavuot*

shfi-chas duhm
Also *she-fi-chat dam.**
Bloodshed, including human contributory negligence leading to the death of innocents.

shihch
Shoes. Plural of *shuch.*

shih-duhch
Also *shi-dooch.**
Also spelled *shiduch.*
1. A match.
2. Engagement, betrothal.
3. An arranged marriage.

shihf
Also spelled *shif.*
A vessel, ship.

---

a as in father; aw as in law; ai as in aisle; ei as in neighbor; e as in bet; i as in vaccine; ih as in tin; o as in solar; oi as in void; oo as in food; u as in put; uh as in but; ch as in chutzpa; zh as in Zhivago.

(a) shihf un a ruder
    1. Literally, "a ship without a rudder."
    2. Poor management.

shihk yihn-gel
    Also spelled *shik yingel*.
    Messenger boy, errand boy.

shihkn
    Also spelled *shiken*.
    To send.

shihkr
    Also *shi-kor.**
    Also spelled *shikur, shikker*.
    1. Intoxicated.
    2. Drunk.

shihk-tse
    Also spelled *shikze, shiktsa, shiksa, shikza, shikse*.
    A non-Jewish woman. The feminine form of *sheigetz*.

shihn
    Also spelled *shin*.
    A letter of the Hebrew alphabet sounded like "sh."

Shihr Ha-ma-a-los
    Also *Shihr Ha-ma-a-lot.**
    Also spelled *Shir Hamaalos*.
    1. Literally, "Song of Ascents," from the Book of Psalms.
    2. The prayer preceding the recital of Grace After Meals.

Shihr Ha-shi-rihm
    Also spelled *Shir Hashirim*.
    The Song of Songs, one of the books of the Bible.

shihsr
    Also spelled *shiser*.
    Shooter, marksman.

shih-vuh
    Also *shih-va,* shihv-aw*.
    Also spelled *shiva*.
    1. Literally, "seven."

---

a as in father; aw as in law; ai as in aisle; ei as in neighbor; e as in bet; i as in vaccine; ih as in tin; o as in solar; oi as in void; oo as in food; u as in put; uh as in but; ch as in chutzpa; zh as in Zhivago.

    2. The seven-day period of mourning for an imme-
diate relative, beginning upon the return from
interment.

shik yingel see *shihk yihngel*

shiken see *shihkn*

shikker see *shihkr*

shiksa see *shihktse*

Shim-shon ha-gi-bor
    1. Literally, "Samson the strongman."
    2. A designation for a very powerful person, de-
rived from the biblical Samson, noted for his
great strength.

shin see *shihn*

Shir Hamaalos see *Shihr Hamaalos*

Shir Ha-shi-rim see *Shihr Hashirihm*

shiser see *shihsr*

shiva see *shihvuh*

shkap-e
    1. A mare.
    2. A nag.
    3. Worthless.

shlachmawnes see *shalachmuhnes*

shlafen see *shlawfn*

shlak
    Also spelled *shlock*.
    1. A stroke.
    2. Shoddy merchandise.
    3. Cheap, inferior, tacky, trashy.
    4. A sloppy, ineffectual person.

shlang
    1. Snake, serpent.
    2. (Slang) penis.

shla-ten sha-mes
    1. Community busybody.
    2. Gossipmonger.

---

a as in father; aw as in law; ai as in aisle; ei as in neighbor; e as in bet; i as in vaccine; ih as in tin; o as in solar; oi as in void; oo as in food; u as in put; uh as in but; ch as in chutzpa; zh as in Zhivago.

shlawfn
> Also spelled *shlafen, shlofen.*
> To sleep.

shlawgn
> Also spelled *shlawgen, shlogen.*
> To beat, hit, slug.

shlawgn kawp ihn vant
> Also spelled *shlogen kop in vant.*
> 1. Literally, "hitting one's head against a wall."
> 2. Trying to do the impossible.
> 3. Wasting time.

shlawg zihch kawp ihn vant
> Also spelled *shlog zich kop in vant.*
> 1. Literally, "beat one's head against the wall."
> 2. Attempt the impossible, but don't bother me!

shlawg zihch miht Gawt aroom
> 1. Literally, "Go fight with God!"
> 2. Fight a losing battle.

shlawsr
> Also spelled *shlosser.*
> Locksmith.

shlecht
> Also spelled *shlehcht.*
> Bad, wicked, mean, evil.

shlemazl see *shlihmazl*

shlemiel see *shlemil*

shle-mil
> Also spelled *shlemiel.*
> 1. A clumsy, ineffectual, bungling person, often victimized.
> 2. A *klawtz.*
> 3. Synonymous with *shlimazl.*

(a) shlep
> 1. Literally, "drag."
> 2. A vacillator.
> 3. An ineffectual person.

shlepen see *shlepn*

---

a as in father; aw as in law; ai as in aisle; ei as in neighbor; e as in bet; i as in vaccine; ih as in tin; o as in solar; oi as in void; oo as in food; u as in put; uh as in but; ch as in chutzpa; zh as in Zhivago.

(a) shlep-er
>   1. Literally, "one who drags."
>   2. A vacillator, an uncertain person.
>   3. One who expects something for nothing.

shlepn
>   Also spelled *shlepen.*
>   To drag, pull, tug, haul.

shli-ach tsi-bur*
>   Also *shaw-li-ach tsi-bur, sha-li-ach tsi-bur.*
>   1. Literally, "community emissary" or "messenger of the populace."
>   2. Leader of a prayer service.
>   3. A cantor.

shlichim see *shelichihm*

shlih-mazl
>   Also spelled *shlimazl, shlimazel, shlemazl.*
>   1. A luckless person.
>   2. A misfit.
>   *Shlemil* is a variant form.

shlihsh-kas
>   Also spelled *shlishkas.*
>   Potato noodles.

shlihsl
>   Also spelled *shlisel.*
>   A key.

shlimazel see *shlihmazl*

shlisel see *shlihsl*

shlock see *shlak*

shlofen see *shlawfn*

shlog see *shlawg*

shlogen see *shlawgn*

shlogen kop in vant see *shlawgn kawp ihn vant*

shloomp
>   Also spelled *shlump.*
>   1. A scatterbrain.
>   2. Someone uncoordinated.

---

a as in father; aw as in law; ai as in aisle; ei as in neighbor; e as in bet; i as in vaccine; ih as in tin; o as in solar; oi as in void; oo as in food; u as in put; uh as in but; ch as in chutzpa; zh as in Zhivago.

3. A dowdy, unkempt person.
4. A slob.

shlosh es-rei mi-dos
Also *sha-losh es-rei mi-dot.**
Literally, "thirteen attributes (of God)."

shlo-shihm
Also spelled *shloshim, sheloshim.*
1. Literally "thirty."
2. The thirty-day mourning period for a close relative.

shlosser see *shlawsr*

shluhb see *zhluhb*

shluhmil see *shlemil*

shlump
1. An ineffectual person.
2. An unkempt person, a slob.

Sh'ma Yisroel see *Shema Yihsrael*

shmad
Apostasy from Judaism.

shmaichl see *shmeichl*

shmaisn
Also spelled *shmeisen.*
To hit, wallop, thrash.

shmaltz
1. Literally, "rendered fat," most often chicken fat.
2. Sweet-talk.
3. Superficiality.
4. Sentimentality.
5. Highly sentimental and banal music and literature.

shmant
Sweet cream.

shman-tzes
1. Trifles.
2. Nonsense.

shma-te
Also *shma-tuh.*

Also spelled *shmatteh.*
A rag.

shma-tes
1. Plural of *shmate.* See above.
2. Old clothes.

shmeer see *shmihr*

shme-ge-gi
1. A fool, jerk.
2. A buffoon.
3. An idiot.

shmeichl
Also *shmaichl.*
Also spelled *shmeichel.*
1. A smile.
2. To ingratiate oneself, fawn, dote.

shmei drei
Baloney, hot air.

shmeisen see *shmaisn*

shmek
1. Sniff.
2. Smell.

(a) shmek ta-bak
1. A pinch of tobacco.
2. Of little value, insignificant.

shmekn ta-bak
To take a sniff of tobacco.

shmen-drihk
Also spelled *shmendrik.*
1. An inept person, a nincompoop.
2. Hero of the satirical comedy *Shmendrik* (1877),
   by Abraham Goldfaden.

shmihr
Also spelled *shmir, shmeer.*
1. Smudge, smear.
2. A swath, an area.
3. A thing, a big thing, as in "the whole *shmihr.*"
4. Bribe.

---

a as in father; aw as in law; ai as in aisle; ei as in neighbor; e as in bet; i as in vaccine; ih as in tin; o as in solar; oi as in void; oo as in food; u as in put; uh as in but; ch as in chutzpa; zh as in Zhivago.

shmihrn
> Also spelled *shmiren.*
> To wipe. See also *shmihr.*

Shmini Atzeres see *Shemini Atseret*

shmi-ras Sha-buhs
> Also *shmi-rat Sha-bat,* shmi-ras Sha-baws.*
> Also spelled *shemiras Shabbos.*
> Literally, "Sabbath observance."

shmirt zihch ois di shihch
> 1. Literally, "Wipe off your shoes!"
> 2. You're welcome in my home!

shmi-tuh
> Also *shmi-ta,* shmi-taw.*
> Also spelled *shemitah.*
> 1. Literally, "to abandon, forsake."
> 2. In the Bible, every seventh year is a Sabbatical year in which all debts are remitted and fields left fallow.

shmo
> A foolish, stupid person.

shmok see *shmuhk*

Shmo-ne Es-rei*
> Also *Shmo-naw Es-rei.*
> Also spelled *Shemoneh Esreh.*
> 1. Literally, "eighteen."
> 2. The *Amida* prayer, which originally consisted of eighteen benedictions, recited at weekday services.

shmoosen see *shmusn*

shmooz
> Also *shmus.*
> To talk, converse idly, chat.

shmuhk
> Also spelled *shmuk, shmuck, shmok.*
> From the German meaning "ornament."
> 1. A contemptible person.
> 2. A foolish person.
> 3. (Slang) penis.

---

a as in father; aw as in law; ai as in aisle; ei as in neighbor; e as in bet; i as in vaccine; ih as in tin; o as in solar; oi as in void; oo as in food; u as in put; uh as in but; ch as in chutzpa; zh as in Zhivago.

shmura matza see *matza shemura*

shmus see *shmooz*

shmusn
>Also spelled *shmoosen*.
>To chat, converse.

shmuts-ihk
>Dirty, soiled.

shmutz
>Dirt, filth.

shnaidr
>Also spelled *shnaider, shneider*.
>Tailor.

shnäps
>Also spelled *shnapps, schnapps*.
>Whiskey, liquor.

shnawr
>Also spelled *shnor*.
>Beg.

shnawr-en
>Also spelled *shnorren*.
>To beg, freeload.

shnawr-er
>Also spelled *schnorrer, shnorrer*.
>A beggar, mendicant.

shneider see *shnaidr*

shnei lu-chos ha-brihs
>Also *shnei lu-chot ha-briht.**
>1. Literally, "The two tablets of the Covenant."
>2. The Decalogue, Ten Commandments.

shnekn
>Also spelled *shneken*.
>Fruit and nut coffee rolls.

shnel
>1. Quick, fast.
>2. Hurry up!

Shnihp-er-shawk
>Also *Shnipishok*.

---

a as in father; aw as in law; ai as in aisle; ei as in neighbor; e as in bet; i as in vaccine; ih as in tin; o as in solar; oi as in void; oo as in food; u as in put; uh as in but; ch as in chutzpa; zh as in Zhivago.

A mythical European city used as the butt of jokes, much like the Chelm humor.

shnook see *shnuk*

shnoor see *shnur*

shnor see *shnawr*

shnorrer see *shnawrer*

shnuhdr
>Also *she-naw-dar, she-na-dar.**
>Also spelled *shnudder.*
>1. Literally, "one who pledged."
>2. A donation pledged at a synagogue service.

shnuk
>Also spelled *shnook.*
>1. A meek, naive, easygoing person.
>2. A gullible person.

shnur
>Also spelled *shnoor.*
>Daughter-in-law.

sho-a*
>Also spelled *shoah.*
>1. Literally, "disaster, destruction, catastrophe."
>2. The Holocaust, decimation of European Jewry under the Nazis from 1933 to 1945.

sho-chuht
>Also *sho-cheit, sho-chet.**
>A person certified to slaughter cattle and fowl in accordance with Jewish law.

shofar see *shofr*

shofr
>Also *sho-fawr, sho-far.**
>A ram's horn, sounded particularly on Rosh Hashanah at the synagogue service.
>*Shofrot** and *shofros* are plural forms.

shoin
>Already, immediately.

shoin far-ges-en
>1. Literally, "already forgotten."

---

a as in father; aw as in law; ai as in aisle; ei as in neighbor; e as in bet; i as in vaccine; ih as in tin; o as in solar; oi as in void; oo as in food; u as in put; uh as in but; ch as in chutzpa; zh as in Zhivago.

2. Did you forget already?
3. Out of sight, out of mind.

shoin gei
>Also spelled *shoin gai.*
>Go already! Beat it! Also expressed in reverse: *gei shoin.*

shoin ge-nug
>That's enough! Enough already!

shokel see *shuhkl*

sho-meir
>Also *sho-mer.**
>1. Guardian.
>2. Watchman, security officer.

sho-meir Sha-baws
>Also *sho-mer Sha-bat.**
>Also spelled *shomeir Shabbat.*
>1. A Sabbath observer.
>2. A religiously observant Jew.

Sho-meir Yihs-raw-eil
>Also *Sho-meir Yihs-ra-el.**
>Also spelled *Shomer Yisrael.*
>1. Literally, "Guardian of Israel."
>2. God.

shomer Shabbat see *shomeir Shabaws*

shom-rihm
>Also spelled *shomrim.*
>Plural of *shomeir.*
>1. Literally, "watchers, guardians."
>2. Policemen.
>3. Name of the New York society of Jewish police officers.
>4. Armed Jewish guards in early agricultural settlements in pre-State Israel.

Shom-ro-nihm
>Also spelled *Shomronim.*
>1. Literally, "Samaritans."
>2. In biblical times, residents of Shomron, the

a as in father; aw as in law; ai as in aisle; ei as in neighbor; e as in bet; i as in vaccine; ih as in tin; o as in solar; oi as in void; oo as in food; u as in put; uh as in but; ch as in chutzpa; zh as in Zhivago.

northern part of Palestine where the Ten Tribes lived.
3. Today, a group of sectarians living on the West Bank of the Jordan who practice a primitive form of Judaism.

sho-teif
Also *sho-tef.**
1. Partner.
2. Associate.

shpai
Literally, "spit."

shpai ois
Literally, "spit out," said to children.

shpa-tsih-ren
Also spelled *shpatziren.*
To walk, stroll, hike.

shpet
Late.

shpetr
Also spelled *shpeter.*
Later.

shpihl-ke
Also spelled *shpilke.*
A pin, a needle.

shpihl-kes
Also spelled *shpilkes.*
1. Literally, "pins and needles."
2. Uneasiness, restlessness.
One who has *shpihlkes* is raring to go and can't sit still. Hyperactive children have *shpihlkes.*

shpihln
To play.

shpihln kawrt-en
To play cards.

shpih-tuhl
Also spelled *shpitol.*
Hospital.

---

shpihtz
>Also spelled *shpitz*.
>1. Peak.
>2. Point.
>3. Tip, top.

shpihtz b'kih-tsur
>Also spelled *shpitz bekitzur*.
>1. Literally, "(Get to) the point briefly."
>2. Make it short and sweet.

shpihtz-fihn-ger
>Also spelled *shpitzfinger*.
>1. Toe.
>2. Fingertip.

shpil
>Also spelled *spiel*.
>A play.

shpilke see *shpihlke*

shpitol see *shpihtuhl*

shpitz see *shpihtz*

shprihch-vawrt
>Also spelled *shprichvort*.
>A proverb, a saying.

shpuh-gel nai
>Also spelled *shpogel nei*.
>1. Literally, "mirror new"
>2. Brand new.

shrai-en
>Also spelled *shreien*.
>To yell, cry out, shout.

shrek-lech
>1. Frightening.
>2. Terrible.

(a) shrek-le-che zach
>A frightening, terrible thing.

shtadln
>Also *shtad-lawn, shtad-lan,* shtad-len*.
>Also spelled *stadlan*.

---

a as in father; aw as in law; ai as in aisle ei as in neighbor; e as in bet; i as in vaccine; ih as in tin; o as in solar; oi as in void; oo as in food; u as in put; uh as in but; ch as in chutzpa; zh as in Zhivago.

In Europe in earlier centuries, a wealthy Jew who was the spokesman of the Jewish community before heads of state.

shtain see *shtein*

shtait geshriben see *shteit geshrihbn*

shtar*
> Also spelled *shetar*.
> 1. A contract.
> 2. A legal Jewish document.

shtarbn
> Also spelled *shtarben*.
> To die.

shtar gei-rus
> Also *shtar gei-rut.**
> Also spelled *shetar gerut*.
> Certificate of conversion to Judaism.

shtark
> Strong, brave.

shtar-ker
> 1. A strong person.
> 2. A tough guy, roughneck.
> 3. A bully.

shtayn see *shtein*

shtein
> Also spelled *shtain, shtayn*.
> Stone.

shtein raich
> Also spelled *shtein reich*.
> 1. Literally, "stone rich."
> 2. Very rich.

shteit ge-shrihbn
> Also spelled *shtait geshriben*.
> 1. Literally, "It is so written."
> 2. It is authoritative.

shtetl
> Also spelled *shtetel*.

---

a as in father; aw as in law; ai as in aisle; ei as in neighbor; e as in bet; i as in vaccine; ih as in tin; o as in solar; oi as in void; oo as in food; u as in put; uh as in but; ch as in chutzpa; zh as in Zhivago.

A small town, particularly in the Jewish communities of Eastern Europe.

shtihk
> Also spelled *shtik*.
> 1. Literally, "a piece, a chunk."
> 2. A game, prank, caprice.
> 3. One's specialty.
> 4. A gimmick.
> See also *shtihkl*.

shtihk hawltz
> Also spelled *shtik holtz*.
> 1. Literally, "a piece of wood."
> 2. A dull, dumb person.

shtihkl
> Also spelled *shtikel*.
> 1. A little piece.
> 2. A trick, prank.
> See also *shtihk*.

shtihk-lach
> 1. Idiosyncracies.
> 2. Pranks.
> See also *shtihk*.

shtihk na-ar
> Also spelled *shtik nar*.
> A bit of a fool.

shtihk na-ches
> Also spelled *shtik naches*.
> 1. Literally "piece of pleasure."
> 2. Great satisfaction, pride, joy.

shtihl
> Also spelled *shtil*.
> Stillness, quiet.

shtihl-ihn-ker-heit
> Also spelled *shtilinkerait*.
> Quietly, unobtrusively.

shtik see *shtihk*

shtil see *shtihl*

---

a as in father; aw as in law; ai as in aisle; ei as in neighbor; e as in bet; i as in vaccine; ih as in tin; o as in solar; oi as in void; oo as in food; u as in put; uh as in but; ch as in chutzpa; zh as in Zhivago.

shtinkn
> Also spelled *shtinken*.
> To stink.

shtoltz see *shtuhltz*

shtoop see *shtup*

shtot see *shtuht*

shtraiml
> Also spelled *shtreimel, streiml*.
> Round, fur-trimmed hats worn by Chassidic Jews on Sabbaths and holidays and said to have originated with the Ba'al Shem Tov, founder of the Chassidic movement.

shtrawfn
> Also spelled *shtrofen*.
> 1. Punish.
> 2. Upbraid.

shtreimel see *shtraiml*

shtrofen see *shtrawfn*

shtrudl
> Also spelled *strudel, shtrudel*.
> A pastry, sweet or savory, most often filled with fruit or cheese.

shtub
> House.

shtuhltz
> Also spelled *shtoltz*.
> 1. Proud.
> 2. An excessive amount of self-esteem.

shtuht
> Also spelled *shtot*.
> 1. City.
> 2. A town.

shtunk
> A stinker.

shtup
> Also spelled *shtoop*.

---

a as in father; aw as in law; ai as in aisle; ei as in neighbor; e as in bet; i as in vaccine; ih as in tin; o as in solar; oi as in void; oo as in food; u as in put; uh as in but; ch as in chutzpa; zh as in Zhivago.

1. Push.
2. Aggression.

shtupn
> Also spelled *shtupen.*
> Push, shove, poke. See also *shtup.*

shtus
> Also *shtut.**
> Nonsense, foolishness.

shuch
> Shoe.

shuh
> Also *sha-a.**
> 1. An hour.
> 2. A moment in time.

shuhkl
> Also spelled *shokel.*
> 1. Shake, sway.
> 2. Nod.

shuhkl mihtn kuhp
> Also spelled *shokel mit dem kop.*
> 1. Literally, "to shake with the head."
> 2. To agree.

shuhlem see *shalom*

shuh-lem ba-yihs
> Also *shaw-lom ba-yihs, sha-lom ba-yiht.**
> Also spelled *shalom bayit.*
> 1. Literally, "household peace."
> 2. Family unity.

shuluhm aleichem see *shawlom aleichem*

shuh-nuh to-vuh
> Also **shaw-na to-vaw, sha-na to-va.***
> 1. Literally, "good year."
> 2. Traditional Jewish New Year greeting.
> 3. New Year greeting card.

shul
> 1. Literally, "school."
> 2. Synagogue.

Shulchn Aw-ruch
>Also *Shul-chan A-ruch.**
>1. Literally, "prepared table."
>2. The name of the code of Jewish law and custom compiled by Joseph Caro in 1565.

shu-le
>School.

shura see *shure*

shu-re
>Also *shu-raw, shu-ra.**
>1. A line.
>2. A row.

shush-ke
>1. Whisper.
>2. An aside.

shushkn
>Also spelled *shushken.*
>To whisper.

shustr
>Also spelled *shuster.*
>Shoemaker.

shvach
>Weak, faint.

shvaig
>Also spelled *shveig.*
>Shut up!

shvaign
>Also spelled *shveigen.*
>To be still, silent.

shvartz
>Black.

shvartz yawr
>1. Literally, "a black year."
>2. A miserable future.
>3. An expression of disappointment and disgust.

shvartz-e
>Also *shvartz-er.*

---

a as in father; aw as in law; ai as in aisle; ei as in neighbor; e as in bet; i as in vaccine; ih as in tin; o as in solar; oi as in void; oo as in food; u as in put; uh as in but; ch as in chutzpa; zh as in Zhivago.

A black person, a Negro.

Shvat*
Also spelled *Shevat*.
The eleventh month of the Jewish religious calendar, fifth of the Civil calendar, corresponding to January-February.

shvawgr
Also spelled *shvoger*.
Brother-in-law.

shve-be-le
1. Literally, "a sulphur match."
2. An excitable person.

shve-ge-rihn
Sister-in-law.

shveig see *shvaig*

shvein-ger
Also spelled *shvenger*.
To be pregnant.

shvein-ger-en
A variant form of *shveinger*. See above.

shven-kechtz
Mouthwash.

shver
1. Difficult, heavy, hard.
2. A father-in-law.

shver tzu ma-chen a le-ben
It's tough to make a living.

shvestr
Also spelled *shvester*.
Sister.

shvihgr
Also spelled *shviger*.
Mother-in-law.

shvihn-del-dihk
Also spelled *shvindeldik*.
Unsteady, dizzy.

---

a as in father; aw as in law; ai as in aisle; ei as in neighbor; e as in bet; i as in vaccine; ih as in tin; o as in solar; oi as in void; oo as in food; u as in put; uh as in but; ch as in chutzpa; zh as in Zhivago.

shvihndl
>Also spelled *shvindel.*
>1. Swindle.
>2. Deception, trickery.
>3. Fraud.
>4. A hoax.

shvihndlt ihn di oign
>Also spelled *shvindelt in di oigen.*
>1. Literally, "dizzy in the eyes."
>2. Staggering.

shvihtz
>Also spelled *shvitz.*
>Sweat, perspire.

shvihtz buhd
>Also spelled *shvitz bod.*
>1. Steambath, sauna.
>2. Turkish bath.

shvihtz-er
>Also spelled *shvitzer.*
>1. Literally, "one who sweats (over nothing)."
>2. A braggart.

shvindel see *shvihndl*

shvoger see *shvawgr*

Shvues see *Shavuot*

Siddur see *Sihdr*

Sidra see *Sedruh*

Sihdr
>Also *Si-door.**
>Also spelled *Siddur.*
>1. Literally, "arrangement, order."
>2. Prayerbook with the daily or Sabbath liturgies.

Sihf-rei To-raw
>Also Sihf-rei To-ra.*
>Plural of *Seifr Toruh.*

simcha see *sihmchuh*

sihm-cha shel mihts-va*
>Also *sihm-chaw shel mihts-vaw.*

---

a as in father; aw as in law; ai as in aisle; ei as in neighbor; e as in bet; i as in vaccine; ih as in tin; o as in solar; oi as in void; oo as in food; u as in put; uh as in but; ch as in chutzpa; zh as in Zhivago.

Also spelled *simcha shel mitzva*.
The joy of performing a *mitzva*.

Sihm-chas To-ruh
Also *Sihm-chat To-ra,* Sihmchas Toraw*.
Also spelled *Simhat Torah, Simchat Torah*.
1. Literally, "Rejoicing in the Law."
2. The festival after Sukkot marking both the completion and beginning of the annual cycle of Torah readings in synagogue.

sihm-chuh
Also *sihm-chaw, sihm-cha.**
Also spelled *simcha, simha, simche*.
1. Joy, rejoicing.
2. A festive celebration.
3. A party.

sihm-chuhs
Also *sihm-chos, sihm-chot.**
Also spelled *simchos, simchot*.
Happy occasions. Plural of *sihmchuh*.

sihn
Also spelled *sin*.
A letter of the Hebrew alphabet sounded like "s."

simcha shel mitzva see *sihmcha shel mihtsva*

Simchat Torah see *Sihmchas Toruh*

simche see *sihmchuh*

simchos see *sihmchuhs*

sihtz-bawd
Also spelled *sitzbod, zihtzbawd*.
Literally, "a sit bath," that is, a hot tub.

sin see *sihn*

Si-van
The third month of the Jewish religious calendar, ninth of the Civil calendar, corresponding to May-June.

si-yum
1. Literally, "completion."
2. The celebration held upon the completion of the study of a tractate of the Talmud.

---

skuhtzl kumt
> Also spelled *skotzel kumt.*
> 1. Well, hello!
> 2. Look who's here!

slihv-uh-vihtz
> Also spelled *slivovitz.*
> A plum brandy popular in Slavic countries.

sme-te-ne
> Sour cream.

smi-chuh
> Also *smi-cha* se-mi-cha.*
> 1. Literally, "laying on of hands."
> 2. Rabbinical ordination involving the laying on of hands by the rabbi performing the ceremony.

snoga
> Ladino for "synagogue."

Sodom see *Sedom*

sof see *suhf*

sofer see *soifr*

sof kol sof see *suhf kuhl suhf*

soifr
> Also *so-fer.**
> Also spelled *sofer.*
> A scribe, especially one who writes Torah Scrolls, *mezuzot,* and *tefilin.*

sondek see *sandek*

s'past niht see *past niht*

spiel see *shpil*

spuh-dek
> Also spelled *spodek.*
> A tall velvet or fur hat worn by Chassidic rabbis, particularly on weekdays.

s'ret zich azoi see *ret zich azoi*

s'shav see *shav*

stadlan see *shtadln*

---

a as in father; aw as in law; ai as in aisle; ei as in neighbor; e as in bet; i as in vaccine; ih as in tin; o as in solar; oi as in void; oo as in food; u as in put; uh as in but; ch as in chutzpa; zh as in Zhivago.

staich
>Also spelled *steitsh*.
>1. What is the explanation?
>2. How is that possible?
>3. What do you mean?

steitsh see *staich*

s'toot mihr laid
>I'm sorry.

strashe mihr niht
>Also spelled *strashe mir nit*.
>Don't threaten me!

strashn
>Also spelled *strashen*.
>1. Intimidate, threaten.
>2. Tease.

strashn di genz
>1. Literally, "threaten the geese."
>2. Frighten.
>3. Tease.

strudel see *shtrudl*

succah see *suka*

Succoth see *Sukos*

sude see *seuda*

suhf
>Also spelled *sof*.
>1. The last letter of the Hebrew alphabet. Without a
>   dot in it, it is sounded like an "s," with a dot, like
>   a "t."
>2. The end, termination, conclusion.

(a) suhf! (a) suhf!
>Also spelled *a sof! a sof!*
>1. Enough!
>2. End it!

suhf kuhl suhf
>Also spelled *sof kol sof*.
>1. Finally.
>2. The end of the matter.

---

a as in father; aw as in law; ai as in aisle; ei as in neighbor; e as in bet; i as in vaccine; ih as in tin; o as in
solar; oi as in void; oo as in food; u as in put; uh as in but; ch as in chutzpa; zh as in Zhivago.

su-ka*

> Also *su-kaw, su-kuh.*
> Also spelled *sukkah, succah.*
> A booth covered with branches, constructed for the festival of Sukkot to commemorate booths lived in by Israelites during their wanderings after the exodus from Egypt.

Sukkot see *Sukos*

Su-kos

> Also *Su-kot.**
> Also spelled *Succoth, Sukkot.*
> 1. Literally, "booths."
> 2. The eight-day festival marking the fall harvest and the wandering of the Israelites in the wilderness of Sinai en route to the Promised Land following the Exodus from Egypt.

sukuh see *suka*

sulze see *p'tcha*

svi-von*

> Also spelled *sevivon.*
> 1. A spinning top.
> 2. A *dreidl* used on Chanukah.

---

a as in father; **aw** as in law; **ai** as in aisle; **ei** as in neighbor; **e** as in bet; **i** as in vaccine; **ih** as in tin; **o** as in solar; **oi** as in void; **oo** as in food; **u** as in put; **uh** as in but; **ch** as in chutzpa; **zh** as in Zhivago.

T

taam see *tam*

ta-am Sha-bat*
Also *tam Sha-buhs*.
The special taste of food on the Sabbath.

ta-a-nihs
Also *ta-a-niht*.*
Also spelled *taanis, taanit*.
A fast.

Ta-a-nihs Es-teir
Also *Ta-a-niht Es-ter**.
Also spelled *Taanit Esther*.
Literally, "the Fast of Esther," observed on the day preceding Purim, recalling Esther's intercession with her husband, King Ahasuerus, to nullify Haman's edict.

Taaniht Yartzait see *Tanihs Yawrtsait*

Tach-a-nun*
Also *Tach-nun*.
Pentitential prayers recited during the weekday service.

tachlihs
Also *tach-liht*.*
Also spelled *tachlis, tachlit*.
1. Purpose, object, practical result.
2. The real thing, the bottom line.

tach-ri-chihm
Also spelled *tachrichim*.
Burial shrouds of white linen.

taf see *tuhf*

tag see *tawg*

tahara see *taharuh*

ta-ha-ras ha-mihsh-paw-chaw
Also *ta-ha-rat ha-mihsh-pa-cha*.*

---

a as in father; aw as in law; ai as in aisle; ei as in neighbor; e as in bet; i as in vaccine; ih as in tin; o as in solar; oi as in void; oo as in food; u as in put; uh as in but; ch as in chutzpa; zh as in Zhivago.

1. Literally, "family purity."
2. Immersion in a *mikva* by married women after menstruation.

ta-ha-ruh
>Also *ta-ha-ra.**
>1. Literally, "purification.
>2. The ritual cleansing of a dead body by the *Chevruh Kadishuh.*

tai see *tei*

tai-er
>Also spelled *teier.*
>1. Expensive.
>2. Valuable.
>3. Costly.

tai-e-re kihnd
>Also spelled *teiere kind.*
>Dear child. Darling child..

tai-er-ihn-ker
>Also spelled *teierinker.*
>1. Sweetheart.
>2. Dearest, darling.

taigechtz see *teigechtz*

taigel see *teigl*

taiglach see *teiglech*

taitsh
>A Yiddish corruption of the German word *Deutsch* ("German").

taivl
>Also *toivl.*
>Also spelled *teivel, teuvel.*
>1. Devil, demon.
>2. Satan.

ta-ka-na*
>Also *ta-kaw-naw, ta-kuh-nuh.*
>Also spelled *takkana.*
>1. Literally, "reform, regulation."
>2. A regulation instituted by a community or congregation.

a as in father; aw as in law; ai as in aisle; ei as in neighbor; e as in bet; i as in vaccine; ih as in tin; o as in solar; oi as in void; oo as in food; u as in put; uh as in but; ch as in chutzpa; zh as in Zhivago.

3. A change in Jewish law instituted by scholars.

ta-ka-not*
Also *ta-kuh-nes, ta-kaw-nos.*
Plural of *takana.*

take see *takuh*

ta-ke a me-tsi-a
Also spelled *takeh a metzia.*
Really, a bargain!

takkana see *takana*

ta-kuh
Also *ta-ke.*
1. Really Is that so?
2. Indeed!
3. You don't say!
4. Are you putting me on?

takuhnes see *takanot*

takuhnuh see *takana*

tal
1. Literally, "dew."
2. The prayer for dew recited on Passover.

ta-lei-sihm
Also *ta-lei-tihm.**
Also spelled *taleisim, talaisim.*
The plural of *talit* in popular use, although *talitot**
is the correct form.

ta-lihs
Also *ta-liht.**
Also spelled *tallis, tallit, talith, talis, talit.*
A rectangular striped prayer shawl with fringes
(tzitziot) attached to the four corners.

ta-lihs kaw-tawn
Also *ta-liht ka-tan*.*
Also spelled *tallit katan.*
1. Literally, "a small *talit.*"
2. An undergarment with fringes *(tzitziot)* attached to its four corners.

talis see *talihs*

---

a as in father; aw as in law; ai as in aisle; ei as in neighbor; e as in bet; i as in vaccine; ih as in tin; o as in
solar; oi as in void; oo as in food; u as in put; uh as in but; ch as in chutzpa; zh as in Zhivago.

talit see *talihs*

ta-li-tot see *taleisihm*

tal-mihd chaw-chuhm
> Also *tal-mihd chaw-chawm, tal-mihd cha-cham.**
> Also spelled *talmid chachem, talmid chacham.*
> 1. Literally, "disciple of the wise."
> 2. Scholar, learned person.

Tal-mud Bav-li
> The Babylonian Talmud.

Tal-mud To-raw
> Also *Tal-mud To-ra.**
> Also spelled *Talmud Torah.*
> 1. Literally, "Torah study."
> 2. An elementary Jewish religious school, some-
> times called *cheder.*

Tal-mud Ye-ru-shal-mi
> The Jerusalem Talmud.

Tal-muhd
> Also *Tal-mud.**
> 1. Literally, "study, learning."
> 2. The compendium of discussions and interpreta-
> tions of the biblical text by the scholars of Pal-
> estine and Babylonia from 500 B.C.E. to 500 C.E.

tam*
> Also *ta-am.*
> 1. Taste, flavor.
> 2. Good taste.
> 3. Zest.

tam me-vate
> Also spelled *tamevate.*
> 1. Literally, "a simpleton expressing himself."
> 2. A naive person.
> 3. A dope.

Tammuz see *Tamuz*

tam Shabuhs see *taam Shabat*

Ta-muz
> Also spelled *Tammuz.*
> The fourth month of the Jewish religious calendar,

---

a as in father; aw as in law; ai as in aisle; ei as in neighbor; e as in bet; i as in vaccine; ih as in tin; o as in solar; oi as in void; oo as in food; u as in put; uh as in but; ch as in chutzpa; zh as in Zhivago.

tenth of the Civil calendar, corresponding to June-July.

tana see *tanuh*

Ta-nach
Also spelled *Tanakh*.
1. The Hebrew Bible.
2. An acronym from the Hebrew initials of *Tora* (Pentateuch), *Nevi'im* (Prophets), *Ketuvim* (Writings).

ta-naw-ihm
Also *ta-na-ihm.**
Also spelled *tanaim*.
Plural of *tanuh*. See below.

tan-det
Inferior, second-rate, cheap, bungled work.

Ta-nihs Yawr-tsait
Also *Ta-a-niht Yar-tzait.**
Also spelled *Taanis Yahrzeit*.
A day of fasting to commemorate the anniversary of the passing of a relative.

tan-sen oif al-e cha-se-nes
1. Literally, "to dance at all weddings."
2. To be involved in everything (even where not invited).

tante see *tantuh*

tan-tuh
Also *tan-te*.
Aunt.

ta-nuh
Also *ta-naw, ta-na.**
Any first or second-century scholar whose teachings on Jewish law and tradition are recorded in the Mishna, the first part of the Talmud.

ta-re-ram
Noise, fuss, hoopla.

Tar-gum
The Aramaic translation or paraphrase of the Hebrew Bible.

---

a as in father; aw as in law; ai as in aisle; ei as in neighbor; e as in bet; i as in vaccine; ih as in tin; o as in solar; oi as in void; oo as in food; u as in put; uh as in but; ch as in chutzpa; zh as in Zhivago.

Targum Onkelos
    The Aramaic translation of the Pentateuch by Aquilas, the convert.

Tash-lihch
    Also spelled *Tashlich.*
    1. Literally, "You will cast out."
    2. Ceremony, held on the first afternoon of Rosh Hashanah, of casting one's sins symbolically into a stream or river, usually by throwing crumbs into the water.
    3. The prayer recited during the above ceremony.

Tat
    A Persian dialect spoken by the "Mountain Jews" of the Caucasus.

ta-te
    Also *ta-tuh.*
    Also spelled *tata.*
    Father, dad, papa.

ta-te-le
    Also spelled *tateleh.*
    An affectionate form of *tate*. See *tate.*

ta-te ma-me
    1. Literally, "father-mother."
    2. A cry of anguish and despair.

(a) ta-tens a kihnd
    Also spelled *a tatens a kind.*
    1. Literally, "a father's child."
    2. Someone who takes after father.
    3. Child of a good family.

ta-ten-yoo
    Also spelled *tatenyu.*
    1. Literally, "father dear."
    2. An intimate manner of addressing God.

ta-ten-yoo fatr
    Also spelled *tatenyoo fatr.*
    1. Papa-father.
    2. God.

---

a as in father; aw as in law; ai as in aisle; ei as in neighbor; e as in bet; i as in vaccine; ih as in tin; o as in solar; oi as in void; oo as in food; u as in put; uh as in but; ch as in chutzpa; zh as in Zhivago.

ta-tihn-ke
>Also spelled *tatinke*.
>An affectionate form of *tate*. See *Tate*.

tav see *tuhf*

taw-ches lekr
>Also spelled *toches leker*.
>1. Literally, ""buttocks-licker."
>2. One who fawns over another person.

taw-ches oifn tihsh
>Also spelled *toches oifn tish*.
>1. Literally, "buttocks on the table."
>2. Get down to business!
>3. Put up or shut up!

tawchtr
>Also spelled *tochter*.
>Daughter.

tawg
>Also spelled *tog, tag*.
>Day.

tawg shu-le
>Also spelled *tog shule*.
>Day school.

tawg teg-lech
>Also spelled *tog teglech*.
>Day-to-day, daily.

tay see *tei*

t'chi-yas ha-meis-ihm
>Also *te-chi-yat ha-mei-tihm.**
>Also spelled *t'chias hameisim, techiat hametim*.
>The resurrection of the dead, associated in Orthodox Judaism with the coming of the Messiah.

tcholent see *tshawlent*

teba
>The Sephardic word for *teva*. See *teva*.

Tebeth see *Teiveis*

tefila see *t'filuh*

---

a as in father; aw as in law; ai as in aisle· ei as in neighbor; e as in bet; i as in vaccine; ih as in tin; o as in solar; oi as in void; oo as in food; u as in put; uh as in but; ch as in chutzpa; zh as in Zhivago.

tefilin see *t'filihn*

tehila see *t'hilaw*

Tehillim see *T'hihlihm*

tehi nihshmata see *t'hi nihshmawsaw*

tehi nihshmato see *t'hi nishmawso*

tei
> Also spelled *tai, tay.*
> Tea.

teier see *taier*

teiere kind see *taiere kihnd*

teierinker see *taierihnker*

tei-gechtz
> Also spelled *taigechtz.*
> A baked pudding made of rice, noodles, barley, or mashed potatoes.

teigl
> Also spelled *teigel, taigel.*
> A small cake filled with nuts and fruit and dipped in honey. A popular Rosh Hashanah delicacy.

teig-lech
> Also *teig-lach.*
> Also spelled *taiglech, taiglach.*
> Plural of *teigl. See above.*

Teitsh Chu-mesh
> Also spelled *Taitsh Chumash.*
> Yiddish translation of the Torah, read mostly by women who were not afforded a Hebrew education.

tei-va*
> Also *tei-vaw.*
> Also spelled *teva.*
> The *bima,* or platform, in the synagogue.

Tei-veis
> Also spelled *Tevet,* Tebeth.*
> The tenth month of the Jewish religious calendar, fourth of the Civil calendar, corresponding to December-January.

---

teivel see *taivl*

tekia see *tekiuh*

te-ki-uh
>   Also *te-ki-a,* te-ki-aw.*
>   Also spelled *t'kiah, tekiah.*
>   An unbroken *shofar* blast sounded in the synagogue on Rosh Hashanah.

tel-e-rel fun hihml
>   Also spelled *telerel fun himmel.*
>   1. Literally, "saucers from heaven."
>   2. Something unattainable (the moon on a plate).

temp
>   Dull, dense.

tenaim see *t'nawihm*

terefah see *treif*

te-roo-aw
>   Also *te-roo-a.**
>   Also spelled *teruah, t'ruah, terua.*
>   A wavering *shofar* sound consisting of nine staccato notes.

te-roo-maw
>   Also *te-roo-ma.**
>   Also spelled *terumah, t'rumah.*
>   1. Offering.
>   2. Gift.
>   3. An offering of a product of the field, brought to the priests in the Temple in Jerusalem.

tes
>   Also *tet.**
>   The ninth letter of the Hebrew alphabet, corresponding in sound to "t."

te-shoo-vos
>   Also *te-shoo-vot.**
>   Also spelled *teshuvos, t'shuvot.*
>   Plural of *teshoova (t'shoovuh).*

teshuva see *t'shoovuh*

tet see *tes*

Tevet see *Teiveis*

t'fih-lihn*
>   Also *te-fi-lihn*.
>   Also spelled *t'filin, tefilin*.
>   Phylacteries, small boxes mounted on leather straps, worn by male Jews during weekday morning prayers. One, worn on the arm, is called *t'filihn shel yad;* the other, worn on the forehead, is called *t'filihn shel rosh*. Verses from the Bible, handwritten on parchment, are enclosed in each box.

t'fila see *t'filuh*

T'fi-las Ha-de-rech
>   Also *Te-fi-lat Ha-de-rech.**
>   1. Literally, "prayer (for) the road."
>   2. A prayer recited before commencing a journey.

t'filaw see *t'filuh*

t'fi-luh
>   Also *t'fi-la,** *t'fi-law*.
>   Also spelled *tefila, tefilaw, tefillah*.
>   1. Prayer.
>   2. In the Mishna the word refers to the *Amida* prayer, also known as the *Shemone Esrei*.

t'hih-lihm
>   Also *te-hi-lihm.**
>   Also spelled *tehillim*.
>   1. Psalms.
>   2. The Book of Psalms.

t'hi-law
>   Also *te-hi-la,** *te-hilaw*.
>   Also spelled *t'hila, tehilah*.
>   1. Psalm.
>   2. The singular of *t'hihlihm*.

tihk-vaw
>   Also *tihk-va.**
>   Also spelled *tikvaw, tikva*.
>   1. Hope.
>   2. "The Hope" *(Hatikva)*, the Israeli national anthem.

---

a as in father; aw as in law; ai as in aisle; ei as in neighbor; e as in bet; i as in vaccine; ih as in tin; o as in solar; oi as in void; oo as in food; u as in put; uh as in but; ch as in chutzpa; zh as in Zhivago.

tihmtum
>Also spelled *timtum*.
>1. A simple child, derived from the Hebrew *tam*.
>2. A bisexual person.
>3. An effeminate man.

tihsh
>Also spelled *tish*.
>Table.

Tihsh-aw B'Awv
>Also *Tihsh-a B'Av*.*
>Also spelled *Tisha B'Av, Tisha B'ov*, and *Tisha Be'av*.
>1. Literally, "the ninth of (the Hebrew month of) Av."
>2. The name of a fast day marking the destruction of the First (586 B.C.E.) and Second (70 C.E.) Temples in Jerusalem.

Tihsh-ri
>Also *Tihsh-rei*.*
>Also spelled *Tishri*.
>The seventh month of the Jewish religious calendar, first of the Civil calendar, corresponding to September-October. The first two days of Tihshri are the Jewish New Year. The tenth day is the Day of Atonement.

Ti-kun*
>Also spelled *Tikkun*.
>A devotional prayer service.

tikva see *tihkvaw*

timtum see *tihmtum*

tish see *tihsh*

Tisha B'Av see *Tihshaw B'Awv*

Tishri see *Tihshri*

t'kiah see *tekiuh*

t'naw-ihm
>Also *te-na-ihm*.*
>Also spelled *tenaim*.
>1. Literally, "conditions," referring particularly to

---

a as in father; aw as in law; ai as in aisle; ei as in neighbor; e as in bet; i as in vaccine; ih as in tin; o as in solar; oi as in void; oo as in food; u as in put; uh as in but; ch as in chutzpa; zh as in Zhivago.

the document spelling out the agreement for
marriage.
2. The betrothal ceremony.

toches see *tuhches*

toches leker see *tawches lekr*

toches oifn tish see *tawches oifn tihsh*

tochis see *tuhches*

to-cho k'va-ro
1. Literally, "His interior is as his exterior."
2. A sincere, open, and honest individual.

tochter see *tawchtr*

tog see *tawg*

togshule see *tawg shule*

tog teglech see *tawg teglech*

toign
Also spelled *toigen*.
Fit for, good for.

toign oif ka-paw-res
Also *toi-gen oif ka-po-res*.
1. Literally, "suitable for *kapores*," the atonement
fowl used before Yom Kippur to take away one's
sins and which is then slaughtered.
2. To be worthless.

Toi-ras luhkshn
Also spelled *Toras lukshen*.
1. Literally, "noodle Torah."
2. Learning of no consequence.
3. Faulty scholarship.

Toiruh see *Toruh*

Toi-ruh ihz di bes-te s'choi-re
Also spelled *Torah iz di beste s'chorah*.
Literally, "Torah is the best merchandise."

toit
Also *tot*.
Dead, deceased.

toit hun-ge-rihk
Also spelled *toit hungerik*.

---

a as in father; aw as in law; ai as in aisle; ei as in neighbor; e as in bet; i as in vaccine; ih as in tin; o as in
solar; oi as in void; oo as in food; u as in put; uh as in but; ch as in chutzpa; zh as in Zhivago.

1. Literally, "dead hungry."
2. Starved.

(a) toitn ban-kes

Also spelled *a toyten bankus*.
Literally, "(it will have as little avail as treating) a dead person with cupping."

toi-veh

Also *to-vaw, to-va,* toi-vuh*.
1. Good.
2. (To do) a favor.

too-be-ta-ka

Also spelled *tubetaka*.
A multicolored skullcap worn by Russian Jews.

too-en-vei

Also *tu-en vai*.
To hurt, pain.

toonkel see *tunkl*

(es) toot mihr laid

1. Literally, "It causes me pain."
2. I'm sorry.
Sometimes written as *s'toot mihr laid*.

(es) toot mihr vei

Literally, "It hurts me." Sometimes written as *s'toot mihr vei*.

(es) toot vei dem hartz

1. Literally, "The (my) heart hurts."
2. I'm heartbroken.
Sometimes written as *s'toot vei dos* (or *dem*) *hartz*.

Tora see *Toruh*

Torah see *Toruh*

Torah iz di beste s'chorah see *Toiruh ihz di beste s'choire*

To-ruh

Also *Toi-ruh, To-raw, Tora.**
Also spelled *Torah*.
1. Teaching.
2. The Law.

---

a as in father; aw as in law; ai as in aisle; ei as in neighbor; e as in bet; i as in vaccine; ih as in tin; o as in solar; oi as in void; oo as in food; u as in put; uh as in but; ch as in chutzpa; zh as in Zhivago.

    3. Pentateuch
    4. The totality of traditional Jewish wisdom, literature, culture.

To-ruh lih-shmaw
    Also *To-ra lih-shma.**
    Also spelled *Torah lishma.*
    Literally, "(the study of) Torah for its own sake."

To-ruh mi-Si-nai
    Also *To-ra mi-Si-nai,** *To-raw mi-Si-nai.*
    Also spelled *Torah mi-Sinai.*
    1. Literally, "Torah from (Mt.) Sinai."
    2. Revelation.

To-ruh she-b'al pe
    Also *To-raw she-b'al pe, To-ra she-b'al pe.**
    Also spelled *Torah she-b'al pe.*
    The unwritten Torah, the Oral Law as recorded in the Talmud.

To-ruh she-bihk-sav
    Also *To-ra she-bihk-tav.**
    1. Literally, "written Torah."
    2. The Bible.

Tosafists
    1. Literally, "supplementers, adders."
    2. A group of scholars who added explanations to the Talmud. The earliest and more important ones were descendants of Rashi, living from the twelfth to fourteenth centuries.

To-sa-fot*
    Also *Tos-fos.*
    Notes and comments of the Tosafists. See above.

To-sef-taw
    Also *To-sef-ta,** *To-sihf-ta.*
    Also spelled *Tosifta.*
    1. Literally, "supplement."
    2. A collection of Jewish law similar to the Mishna but containing additional material. Its editors are believed to be the third-century scholars Oshaya and Rabbah.

tot see *toit*

---

a as in father; aw as in law; ai as in aisle; ei as in neighbor; e as in bet; i as in vaccine; ih as in tin; o as in solar; oi as in void; oo as in food; u as in put; uh as in but; ch as in chutzpa; zh as in Zhivago.

tova see *toiveh*

traibr see *treibr*

traif see *treif*

traife see *treif*

traifener bain see *treifener bein*

tran-te
>   1. Rag
>   2. Decrepit, worn out.

traw-ge-dihk
>   Also spelled *trogedik*.
>   1. Literally, "carrying."
>   2. Pregnant.

trawg ge-zunt-er-heit
>   Also spelled *trog gezunterhait*.
>   1. Literally, "Carry (wear) it in good health."

trawgn
>   Also spelled *trogen*.
>   1. To carry.
>   2. To bear.

trayf see *treif*

trefn
>   Also spelled *trefen*.
>   1. To meet.
>   2. To encounter, run across.
>   3. To guess right.

treibr
>   Also *traibr*.
>   Also spelled *treiber, traiber*.
>   To remove the sciatic nerve and certain other vessels and tendons from the hindquarter of an animal, rendering it kosher.

treif
>   Also *trei-fa,* trei-faw, treifuh*.
>   Also spelled *trayf, traif, traife, tref, trefa*.
>   1. Literally, "torn," a torn animal.
>   2. A nonkosher animal.
>   3. Nonkosher food.

---

a as in father; aw as in law; ai as in aisle; ei as in neighbor; e as in bet; i as in vaccine; ih as in tin; o as in solar; oi as in void; oo as in food; u as in put; uh as in but; ch as in chutzpa; zh as in Zhivago.

trei-fe-ne bihch-er
> Also spelled *traifene bicher.*
> 1. Literally, "nonkosher books."
> 2. Forbidden literature.

trei-fe-ner bein
> Also spelled *traifener bain.*
> 1. Literally, "nonkosher bone."
> 2. A nonobservant Jew.

treif puhsl
> Also spelled *traif posel.*
> 1. Literally, "unfit and unqualified."
> 2. Defective.
> 3. Absolutely not kosher.

trihnkn
> Also spelled *trinken.*
> 1. To drink.
> 2. To imbibe.

trogedik see *trawgedihk*

trogen see *trawgn*

trog gezunterhait see *trawg gezunterheit*

trombenik see *truhmbenihk*

t'ruah see *terooaw*

truhm-be-nihk
> Also spelled *trombenik.*
> 1. A lazy person.
> 2. A ne'er-do-well.

t'rumah see *teroomaw*

tsa-ar ba-alei cha-yihm*
> Also spelled *tza'ar ba'ale chayim.*
> 1. Literally, "the pain (suffering) of living things."
> 2. The concept of kindness to animals in Jewish tradition.
> 3. The Jewish aversion to and ban on hunting and on fishing with a hook.

tsa-ar gi-dul baw-nihm
> Also *tza-ar gi-dul ba-nihm.**
> Literally, "the pain (difficulty) of raising children."

---

a as in father; **aw** as in law; **ai** as in aisle; **ei** as in neighbor; **e** as in bet; **i** as in vaccine; **ih** as in tin; **o** as in solar; **oi** as in void; **oo** as in food; **u** as in put; **uh** as in but; **ch** as in chutzpa; **zh** as in Zhivago.

tsa-di*
> Also *tsa-dihk, tsa-dei.*
> Also spelled *tzadi.*
> The eighteenth letter of the Hebrew alphabet, corresponding to "ts" in sound.

tsa-dihk
> Also spelled *tzaddik, tzadik, zaddik.*
> 1. Literally, "a righteous person."
> 2. Pietist.
> 3. Saint.
> 4. A Chassidic rabbi or leader.
> 5. The popular pronunciation of the eighteenth letter of the Hebrew alphabet. See *tsa-di.*

tsait
> Also spelled *tzeit.*
> 1. Time.
> 2. Era.

tsap mihr niht main blut
> Also spelled *tzap mir nit mein blut.*
> 1. Literally, "Don't bleed me!"
> 2. Don't aggravate me!

tsarot see *tzuhruhs*

tsats-ke-le di ma-mes
> Also spelled *tzatzkele di mames.*
> Mama's pet.

tsatz-ke
> Also spelled *tzatzke, tshatshke, chachke, chatshke.*
> 1. A bauble, plaything, trinket.
> 2. Something cute.
> 3. A doll.

tsa-vuh-uh
> Also *tza-va-a,* tzeva'a.*
> Last will and testament.

tsawn
> Also spelled *tzon.*
> Tooth.

---

a as in father; aw as in law; ai as in aisle; ei as in neighbor; e as in bet; i as in vaccine; ih as in tin; o as in solar; oi as in void; oo as in food; u as in put; uh as in but; ch as in chutzpa; zh as in Zhivago.

tsawres see *tzuhruhs*

tse-brech a fus
    1. Literally, "Break a foot!"
    2. Break a leg!

tsedaka see *tseduhkuh*

tse-dreit
    Also *tse-drait*.
    1. Literally, "turned, twisted, distorted."
    2. Mixed up, confused.
    3. Nutty, crazy.

tse-du-delt
    Mixed up.

tse-duh-kuh
    Also *tse-da-ka,** *tse-daw-kaw*.
    Also spelled *tsedakah, tzedaka*.
    1. Philanthropy, charity, benevolence.
    2. Justice.

tse-geit zihch ihn moil
    Also spelled *tzegait zich in moil*.
    1. Literally, "It melts in the mouth."
    2. Delicious.

tsein
    Also spelled *tzain*.
    Teeth. The plural of *tsawn*.

tsein duhktr
    Also spelled *tzain dokter*.
    Literally, "tooth doctor," a dentist.

tse-kawcht
    Also spelled *tzekocht*.
    1. Literally, "overboiled."
    2. Excited, furious.

tse-lem
    Also spelled *tzelem*.
    1. An image.
    2. A crucifix.

tse-mihsh-e-nihsh
    Also spelled *tzemishenish*.
    Confusion.

---

a as in father; aw as in law; ai as in aisle; ei as in neighbor; e as in bet; i as in vaccine; ih as in tin; o as in solar; oi as in void; oo as in food; u as in put; uh as in but; ch as in chutzpa; zh as in Zhivago.

tse-mihsht
> Also *tsu-mihsht*.
> Also spelled *tsemisht, tzemisht*.
> Mixed-up, confused, befuddled.

tse-rais ge-zunt-er-heit
> Also spelled *tzereis gezunterhait*.
> Literally, "Tear (it) in good health," addressed to one who purchased a new garment.

tse-traw-gen
> Also spelled *tzetrogen*.
> Absent-minded.

tse-tu-melt
> Also *tsu-tu-melt*.
> Also spelled *tzetumelt*.
> Mixed up, confused, befuddled.

tse-vihl-de-ter
> Also spelled *tzevildeter*.
> 1. A wild person.
> 2. A misbehaving child.

tshai-nihk
> Also spelled *tsheinik.*.
> Teapot.

tshatshke see *tsatzke*

tshav see *shav*

tshaw-lent
> Also spelled *tsholent, tcholent, cholent*.
> A dish consisting of meat, potatoes, and legumes, baked before sunset Friday and kept warm on Saturday to avoid cooking on the Sabbath. Also called *shalet* and *sholet* by German-speaking Jews and *adafino* and *chamin* by Sephardic Jews.

tsheinik see *tshainihk*

tshe-pe
> Also spelled *tcheppeh*.
> 1. To pick on (someone).
> 2. To tease.
> 3. To annoy, bother, pester, irk, harass.

---

a as in father; aw as in law; ai as in aisle; ei as in neighbor; e as in bet; i as in vaccine; ih as in tin; o as in solar; oi as in void; oo as in food; u as in put; uh as in but; ch as in chutzpa; zh as in Zhivago.

tshe-pe zihch niht tsu mihr
>   Also spelled *tzhepe zich nit tzu mir.*
>   Don't annoy me!

tshe-pe zihch uhp fun mihr
>   Also spelled *tzhepe zich op fun mir.*
>   1. Get away from me!
>   2. Leave me alone!

tshepn
>   Also *tze-pen.*
>   Also spelled *tzhepen.*
>   1. Annoy, harass.
>   2. Touch.

tsholent see *tshawlent*

t'shoo-vuh
>   Also *te-shoo-vaw, te-shoo-va.**
>   Also spelled *t'shuvuh, teshuvaw, teshuva.*
>   1. Literally, "a turning, returning."
>   2. Repentance.
>   3. An answer, retort.

tsi
>   Also *tsu.*
>   Also spelled *tzi.*
>   1. If.
>   2. Whether.

tsi bihst du me-shih-ge?
>   Also spelled *tzi bistu meshuge?*
>   (I wonder) are you crazy?

tsih-be-le
>   Also spelled *tzibele.*
>   Onion.

tsihkln zihch
>   Also spelled *tziklen zich.*
>   A cantor's falsetto repetition of a musical phrase.

tsih-mes
>   Also *tsih-muhs.*
>   Also spelled *tsimmes, tzimmes.*
>   1. A compote, usually of cooked fruit such as plums
>   or prunes.

---

a as in father; aw as in law; ai as in aisle; ei as in neighbor; e as in bet; i as in vaccine; ih as in tin; o as in solar; oi as in void; oo as in food; u as in put; uh as in but; ch as in chutzpa; zh as in Zhivago.

2. A vegetable stew of carrots and sweet potatoes, well spiced.

The word *tsihmes* may derive from the German *zum Essen,* "to eat."

tsihmr

Also spelled *tzimmer.*

Room.

tsimmes see *tsihmes*

tsi-rung

Also spelled *tzirung.*

1. Jewelry.
2. Earrings.

tsi-tsiht*

Also *tsih-tshihs.*

Also spelled *tzitzit, tsitsit, tsitsis.*

Fringes attached to the four corners of the prayer shawl.

tsitzel

Heavy rye bread with a thick crust, the bottom coated with cornmeal. Also known as corn bread.

tsnies see *tsnius*

tsni-us

Also *tsni-es, tzni-ut.**

Modesty, humility.

tsnu-aw

Also *tse-nu-a.**

Also spelled *tzenuah.*

1. A chaste woman.
2. A modest woman.

tsouris see *tzuhruhs*

tsu see *tsi*

tsu fihl

Also *tzi fihl.*

Also spelled *tzu fil.*

1. Literally, "too much."
2. Too costly.

---

a as in father; aw as in law; ai as in aisle; ei as in neighbor; e as in bet; i as in vaccine; ih as in tin; o as in solar; oi as in void; oo as in food; u as in put; uh as in but; ch as in chutzpa; zh as in Zhivago.

tsu-frih-den
> Also spelled *tzufriden.*
> Content, satisfied.

tsu ge-zunt
> Also spelled *tzu gezunt.*
> Literally, "to health," said when another sneezes.

tsu kumn oifn zihn-en
> Also spelled *tzu kumen oifen zinen.*
> 1. Literally, "to come upon the senses."
> 2. To come to mind, to occur to someone.

tsukr
> Also spelled *tzuker.*
> Sugar.

tsu-lihb
> Also spelled *tzulib.*
> On account of, because of, for the sake of.

tsum glihk, tsum shlih-mazl
> Also spelled *tzum glik, tzum shlimazel.*
> For better, for worse.

tsumihsht see *tsemihsht*

tsuris see *tzuhruhs*

tsu shand un tsu shpuht
> 1. Literally, "to shame and to mock."
> 2. To be disgraced.

tsu tai-er
> Also spelled *tzu teier.*
> Too costly.

tsu-tshep-e-nihsh
> Also spelled *tzutzhepenish.*
> 1. A nuisance, pest.
> 2. An unwanted person.
> 3. A hanger-on.

tsutumelt see *tsetumelt*

tsvi-bak
> Also spelled *zweiback.*
> A type of toast that has been baked twice.

tubetaka see *toobetaka*

---

a as in father; aw as in law; ai as in aisle; ei as in neighbor; e as in bet; i as in vaccine; ih as in tin; o as in solar; oi as in void; oo as in food; u as in put; uh as in but; ch as in chutzpa; zh as in Zhivago.

Tu Bi-Shvat
>Also spelled *Tu BiShevat*.
>The fifteenth day of the Hebrew month Shvat, also called "New Year for Trees" or "Arbor Day."

tuch
>1. A kerchief.
>2. A headcovering used by Orthodox Jewish married women.

tuchis see *tuhchuhs*

tuen see *tuhn*

tuen vai see *tooen vei*

tuh-chuhs
>Also spelled *toches, tochis, tuchis, tuches*.
>1. Literally, "bottom."
>2. The buttocks, the behind.

tuhf
>Also *taf, tav*.
>The twenty-second and final letter of the Hebrew alphabet, sounded like "s" or "t."

tuhn
>Also *tu-en*.
>Do, to do.

tumel see *tuml*

tu mihr a toi-ve
>Also spelled *tu mir a toyve*.
>Do me a favor.

tu mihr niht kain toi-ves
>Also spelled *tu mir nit kein toives*.
>Don't do me any favors.

tu mihr tzu-lihb
>Also spelled *tu mir tzulib*.
>1. Do it for my sake.
>2. Do me a favor.

tuml
>Also spelled *tumel*.
>Confusion, din, uproar, noise.

a as in father; aw as in law; ai as in aisle; ei as in neighbor; e as in bet; i as in vaccine; ih as in tin; o as in solar; oi as in void; oo as in food; u as in put; uh as in but; ch as in chutzpa; zh as in Zhivago.

tun-ked
Dipped, dunked.

tunkl
Also spelled *toonkel.*
1. Dark, shadowy, dim.
2. Shady (affairs), sinister.

tza-ar ba'ale chayim see *tsaar baalei chayihm*

tza'ar gidul banihm see *tsaar gidul bawnihm*

tzadi see *tsadi*

tzaddik see *tsadihk*

tzain see *tsein*

tzain dokter see *tseinduhktr*

tzarot see *tzuhruhs*

tzatzke see *tsatzke*

tzedaka see *tseduhkuh*

tzegait zich in moil see *tsegeit zihch ihn moil*

tzeit see *tsait*

tzekocht see *tsekawcht*

tzelem see *tselem*

tzemisht see *tsemihsht*

tzenuah see *tsnuaw*

tzepen see *tshepn*

tzereis gezunterhait see *tserais gezunterheit*

tzetrogen see *tsetrawgen*

tzetumelt see *tsetumelt*

tzeva'a see *tsavuhuh*

tzevildeter see *tsevihldeter*

tzhepen see *tshepn*

tzhepe zich nit tzu mir see *tshepe zihch niht tsu mihr*

tzi see *tsi*

tzibbeles see *tsihbeles*
Onions.

Tzi-duk Ha-Dihn
Also spelled *Tzidduk Hadin.*

---

a as in father; aw as in law; ai as in aisle; ei as in neighbor; e as in bet; i as in vaccine; ih as in tin; o as in solar; oi as in void; oo as in food; u as in put; uh as in but; ch as in chutzpa; zh as in Zhivago.

1. Literally, "Justification of the (Divine) Judgment."
2. A prayer recited at the Jewish burial service.

tzihtr
Also spelled *tziter.*
To tremble, to shake, to be nervous.

tziklen zich see *tsihkln zihch*

tzimmer see *tsihmr*

tzimmes see *tsihmes*

tzi-rung see *tsi-rung*

tziter see *tzihtr*

tzitzit see *tsitsiht*

Tzi-yon*
Also *Tzi-yoin.*
1. Zion.
2. Originally, a Canaanite fortress in Jerusalem captured by David.
3. The biblical city of David.

tzniut see *tsnius*

tznua see *tsnuan*

tzom
A fast.

Tzom Ge-dal-yuh
Also *Tzom Ge-dal-ya.**
Also spelled *Tzom Gedaliah, Zom Gedalia.*
The Fast of Gedalia observed the day after Rosh Hashanah. On this day Gedaliah, the Babylonian-appointed governor of Judea, was murdered in 582 B.C.E.

tzon see *tsawn*

tzoo-tzoo klepn
To adhere to.

tzu
1. To.
2. Too, excessive.

tzu fil see *tsu fihl*

---

a as in father; aw as in law; ai as in aisle; ei as in neighbor; e as in bet; i as in vaccine; ih as in tin; o as in solar; oi as in void; oo as in food; u as in put; uh as in but; ch as in chutzpa; zh as in Zhivago.

tzufriden see *tsufrihden*

tzug
1. A draft of wind.
2. Pull.
3. Move.

tzu gezunt see *tsu gezunt*

tzuh-luh-ches
To make one angry. A distortion of two words: *tzoo* (Yiddish, "to") and *lehachihs* (Hebrew, "anger").

tzuh-ruhs
Also *tzaw-ros, tza-rot,* tsaw-res.*
Also spelled *tzures, tsuris, tsouris.*
1. Troubles.
2. Aggravation.
3. Sufferings.
4. Distress.

tzuker see *tsukr*

tzu kumen oifen zinen see *tsu kumn oifn zihnen*

tzulib see *tsulihb*

tzum glik, tzum shlimazel see *tsum glihk, tsum shlihmazl*

tzung
Tongue.

tzures see *tzuhruhs*

tzu teier see *tsu taier*

tzutzhepenish see *tsutshepenihsh*

U

uh-ber
> Also spelled *ober, uhbr.*
> 1. However.
> 2. But

uhch see *och*

uh-der
> Also spelled *oder.*
> 1. Either.
> 2. Or.

uh-huh
> Also spelled *oho.*
> 1. Yes.
> 2. Wow!

uhn
> Also spelled *on.*
> Without, sans.

uhn-ge-patsh-ket
> Also spelled *ungepotchket.*
> 1. Cluttered, disordered, sloppy, littered, muddled, messed up.
> 2. Overdone, overdecorated.

uhn lang-e hak-daw-mes
> Also spelled *on lange hakdomes.*
> 1. Literally, "without a long introduction."
> 2. Keep it short.
> 3. Get to the point.

uhvl
> Also *aw-veil, a-vel.**
> Also spelled *ovel.*
> A mourner after the funeral.

ul-pan
> 1. Instruction, teaching.

---

a as in father; aw as in law; ai as in aisle; ei as in neighbor; e as in bet; i as in vaccine; ih as in tin; o as in solar; oi as in void; oo as in food; u as in put; uh as in but; ch as in chutzpa; zh as in Zhivago.

2. In modern Israel, a school for the intensive study of Hebrew.

um-be-ru-fen
1. Uncalled for.
2. God forbid!

um-be-shri-en
1. God forbid!
2. May it not happen.!

um-ge-dul-dihk
Also spelled *umgeduldik*.
Petulant, impatient.

um-glihk
Also spelled *umglik*.
1. Literally, "without luck."
2. Misfortune.
3. Tragedy.

um-glihk-lihch-er mentsh
1. An unfortunate, unlucky person.
2. A born loser.

um-meg-lihch
Impossible.

u-mos haw-o-lawm
Also *u-mot ha-o-lam.**
1. Literally, "the peoples of the world."
2. Gentiles.

um-zihst
Also spelled *umzist*.
1. Free.
2. Useless.

un a zawrg
Without a worry.

ungepotchket see *uhngepatshket*

un-ter-fihr-er
Also spelled *unterfirer*.
Escort at a wedding.

un-ter-koi-fen
1. Literally, "to buy from under."

---

a as in father; aw as in law; ai as in aisle; ei as in neighbor; e as in bet; i as in vaccine; ih as in tin; o as in solar; oi as in void; oo as in food; u as in put; uh as in but; ch as in chutzpa; zh as in Zhivago.

2. To bribe.

un-ter-shmeich-len

To cater to someone, curry favor, fawn upon.

un-ter-shte shu-re

Also *un-ter-shte shuruh*.

1. Literally, "the bottom line."

2. The essence.

un-ter-velt mentsh

1. Literally, "underworld man."

2. Racketeer.

ush-pi-zihn

Also spelled *ushpizin*.

1. Guest.

2. Prayers said to welcome the patriarchs into the *suka*.

utsn

Also spelled *utzen*.

To goad, needle.

a as in father; aw as in law; ai as in aisle; ei as in neighbor; e as in bet; i as in vaccine; ih as in tin; o as in solar; oi as in void; oo as in food; u as in put; uh as in but; ch as in chutzpa; zh as in Zhivago.

V

V'Adar see *VeAdar*

vai see *vei*

vaib
>   Also spelled *veib*.
>   Wife.

vai-ber-nihk
>   Also spelled *veibernik*.
>   1. Literally, "womanizer."
>   2. Lady-killer, debauchee.

vai iz mir see *vei ihz mihr*

vainen see *veinen*

vainik see *veinihk*

vainik vos see *veinihk vaws*

vais
>   Also spelled *weiss, veis*.
>   White

vais-e ze-ke-lach
>   Also spelled *weisse zekelach*.
>   Literally, "white stockings," worn by some *chasidim*.

vais ich vos? see *veis ihch vaws?*

vais-e ze-ke-lach
>   Also spelled *weisse zekelach*.
>   Literally, "white stockings," worn by some Chasidim.

vaist vos? see *veist vaws?*

vaist zihch mihr ois
>   It seems to me.

vaitr
>   Also spelled *veiter*.

---

1. Further.
2. Next.

vaizn
Also spelled *veizen*.
1. To show, display.
2. To point to.

vaksn vi a tzih-be-le
Grow like an onion.

val-ge-ren
Also spelled *volgeren*.
To roam, wander.

val-ger-en zihch
1. Literally, "roll oneself around."
2. To roam around aimlessly.
3. To be homeless.

val-ger-er
1. One who wanders about.
2. A homeless person.

va-ne
Also spelled *vaneh*.
1. Bath.
2. Bathtub.

vant
Wall.

vantz
1. A bedbug.
2. A nobody.

va-re-nih-kes
Also spelled *varenikes*.
Dumplings filled with jelly, fruit, or cheese.

var-en-ya
Preserves.

varfn an oig
Also spelled *varfen an oig*.
1. Literally, "to cast an eye."
2. Watch out for, guard.
3. Attract.

a as in father; aw as in law; ai as in aisle; ei as in neighbor; e as in bet; i as in vaccine; ih as in tin; o as in solar; oi as in void; oo as in food; u as in put; uh as in but; ch as in chutzpa; zh as in Zhivago.

var-nihsh-kes
>Also spelled *varnishkes.*
>1. Stuffed potato cakes.
>2. Kasha with noodles.

vart a mih-nut
>Also spelled *vart a minut.*
>1. Wait a minute!
>2. Hold on!

vartn
>Also spelled *varten.*
>Await, wait for.

vas failt zai? see *vuhs feilt zei*

vash tsih-mer
>Also spelled *vash tzimmer.*
>Washroom, bathroom.

vasr
>Also spelled *vasser.*
>Water.

vater see *fawtr*

vav see *vuhv*

vawch
>Also spelled *voch.*
>Week.

vaws hert zihch
>1. Literally, "What is heard?"
>2. What's new?

vay see *vei*

Ve-A-dar*
>Also *Ve-A-dawr.*
>Also spelled *V'Adar.*
>Literally, "and (plus) Adar," the second Adar, an
>extra month added to the calendar on leap years in
>order to reconcile the lunar and solar calendars.
>Also called *Adar Sheni,* meaning Adar II.

vechtr
>Also spelled *vechter.*
>A watchman, guard.

---

veg
> Way, path, road.

vei
> Also spelled *vai, vay.*
> Woe, alas.

veib see *vaib*

veibernik see *vaibernihk*

vei ihz mihr
> Also spelled *vai iz mir.*
> Woe is me.

vei-nen
> Also spelled *vainen.*
> To cry, weep.

vei-nihk
> Also *vei-nihg.*
> Also spelled *vainik.*
> 1. Few.
> 2. A little.

vei-nihk vaws
> Also spelled *vainik vos.*
> Not enough.

veis see *vais*

veis ihch vaws
> Also spelled *vais ich vos*
> 1. Literally, "I know not what."
> 2. I couldn't care less.

veis vi kalch see *vais vi kalch*

veist vaws?
> Also spelled *vaist vos?*
> 1. Literally, "Do you know what?"
> 2. Who says?
> 3. Stuff and nonsense!

veiter see *vaitr*

vei-tig
> Also *vei-tihk, vei-tuhg.*
> Ache, pain, hurt.

veizen see *vaizn*

---

a as in father; aw as in law; ai as in aisle; ei as in neighbor; e as in bet; i as in vaccine; ih as in tin; o as in solar; oi as in void; oo as in food; u as in put; uh as in but; ch as in chutzpa; zh as in Zhivago.

vekn
> Also spelled *veken*.
> Awaken.

vekr
> Also spelled *veker*.
> 1. Literally, "awaker."
> 2. Alarm clock.

vek-zeigr
> Also spelled *vekzaiger*.
> Alarm clock.

velt
> World.

vemn
> Also spelled *vemen*.
> Whom.

vemn nar-stu?
> Also spelled *vemen narstu?*
> 1. Literally, "Whom are you fooling?"
> 2. Whom are you kidding?

ven
> When.

ven ihch es, huhb ihch zei a-le ihn drerd
> Also spelled *ven ich es, hob ich zai alle in drerd*.
> 1. Literally, "When I am eating, they can all go to hell!"
> 2. Don't bother me when I'm eating!

ver der-har-get
> 1. Literally, "Get killed!"
> 2. Drop dead!

ver-en a teil
> Also spelled *veren a tail*.
> To be ruined.

verenikes see *varenihkes*

ver far-bluhn-jet
> Also spelled *ver farblunzhet*.
> 1. Literally, "Get lost!"
> 2. Leave me alone!

---

a as in father: aw as in law; ai as in aisle; ei as in neighbor; e as in bet; i as in vaccine; ih as in tin; o as in solar; oi as in void; oo as in food; u as in put; uh as in but; ch as in chutzpa; zh as in Zhivago.

ver-fe-nyihf-kiht
Dead drunk.

ver veis?
Also spelled *ver vais?*
Who knows?

ver vuhlt daws ge-gleibt?
Also spelled *ver volt dos geglaibt?*
Literally, "Who would have believed it?"

vi
1. How.
2. As.

vi a barg
As (large) as a mountain.

vi a lawch ihn kuhp
Also spelled *vi a loch in kop.*
1. Literally, "like a hole in the head."
2. Something unnecessary.

vi a loong oon leibr oifn nawz
Also spelled *vi a lung un leber oifn noz.*
1. Literally, "like a lung and liver on my nose."
2. Like a useless thing.
3. Something uncalled for.

vi a toitn ban-kes see *(a) toitn bankes*

vi a-zoi?
How so? How come?

vidder see *vihdr*

Vi-dui
Also spelled *Viddui.*
The confession of sins made to God on Yom Kippur
and on the deathbed.

vifil see *vihfihl*

vi geit duhs ge-sheft?
Also spelled *vi gait dos gesheft?*
1. Literally, "How's business?"
2. How are things?

vi geit es aich?
Also spelled *vi gait es eich?*

---

a as in father; aw as in law; ai as in aisle; ei as in neighbor; e as in bet; i as in vaccine; ih as in tin; o as in solar; oi as in void; oo as in food; u as in put; uh as in but; ch as in chutzpa; zh as in Zhivago.

1. Literally, "How goes it with you?"
2. How are you?

vihdr
>Also spelled *vidder.*
>Again.

vi heist du?
>Also spelled *vi haistu?*
>1. Literally, "How are you called?"
>2. What's your name?

vi heist duhs?
>Also spelled *vi haist dos?*
>Literally, "What is this called?"

vihfihl
>Also *vi-fihl, vifl.*
>Also spelled *vifil.*
>1. How much?
>2. How many?

vihld
>Also spelled *vild.*
>Wild, savage.

vihl-de cha-ye
>Also spelled *vilde chaya.*
>Wild animal.

vihldr mensh
>Also spelled *vilder mentsh.*
>Wild person, savage person.

vihl-stu?
>Do you want? Do you want to?

vihs-en-dihk
>Also spelled *vissendik.*
>With foreknowledge, knowingly.

vihsh-ni-ak
>Also spelled *wishniak, vishnik.*
>Cherry brandy.

vihsn
>Also spelled *vissen.*
>1. Know.
>2. Learn.

vihtz
> Also spelled *vitz.*
> A joke, wisecrack.

vi-ku-ach
> 1. Controversy.
> 2. Debate.

vild see *vihld*

vilde chaya see *vihlde chaye*

vilder mentsh see *vihldr mensh*

vishnik see *vihshniak*

vissen see *vihsn*

vissendik see *vihsendihk*

vitz see *vihtz*

voch see *vawch*

vo den see *vuh den*

voi-ler yung
> Mischievous youth, roughneck.

volgeren see *valgeren*

vortshpiel see *vuhrtshpil*

vos see *vuhs*

vu?
> Where? In what place?

vuh den?
> Also spelled *vo den.*
> What else?

vu hihn geist du?
> Also spelled *vuhin gaistu?*
> Literally, "Where are you going?"

vuhrt-shpil
> Also spelled *vortshpiel.*
> 1. Literally, "word play, play on words."
> 2. A pun.
> 3. A witticism.

vuhs?
> Also spelled *vos.*
> What?

---

a as in father; aw as in law; ai as in aisle; ei as in neighbor; e as in bet; i as in vaccine; ih as in tin; o as in solar; oi as in void; oo as in food; u as in put; uh as in but; ch as in chutzpa; zh as in Zhivago.

vuhs bai a nihch-te-ren oifn lung, ihz bai a shihk-er-en oifn tsung
Also spelled *vos bei a nichteren oifn lung, iz bei a shikkeren oifn tzung.*
Literally, "What a sober person has on the lung (mind), a drunk has on the tongue."

vuhs far a me-chutn bihn ihch dihr?
Also spelled *vos far a mechutan bin ich dir?*
1. Literally, "What kind of an in-law am I to you?"
2. What am I to you, anyway?

vuhs feilt zei
Also spelled *vas failt zai?*
1. What are they lacking?
2. What do they want?

vuhs gihchr als besr
Also spelled *vos gicher altz besser.*
Literally, "the quicker the better."

vuhs hakst du mihr ihn kuhp
Also spelled *vos hakst du mir in kop?*
1. Literally, "For what are you chopping my head off?"
2. Why are you talking me to death?

vuhs heist es?
Also spelled *vos haist es?*
What is it called? What's its name?

vuhs hert zihch?
Also spelled *vos hert zich?*
1. Literally, "What is heard?"
2. What's new?

vuhs hert zihch ep-es nai-es?
Also spelled *vos hert zich epes neies?*
1. Literally, "What of something new is heard?"
2. What's new?

vuhs huhb ihch duhs ge-darft?
Also spelled *vos hob ich dos gedarft?*
Literally, "For what did I need that?"

vuhs ihn der kuhrt
Also spelled *vos in der kort.*

1. Literally, "whatever is in the cards."
2. Whatever fate brings.

vuhs ihz?
>Also spelled *vos iz?*
>1. Literally, "What is?"
>2. What's the matter?

vuhs ihz der chih-lek?
>Also spelled *vos iz der chilek?*
>Literally, "What's the difference?"

vuhs ihz der tach-lihs?
>Also spelled *vos iz der tachlis?*
>1. Literally, "What is the purpose?"
>2. To what does it lead?
>3. What's the end result?

vuhs ihz di chawch-me?
>Also spelled *vos iz di chochma?*
>1. What's the rationale (joke)?
>2. What's the trick?
>3. What's so clever?

vuhs ihz di un-ter-shte shu-re?
>Also spelled *vos iz di untershte shure?*
>1. Literally, "What is the bottom line?"
>2. What's the point?
>3. What's the end result?

vuhs ihz miht dihr?
>Also spelled *vos iz mit dir?*
>Literally, "What's wrong with you?"

vuhs ihz oifn kuhp ihz oifn tsung
>Also spelled *vos iz oifen kop iz oifen tzung.*
>1. Literally, "Whatever is on the head (mind) is on the tongue."
>2. A talkative person.
>3. An uninhibited person.
>4. One who can't keep a thing to him/herself.

vuhs ihz oifn lung ihz oifn tsung
>Also spelled *vos iz oifen lung iz oifen tzung.*
>1. Literally, "Whatever is on the lung is on the tongue."
>2. One who can't keep a thing to him/herself.

a as in father; aw as in law; ai as in aisle: ei as in neighbor; e as in bet; i as in vaccine; ih as in tin; o as in solar; oi as in void; oo as in food; u as in put; uh as in but; ch as in chutzpa; zh as in Zhivago.

vuhs kuhcht zihch ihn tepl?
> Also spelled *vos kocht in teppel?*
> 1. Literally, "What's cooking in the pot?"
> 2. What's new?
> 3. What's happening?

vuhs macht duhs oif?
> Also spelled *vos macht dos ois?*
> What difference does it make?

vuhs macht duhs ois?
> Also spelled *vos macht dos ois?*
> What difference does it make?

vuhs macht ihr?
> Also *vuhs machst du?*
> 1. How do you feel?
> 2. How do you do?

vuhs meint es?
> Also spelled *vos maint es?*
> What does it mean?

vuhs nawch?
> Also spelled *vos noch?*
> 1. What else?
> 2. What then?
> 3. What further?

vuhs ret ihr e-pes?
> Also spelled *vos ret ir epes?*
> What are you talking about anyway?

vuhs rets du?
> Also spelled *vos redstu?*
> 1. Literally, "What are you saying?"
> 2. What are you talking about?
> 3. No kidding?

vuhs tut zihch duh?
> Also spelled *vos tut zich do?*
> What's going on here?

vuhs vet zain?
> Also spelled *vos vet zein?*
> 1. Literally, "What will be?"
> 2. What will happen?

---

a as in father; aw as in law; ai as in aisle; ei as in neighbor; e as in bet; i as in vaccine; ih as in tin; o as in solar; oi as in void; oo as in food; u as in put; uh as in but; ch as in chutzpa; zh as in Zhivago.

vuhs vet zain, vet zain
> Also spelled *vos vet zein, vet zein.*
> Literally, "What will be, will be."

vuhs zawgt ihr?
> Also spelled *vos zogt ir?*
> 1. Literally, "What are you saying?"
> 2. What do you mean?
> 3. You don't mean it!

vuhv
> Also *vav.**
> The sixth letter of the Hebrew alphabet, corresponding in sound to "v."

vund
> Wound

vursht
> Also spelled *wurst.*
> 1. Delicatessen.
> 2. Salami.
> 3. Sausage.

vu tut dihr vei?
> Also spelled *vu tut dir vai?*
> Where does it hurt you?

---

a as in father; aw as in law; ai as in aisle: ei as in neighbor; e as in bet; i as in vaccine; ih as in tin; o as in solar; oi as in void; oo as in food; u as in put; uh as in but; ch as in chutzpa; zh as in Zhivago.

W

weiss see *vais*
weisse zekelach see *vaise zekelach*
wishniak see *vihshniak*
wurst see *vursht*

Y

Ya-a-le V'ya-vo*

Also *Ya-a-le V'yaw-vo.*

1. Literally, "May our hopes and prayers go up (before God)."
2. A prayer inserted in the *Amidah* and in the Grace After Meals on holidays and New Moons.

yach-ne

Also *yach-na, yach-nuh.*

1. A strident, blabbermouth woman.
2. A gossip.

yach-sen

Also *yach-suhn, yach-san.**

1. A person of distinguished lineage.
2. Privileged character.

yad see *yawd*

Yad Va-shem*

Also *Yad Vaw-sheim.*

1. Literally, "a monument and a name" (Isaiah 56:5).
2. The State of Israel's Martyrs' and Heroes' Remembrance Authority.
3. A memorial museum of the Holocaust in Jerusalem.

yahrzeit see *yartsait*

yahrzeit licht see *yartsait lihcht*

Yahud

In the Koran, a name used contemptuously by Muhammed for Jews of his age.

Yahve

Also spelled *Yahwe, YHVH.*

The equivalent of Jehovah (God).

yam see *yuhm*

Yamin Noraim see *Yawmihm Norawihm*

---

a as in father; aw as in law; ai as in aisle; ei as in neighbor; e as in bet; i as in vaccine; ih as in tin; o as in solar; oi as in void; oo as in food; u as in put; uh as in but; ch as in chutzpa; zh as in Zhivago.

yar-muhl-ke

Also spelled *yamulke, yarmulka, yarmulke.*

A skullcap, worn by Orthodox and Conservative Jewish men at prayer, and at all times by observant Orthodox males.

yar-tsait

Also spelled *yahrtzeit, yohrtzeit, yortzeit, yartzeit, yahrzeit, jahrzeit.*

1. Literally, "year's time."
2. The anniversary of a death, observed by the lighting of a memorial lamp for twenty-four hours.

yar-tsait lihcht

Also spelled *yahrzeit licht.*

1. Literally, "annual light."
2. The memorial candle lit on the anniversary of a person's death and on the eve of the Day of Atonement.

yasher koi-ach

1. Literally, "May your strength increase!"
2. Congratulations!

ya-te-be-dam

1. A blusterer.
2. An intimidator.
3. A self-designated bigshot.

yatom see *yuhsuhm*

yawd

Also *yud, yad.**

Also spelled *yod.*

The tenth letter of the Hebrew alphabet, corresponding in sound to the letter "y."

yawgn

Also spelled *yogen.*

1. To hurry.
2. To chase.
3. To speed.

Yaw-mihm No-raw-ihm

Also *Ya-mihm No-ra-ihm.**

---

a as in father; aw as in law; ai as in aisle; ei as in neighbor; e as in bet; i as in vaccine; ih as in tin; o as in solar; oi as in void; oo as in food; u as in put; uh as in but; ch as in chutzpa; zh as in Zhivago.

Also spelled *Yamim Noraim* and *Yomim Noraim.*
1. Literally, "Days of Awe.
2. The ten-day Jewish High Holy Day period, beginning with Rosh Hashanah and ending with Yom Kippur.

yawr
Also spelled *jahr, yor.*
Year.

(a) yawr miht a miht-vawch
Also spelled *a yor mit a mitvoch.*
1. Literally, "a year plus a Wednesday."
2. A long, long time.

yawsom see *yuhsuhm*

ya-yihn ne-sech
Nonkosher wine.

y'dies see *yediuhs*

ye-der
Also *yeidr.*
Every, each.

yeder mentsh hot zein aigene meshugaas see *yeidr mensh hawt zain eigene m'shugaas*

yediot see *yediuhs*

Ye-di-ot Ach-ro-not*
Also *Ye-di-os Ach-ro-nos.*
1. Literally, "last news."
2. The name of a daily afternoon Hebrew newspaper in Israel.

ye-di-uhs
Also *ye-di-ot,* *y'di-es.*
1. News.
2. Announcements.

yefaifia see *y'feifiya*

Ye-hoo-di
Also spelled *Yehudi.*
1. A citizen of Judah in Bible days.
2. A Jew, a person born of a Jewish mother.
3. A person converted to Judaism.

---

a as in father; aw as in law; ai as in aisle ei as in neighbor; e as in bet; i as in vaccine; ih as in tin; o as in solar; oi as in void; oo as in food; u as in put; uh as in but; ch as in chutzpa; zh as in Zhivago.

Yehudi see *Yehoodi*

yeidr see *yeder*

yeidr mensh hawt zain ei-ge-ne m'shu-ga-as
>Also spelled *yeder mentsh hot zein aigene mesh-ugaas.*
>Literally, "Every person has his own idio-syncrasies."

Yeishoo
>Also spelled *Yeshu.*
>Jesus.

yeitsr haw-raw
>Also *yei-tser ha-ra*.*
>Also spelled *yetzer hara.*
>1. Literally, "evil inclination."
>2. A negative impulse, a compulsion.

yeitsr tov
>Also spelled *yetzer tov.*
>The good inclination in man.

ye-ke
>Also spelled *yekke.*
>1. A Jew from Germany.
>2. A "greenhorn" in Israel.

ye-nemz
>1. Literally, "the other's."
>2. Belonging to another person.

ye-ne velt
>1. Literally, "the other world."
>2. The world-to-come.

yenta see *yentuh*

yen-tuh
>Also spelled *yenta, yente.*
>A blabbermouth, a gossipy woman. A distortion of the Spanish name Juanita or, more likely, of the French name Gentille.

yentz
>1. To fornicate, copulate.
>2. To swindle, defraud.

---

a as in father; aw as in law; ai as in aisle; ei as in neighbor; e as in bet; i as in vaccine; ih as in tin; o as in solar; oi as in void; oo as in food; u as in put; uh as in but; ch as in chutzpa; zh as in Zhivago.

yentz-er
1. A promiscuous person.
2. A crook, swindler.

Ye-roo-shaw-la-yihm
Also *Ye-ru-sha-la-yihm.**
Also spelled *Y'rushawlayim.*
1. Literally, "city of peace."
2. Jerusalem.

Yerushalayihm see *Yerooshawlayihm*

ye-shihv-uh buhchr
Also spelled *yeshivah bawcher, yeshiva bocher.*
1. Literally*"yeshiva youth."*
2. A parochial school student.
3. A student at a Talmudic academy.

yeshiva see *y'shivuh*

yeshivot
Plural of *yeshiva.*

Yeshu see *Yeishoo*

ye-shuv-nihk
Also spelled *yeshuvnik.*
1. A farmer, a rustic.
2. An uncouth person.

yetzer hara see *yeitzr hawraw*

yetzer tov see *yeitsr tov*

yetzt see *ihtst*

y'fei-fi-ya*
Also *y'fei-fi-yaw.*
Also spelled *yefaifia.*
A beautiful woman, a belle.

yi-boom*
Also spelled *yibum.*
1. A Levirate marriage.
2. In the Bible, the obligation of a dead man's
   brother to marry the widow if there are no sons
   (Deuteronomy 25:5-10).

yiches see *yihchus*

---

a as in father; aw as in law; ai as in aisle; ei as in neighbor; e as in bet; i as in vaccine; ih as in tin; o as in
solar; oi as in void; oo as in food; u as in put; uh as in but; ch as in chutzpa; zh as in Zhivago.

yi-chud*
>   Also spelled *yihud*.
>   1. Literally, "union."
>   2. The consumation of a marriage.
>   3. The mystical concept of Divine union.

yichus see *yihchuhs*

Yid see *Yihd*

Yidden see *Yidn*

Yiddene see *Yihdene*

Yiddish see *Yihdihsh*

Yidn
>   Also spelled *Yidden*.
>   Plural of *Yid*.

yigdal see *yihgdal*

yih-chuhs
>   Also *yi-chus*.*
>   Also spelled *yiches*.
>   1. Lineage, pedigree, ancestry.
>   2. Status (achieved through scholarship, money or family).

Yihd
>   Also spelled *Yid*.
>   A male Jew.

Yihd-e-ne
>   Also spelled *Yiddene*.
>   A female Jew.

Yihd-ihsh
>   Also spelled *Yiddish*.
>   1. Literally, "Jewish."
>   2. The mother-tongue of Ashkenazic (East European) Jews and their descendants in other countries, derived from approximately 75 percent medieval High German and 25 percent Hebrew and written in Hebrew characters.

Yihg-dal
>   Also spelled *Yigdal*.
>   1. Literally, "May He be magnified."

---

a as in father; aw as in law; ai as in aisle; ei as in neighbor; e as in bet; i as in vaccine; ih as in tin; o as in solar; oi as in void; oo as in food; u as in put; uh as in but; ch as in chutzpa; zh as in Zhivago.

2. The title and opening words of a Hebrew hymn embodying Maimonides' Thirteen Articles of Faith. Attributed to Daniel ben Judah of early fourteenth-century Rome.

yihn-ge-le
Also spelled *yingele.*
A pet form of *yihngl.*

yihngl
Also spelled *yingel.*
Young boy.

yihr-as shaw-ma-yihm
Also *yihr-at sha-ma-yihm.**
Also spelled *yirat shamayim.*
1. Literally, "the fear of heaven."
2. Fear of God.
3. According to Psalm 111:10, the beginning of wisdom.

yihs-ga-dal v'yihs-ka-dash
Also *yiht-ga-dal v'yiht-ka-dash.**
Also spelled *yitgadal v'yitkadash.*
1. Literally, "May [God's great Name] be extolled and hallowed."
2. The opening words of the *Kaddish* prayer.

Yihs-raw-eil
Also *Yihs-ra-el.**
Also spelled *Yisroel, Yisrael*
1. Israel.
2. Another name for the biblical Jacob (Genesis 32:29)
3. A name for the Jewish people.
4. The state created in 1948.

yihud see *yichud*

Yihz-kuhr
Also *Yihz-kor.**
Also spelled *Yizkor.*
1. Literally, "May He remember."
2. The opening of the memorial prayer recited at the service for the dead held on Yom Kippur and

on the concluding days of Passover, Shavuot, and Sukkot.

yi-mach sh'mo
Literally, "May his name be erased." An epithet added when the name of an enemy of Jews is mentioned.

yingel see *yihngl*

yingele see *yihngele*

yirat shamayim see *yihras shawmayihm*

yi-shuv
1. Literally, "settlement."
2. The name of the Jewish community in Israel before the proclamation of the State in 1948.

yi-shuv ba-a-retz*
The religious obligation of residing in Israel.

yi-shuv-nihk
Also spelled *yishuvnik*.
One who lives on a *yishuv* in Israel.

Yisrael see *Yihsraweil*

yitgadal v'yitkadash see *yihsgadal v'yihskadash*

Yizkor see *Yihzkuhr*

yo see *yuh*

yod see *yawd*

yogen see *yawgn*

yohrtzeit see *yartsait*

yoich
Soup.

yoishr
Also *yo-sher*.*
Also spelled *yoi-sher*.
Justice, fairness, integrity.

yoiveil see *yoveil*

yold see *yuhld*

yom
Day.

---

a as in father; aw as in law; ai as in aisle; ei as in neighbor; e as in bet; i as in vaccine; ih as in tin; o as in solar; oi as in void; oo as in food; u as in put; uh as in but; ch as in chutzpa; zh as in Zhivago.

Yom ha-Atz-ma-ut*
Also *Yom haw-Atz-maw-oos.*
Israel Independence Day, observed on the fifth day of Iyar.

Yom ha-Dihn
Also spelled *Yom ha-Din.*
1. Literally, "judgment day."
2. Yom Kippur, the Day of Atonement.

Yom ha-Sho-a*
Also *Yom ha-Sho-aw.*
Literally, "Holocaust Day," observed on the twenty-seventh day of Nisan as a memorial to the six million Jews who perished during the Nazi era.

Yom ha-Zi-kaw-ron
Also *Yom ha-Zi-ka-ron.**
1. Literally, "day of remembrance."
2. Rosh Hashanah, the Jewish New Year.

Yomim Noraim see *Yawmihm Norawihm*

Yom Kihpr
Also *Yom Ki-poor.**
Also spelled *Yom Kippur.*
Literally, "Day of Atonement," observed on the tenth day of Tishri as a day of fasting and prayer.

Yom Kippur see *Yom Kihpr*

Yom Te-roo-a*
Also *Yom Te-roo-aw.*
Also spelled *Yom Teruah.*
Literally, "a day of sounding the *shofar*," one of the designations for Rosh Hashanah used in the liturgy.

yom tov*
1. Literally, "good day."
2. Synonym for Jewish holiday.

Yom Ye-ru-sha-la-yihm*
Also *Yom Ye-roo-shaw-law-yihm.*
Literally, "Jerusalem Day," observed on the twenty-eighth of the month of Iyar in commemoration of the unification of Jerusalem in 1967.

---

a as in father; **aw** as in law; **ai** as in aisle; **ei** as in neighbor; **e** as in bet; **i** as in vaccine; **ih** as in tin; **o** as in solar; **oi** as in void; **oo** as in food; **u** as in put; **uh** as in but; **ch** as in chutzpa; **zh** as in Zhivago.

yontif see *yuhntihf*

yontifdik see *yuhntihfdihk*

yor see *yawr*

(a) yor mit a mitvoch see *(a) yawr miht a mihtvawch*

yortzeit see *yartsait*

yosher see *yoishr*

yo-tzeir
> Also *yo-tzer.**
> 1. Literally, "creation."
> 2. A prayer in the morning service lauding God as the Creator.
> *Yotzrot* is the plural form.

yo-veil*
> Also *yoi-veil, yoivl.*
> Also spelled *yovel.*
> 1. Literally, "jubilee."
> 2. Jubilation, gaiety, merriment.
> 3. In the Bible, a celebration every fiftieth year in which all lands were returned to the original owners.

Y'ru-shaw-la-yim see *Yerooshawlayihm*

y'shi-vuh
> Also *ye-shi-va,** ye-shi-vaw.*
> Also spelled *yeshibah, yeshivah.*
> 1. Literally, "a sitting place."
> 2. An academy of Jewish learning for elementary, secondary, or higher learning.
> 3. A parochial school.

yud see *yawd*

yuh
> Also spelled *yo.*
> Yes, affirmative.

yuhkl
> Also *yu-kel.*
> A buffoon.

yuhld
> Also spelled *yold.*

---

a as in father; aw as in law; ai as in aisle; ei as in neighbor; e as in bet; i as in vaccine; ih as in tin; o as in solar; oi as in void; oo as in food; u as in put; uh as in but; ch as in chutzpa; zh as in Zhivago.

1. A dope.
2. A boor.
3. A chump.

yuhm
Also spelled *yam.**
Sea, ocean.

yuhn-tihf see *yom tov*

yuhn-tihf-dihk
Also spelled *yontifdik.*
1. In a holiday mood.
2. Jovial.

Yuhsh-ke
Jesus.

yuh-suhm
Also *yaw-som, ya-tom.**
Orphan.

yukel see *yuhkl*

yung
1. Young.
2. Youth.

yun-gatsh
1. A coarse person.
2. Street urchin, brat, young rogue.

yun-ger-man-tshihk
1. A young, vigorous lad.
2. A newlywed.

(a) yung miht beinr
Also spelled *(a) yung mit bainer.*
1. Literally, "a lad with (sturdy) bones."
2. A strongly-built person.

Z

zach
   A thing.

zaddik see *tsadihk*

zaft
   Juice.

zaf-tihk
   Also *zaf-tihg*.
   Also spelled *zaftik, zaftig, zoftik, zoftig, saftig.*
   1. Literally, "juicy, succulent."
   2. Shapely, full-bodied, referring to the female figure.

zai a-zoi gut
   Also spelled *zei azoi gut.*
   1. Literally, "Be so good (as to . . .)!"
   2. Please!

zaicher see *zeicher*

zaide see *zeiduh*

zaier see *zeir*

zaiger see *zeigr*

zai ge-zunt
   Also spelled *zei gezunt.*
   1. Literally, "Be well!"
   2. Sometimes said in place of goodbye.

zai mihr frei-lach
   Also spelled *zei mir frailech.*
   Be happy!

zai mihr ge-zunt
   Also spelled *zei mir gezunt.*
   Literally, "Be healthy!" with the implication "and leave me alone!"

---

a as in father; aw as in law; ai as in aisle; ei as in neighbor; e as in bet; i as in vaccine; ih as in tin; o as in solar; oi as in void; oo as in food; u as in put; uh as in but; ch as in chutzpa; zh as in Zhivago.

zai mihr moichl
>Also spelled *zei mir moichel*.
>Pardon me. Excuse me.

zain
>To be.

zai niht a nar
>Also spelled *zei nit a nar*.
>Don't be a fool!

zai niht a vai-zaw-suh
>Also spelled *zei nit a vayzoso*.
>1. Literally, "Don't be a Vaizata!" Vaizata is Haman's youngest son in the story of Purim.
>2. Don't be an idiot!

zai niht kein goi-lem
>Also spelled *zei nit kain golem*.
>1. Literally, "Don't be a robot!"
>2. Don't be a dummy!

zai zihch mat-ri-ach . . .
>Also spelled *zei zich matriach . . .*
>1. Take the trouble to. . .
>2. Be so kind as to . . .

zak
>A sack, a bag.

zakain see *zawkein*

zalaven see *zhalevn*

zaltz
>Salt.

zawgn
>Also spelled *zogen*.
>1. To say.
>2. To tell.

zawgn a lihgn
>Also spelled *zogen a ligen*.
>To tell a lie.

zawgn a pawr ver-ter
>Also spelled *zogen a por verter*.
>1. To say a few words.
>2. To make a brief speech.

---

a as in father; aw as in law; ai as in aisle: ei as in neighbor; e as in bet; i as in vaccine; ih as in tin; o as in solar; oi as in void; oo as in food; u as in put; uh as in but; ch as in chutzpa; zh as in Zhivago.

zaw-guhr-ke
>Also spelled *zogerke.*
>1. Literally, "a female communicator."
>2. The woman who led prayers in the section of Orthodox synagogues reserved for ladies, particularly in pre-World War II Eastern Europe.

zaw-kein
>Also *za-kein, za-ken.**
>Also spelled *zakain.*
>Old man.

zawl
>Also spelled *zol.*
>1. Should.
>2. May.
>3. Let.

zawl dihch chapn baim boich
>Also spelled *zol dich chapen beim boich.*
>You should get a stomach cramp!

zawl dihr grih-men ihn boich
>May you get a cramp in your stomach!

zawl dihr klapn ihn kuhp
>Also spelled *zol dir klappen in kop.*
>It should bang in your head (that which is annoying me)!

zawl er tsu-brechn a fus
>Also spelled *zol er tsebrechen a fus.*
>May he break a leg!

zawl es bren-en
>Also spelled *zol es brenen.*
>1. Let it burn!
>2. The hell with it!

zawl Gawt mihr helfn
>Also spelled *zol Gott mir helfen.*
>May God help me!

zawl Gawt uhp-hihtn
>Also spelled *zol Gott ophiten.*
>May God prevent (it)!

---

a as in father; aw as in law; ai as in aisle; ei as in neighbor; e as in bet; i as in vaccine; ih as in tin; o as in solar; oi as in void; oo as in food; u as in put; uh as in but; ch as in chutzpa; zh as in Zhivago.

zawl ihch a-zol vihsn fun tsuh-res
> Also spelled *zol ich azoi vissen fun tsores.*
> 1. Literally, "I should so know from trouble (as I know about this matter)."
> 2. I haven't the faintest idea.

zawlst du a-zoi leibn
> Also spelled *zolstu azoi leben.*
> Literally, "You should live so (long)!"

zawlst ge-shvawln ve-ren vi a barg
> Also spelled *zolst geshvollen veren vi a barg.*
> Literally, "May you swell up (as big) as a mountain!"

zawlst leibn oon zain ge-zunt
> Also spelled *zolst leben un zein gezunt.*
> Literally, "May you live and be well!"

zawlst lihgn ihn der erd
> Also spelled *zolst ligen in drerd.*
> 1. Literally, "You should lay in the earth!"
> 2. Drop dead!

zawlst niht vihsn fun kein shlechtz
> Also spelled *zolst nit vissen fun kain shlechts.*
> Literally, "You shouldn't know from anything bad!"

zawl vaksn tsih-be-les fun pu-pihk
> Also spelled *zol vaksen tzibeles fun pupik.*
> Literally, "May onions sprout from your navel."

zawl zain
> Also spelled *zol zein*
> 1. Literally, "Let it be!"
> 2. That's it!

zawl zain a-zoi
> Also spelled *zol zein azoi.*
> 1. Literally, "Let it be so!"
> 2. O.K.

zawl zain ge-zunt
> Also spelled *zol zein gezunt.*
> Let everything (everyone) be well!

---

a as in father; aw as in law; ai as in aisle: ei as in neighbor; e as in bet; i as in vaccine; ih as in tin; o as in solar; oi as in void; oo as in food; u as in put; uh as in but; ch as in chutzpa; zh as in Zhivago.

zawl zain miht glihk
>Also spelled *zol zein mit glik.*
>1. Literally, "Let it be with luck."
>2. May you have luck!
>3. May your new venture be successful!

zawl zain sha
>1. Literally, "Let there be silence!"
>2. Keep quiet!

zawl zain shtihl
>1. Literally, "Let there be quiet!"
>2. Keep still!

zawrgn
>Also spelled *zorgen.*
>To worry, be concerned, care about.

zawrg zihch niht
>Also spelled *zorg zich nit.*
>Don't worry!

zayde see *zeiduh*

za-yihn
>Also spelled *zayin.*
>The seventh letter of the Hebrew alphabet, corresponding in sound to "z."

z'chus aw-vos
>Also *ze-chut a-vot.* *
>Literally, "merit of the fathers." According to tradition, the good deeds of the patriarchs—Abraham, Isaac, and Jacob—win favor for their descendants.

zecher see *zeicher*

ze-chus
>Also *ze-chut,* * *z'chus.*
>Merit.

zechut avot see *z'chus awvos*

zeh nor see *zei nawr*

zei azoi gut see *zai azoi gut*

zei-cher li-tsi-as Mihtz-ra-yihm
>Also *ze-cher li-ye-tzi-at Mihtz-ra-yihm.* *
>Also spelled *zaicher litzias Mitzraim.*

---

a as in father; aw as in law; ai as in aisle; ei as in neighbor; e as in bet; i as in vaccine; ih as in tin; o as in solar; oi as in void; oo as in food; u as in put; uh as in but; ch as in chutzpa; zh as in Zhivago.

Literally, "in remembrance of the Exodus from
Egypt," a phrase that is part of the *Kiddush* recited
on the Sabbath and holidays.

zei-chr tza-dihk lihv-raw-chaw
>Also *zeicher tzadihk livracha.**
>Also spelled *zecher tzaddik livrachah.*
>Literally, "The memory of the righteous is a bless-
>ing!"

zeide see *zeiduh*

zei-duh
>Also spelled *zaide, zeide, zayde.*
>Grandfather.

zeien see *zein*

zeigel see *zeigl*

zei-ge-lach
>1. Teeth.
>2. Serrated edges.

zei gezunt see *zai gezunt*

zeigr
>Also spelled *zeiger, zaiger.*
>1. A watch.
>2. A clock.

zei-lihg
>Also spelled *zelig.*
>A contraction of *zichrono livracha*, "May his mem-
>ory be blessed."

zei mir see *zai mihr*

zein
>Also *zei-en.*
>1. To look.
>2. To see.

zei nawr
>Also spelled *zeh nor.*
>1. Literally, "Just see!"
>2. Look here!
>3. Well! Well!

zei nit see *zai niht*

zeir
>Also spelled *zaier*.
>1. Very.
>2. Much too much.

zeir gut
>Also spelled *zaier gut*.
>1. Literally, "very good."
>2. O.K.

zeir shein ge-zuhgt
>Also spelled *zaier shain gezogt*.
>1. Literally, "very beautifully stated."
>2. Well said!

zei zich matriach see *zai zihch matriach*

zek
>Plural of *zak*. See above.

zekeinaw see *z'keine*

zelig see *zeilihg*

zel-ten-kait
>Also spelled *zeltenkeit*.
>Exception, rarity.

zeman matan Torateinu see *z'man matan Toraw-seinu*

zemel see *zeml*

ze-mer
>The singular of *zemirot*. See below.

zemirot see *zmiruhs*

zeml
>Also spelled *zemel, zemmel*.
>A crusty roll, soft on the inside.

ze-ro-a*
>Also *z'ro-a*.
>1. The wing or neck of fowl.
>2. The shankbone placed on the *Seder* tray.

zetst zihch a-vek
>Also spelled *zetzt zich avek*.
>Please be seated.

---

a as in father; aw as in law; ai as in aisle; ei as in neighbor; e as in bet; i as in vaccine; ih as in tin; o as in solar; oi as in void; oo as in food; u as in put; uh as in but; ch as in chutzpa; zh as in Zhivago.

zetz
>Punch, bang, hit, slam.

zetzen see *zetzn*

(a) zetz in erd
>Also *a zetz in drerd*.
>1. Literally, "a knock in the ground."
>2. A useless action.
>3. A futile motion.

zetzn
>Also spelled *zetzen*.
>1. To hit.
>2. To place, to seat.
>3. Sexual intercourse.

zetzt zich avek see *zetst zihch avek*

zha-levn
>Also *zal-a-ven*.
>Also spelled *zhaleven*.
>1. Sparing.
>2. Miserly.

zhluhb
>Also spelled *zhlob, shluhb, zhlawb.*
>1. A coarse person.
>2. A slob.

zhu-lihk
>Also spelled *zhulik*.
>Faker, scoundrel.

zhu-met mihr ihn kup
>A buzzing in one's head.

zhu-pe-tze
>A robe worn by *Chasidim*.

zi
>She.

zihch-ro-nos
>Also *zihch-ro-not*.*
>Also spelled *zichronot*.
>1. Literally, "memories."
>2. A portion of the Rosh Hashanah *musaf* service.

---

a as in father; aw as in law; ai as in aisle: ei as in neighbor; e as in bet; i as in vaccine; ih as in tin; o as in solar; oi as in void; oo as in food; u as in put; uh as in but; ch as in chutzpa; zh as in Zhivago.

zihn-dihk niht

Also spelled *zindik nit.*
1. Don't sin.
2. Don't complain.
3. Don't tempt fate.

zihn-en

Also spelled *zinnen.*
1. Mind.
2. Senses.

zihs

Also spelled *zis.*
Sweet.

zih-se ne-shuh-me

Also spelled *zisse neshama.*
1. Literally, "sweet soul."
2. A sweet person.
3. A saintly person.

zihs-kait

Also spelled *ziskeit.*
1. Sweetness.
2. A sweet thing.
3. A term of endearment, especially for a child.

zihts-fleish

Also spelled *zitsflaish.*
1. Literally, "sitting flesh."
2. Patience.

zihtzen oif shpihl-kes

Also spelled *zitzen oif shpilkes.*
1. To sit on pins and needles.
2. To be nervous about a situation.

zihtzn shih-vuh

Also spelled *zitzen shiva.*
1. Literally, "to sit seven," to stay in one's home for seven days of mourning following the death of an immediate relative.
2. To mourn.

zindik nit see *zihndihk niht*

---

a as in father; aw as in law; ai as in aisle; ei as in neighbor; e as in bet; i as in vaccine; ih as in tin; o as in solar; oi as in void; oo as in food; u as in put; uh as in but; ch as in chutzpa; zh as in Zhivago.

zingn
>   Also spelled *zingen*.
>   To sing.

zinnen see *zihnen*

Zion see *Tziyon*

zis see *zihs*

ziskeit see *zihskait*

zisse see *zihse neshuhme*

zitzen oif shiplkes see *zihtzn oif shpihlkes*

zizit see *tzihtzit*

z'kein-e
>   Also *ze-kei-naw, ze-kei-na.**
>   Old woman.

z'man ma-tan To-raw-sei-nu
>   Also *ze-man ma-tan To-ra-tei-nu.**
>   1. Literally, "the season of the giving of our Torah."
>   2. The festival of Shavuot.

z'mirot see *zmiruhs*

zmi-ruhs
>   Also *zmi-ros, ze-mi-rot, z'mi-rot.**
>   1. Literally, "melodies."
>   2. Sabbath table songs.

zoftig see *zaftihk*

zogen see *zawgn*

zogerke see *zawguhrke*

Zo-har
>   1. Literally, "brightness."
>   2. A commentary on the Pentateuch, the principal source of Jewish mysticism.

zoier zaltz
>   1. Sour salt.
>   2. Citric acid.

zoi-nuh
>   Also *zo-naw, zo-na.**
>   A prostitute.

---

a as in father; aw as in law; ai as in aisle; ei as in neighbor; e as in bet; i as in vaccine; ih as in tin; o as in solar; oi as in void; oo as in food; u as in put; uh as in but; ch as in chutzpa; zh as in Zhivago.

zol see *zawl*

zolst see *zawlst*

Zom Gedalia see *Tzom Gedalyuh*

zona see *zoinuh*

zorg zich nit see *zawrg zihch niht*

zorgen see *zawrgn*

z'roa see *zeroa*

zun
>   1. The sun.
>   2. A son.

zun-ihn-ke
>   Also spelled *zuninke*.
>   Little son, darling son.

zuz
>   The singular of *zuzim*. See below.

zuzim
>   Babylonian coins referred to in the Passover song *Chad Gadya,* "One Only Kid."

zweiback see *tsvibak*

---

a as in father; aw as in law; ai as in aisle; ei as in neighbor; e as in bet; i as in vaccine; ih as in tin; o as in solar; oi as in void; oo as in food; u as in put; uh as in but; ch as in chutzpa; zh as in Zhivago.